INSIGHT GUIDES

BOSTON

APA PUBLICATIONS

L

Part of the Langenscheidt Publishing Group

How to Use This Book

This book is carefully structured both to convey an understanding of the city and its culture and to guide readers through its attractions and activities:

◆ The Best Of section at the front of the book helps you to prioritize. The first spread contains all the Top Sights, while the Editor's Choice details unique experiences, the best buys or other recommendations.

◆ To understand Boston, you need to know something of its past. The city's history and culture are described in authoritative essays written by

specialists in their fields who have lived in and documented the city for many years.

◆ The Places section details all the attractions worth seeing. The main places of interest are coordinated by number with the maps.

◆ Each chapter includes lists of recommended shops, restaurants, bars and cafés.

◆ Photographs throughout the book are chosen not only to illustrate geography and buildings, but also to convey the moods of the city and the life of its people.

◆ The Travel Tips section includes all the practical information you will need, divided into four key sections: transportation, accommodations, activities (including nightlife, events, tours, and sports), and an A–Z of practical tips. Information may be located quickly by using the index on the back cover flap of the book.

◆ A detailed street atlas is included at the back of the book, with all restaurants, bars, cafés and hotels plotted for your convenience.

PLACES AND SIGHTS

Chapters are **color-coded** for ease of use. Each neighborhood has a designated color corresponding to the orientation map on the inside front cover.

A locator map pinpoints the specific area covered in each chapter.

A four-color map shows the area covered in the chapter, with the main sights and attractions coordinated by number with the text.

Margin tips provide extra snippets of information, whether it's a practical tip, a whimsical quote, an historical fact or advice on shopping and eating.

Photo Features

Photo features offer visual coverage of major sights or unusual attractions. Where relevant, there is a map showing the location and essential information on opening times, entrance charges, transport and contact details.

Shopping and Restaurant Listings

Shopping listings provide details of the best shops in each area. **Restaurant listings** give the establishment's contact details, opening times and price category, followed by a useful review. Bars and cafés are also covered here. The colored dot and grid reference refers to the atlas section at the back of the book.

The Daily Catch
323 Hanover St
Tel: 523-8567
www.dailycatch.com
L & D daily $$ ⑬ [p272, F2]
It's calamari all the way at this tiny, hole-in-the-wall institution, which specializes in Sicilian

Travel Tips

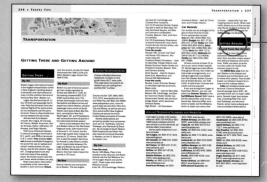

Getting Around

To and from the Airp

ogan, just 3 miles (5km) fr
wntown Boston, is clos
han any other ma

Travel Tips provide all the practical knowledge you'll need before and during your trip: how to get there, getting around, where to stay and what to do. The A–Z section is a handy summary of practical information, arranged alphabetically.

Contents

Maps

THE BEST OF BOSTON: TOP SIGHTS

At a glance, the Boston attractions you can't afford to miss, from the 'Cradle of Liberty' and 'Old Ironsides' to fine art museums, the home of the Red Sox, and historic sites.

◁ **Public Garden.** Boston's lovely central park is America's first public botanical garden. Historic, pedal-powered swan boats – inspired by the medieval German opera *Lohengrin* – offer 15-minute rides in the Lagoon's idyllic setting. See page 148.

▽ **Freedom Trail**. Follow the red-brick road (and red-painted lines) through 2.5 miles (4km) of downtown Boston, exploring the 16 historic sites on the Freedom Trail, including churches, cemeteries, Paul Revere's House, the USS *Constitution*, and the Bunker Hill Monument. See page 40.

◁ **USS *Constitution***. The towering masts of this ship, nicknamed 'Old Ironsides,' dominate the Charlestown Navy Yard. Active-duty US navy sailors escort visitors around the great vessel. See page 139.

△ **Boston Harbor Islands National Recreation Area.** Take a ferry to some of the 34 islands and peninsulas that comprise this area, home to military forts, hiking trails, campsites, and Boston Light – the country's oldest continually used lighthouse. See page 131.

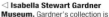

◁ **Isabella Stewart Gardner Museum.** Gardner's collection is displayed in a beautiful Venetian palace, exactly how she left it (plus a 2012 addition that houses special exhibitions, and minus $300 million worth of goods stolen in 1990), with paintings and drawings by Titian, Matisse, Botticelli, Bellini, Whistler, and Sargent. See page 157.

▽ **Museum of Science.** An entertaining and edifying hands-on affair for all ages, containing hundreds of exhibits in fields such as astronomy, computing, energy, anthropology, industry, and nature, along with a planetarium and a giant IMAX dome theater. See page 197.

▷ **Trinity Church.** Henry Hobson Richardson's edifice in Copley Square is one of the country's great ecclesiastical buildings. The stately and striking exterior is beautifully reflected in the mirrored walls of the neighboring John Hancock Tower, and the interior is lavishly decorated with John La Farge frescoes and stained glass. See page 151.

◁ **Harvard Yard.** In the heart of Cambridge, this the walled, leafy campus of America's oldest college, filled with lawns and crisscrossing footpaths and ringed by dignified lecture halls, dormitories, and the Widener Library. See page 179.

▽ **Fenway Park.** Watch the Red Sox try to knock one over left field's looming Green Monster at the country's oldest ballpark. Baseball legends Babe Ruth, Ted Williams, and Cy Young all played here. Guided tours are available. See page 159.

△ **Faneuil Hall Marketplace.** Brimming with restaurants, retail stores, and eclectic entertainers, historic Faneuil Hall is known as the 'The Cradle of Liberty' for the pre-revolutionary activities it hosted, including speeches by Samuel Adams. See page 108.

THE BEST OF BOSTON: EDITOR'S CHOICE

The very best of Boston for all kinds of travelers: from festivals to family-oriented attractions, markets to money-savers.

BEST FOR FAMILIES

Boston by Little Feet. An hour-long walking tour of the Freedom Trail for ages 6–12. See page 258.
Boston Common splash pad and Frog Pond. Skating in winter. See page 90.
Boston Duck Tours. Tours of Boston and the Charles River aboard World War II amphibious vehicles. See page 255.
Children's Museum. A hands-on place mixing educational and fun activities. See page 250.
Franklin Park Zoo. Exotic animals, a tropical rain forest and a petting zoo. See page 250.
Museum of Science and Hayden Planetarium. World-class, exciting look-and-touch museum. See page 197.
New England Aquarium. Sea otters, penguins, dolphins, a giant tank, plus live shows. See page 124.
Swan Boats. Since 1877, these pedal-powered boats have plied the Public Garden lagoon. Enjoy fifteen-minute rides from mid-April to September. See page 148.
USS _Constitution_. 'Old Ironsides,' the oldest commissioned ship in the US Navy, is a floating antidote to dry textbook history. See page 139.
Whale Watch. Cruise lines set sail in the hope of sighting the mammals. See pages 134.

BEST FESTIVALS AND EVENTS

Boston Marathon. A famous, grueling, 26-mile-run on the third Monday in April. See page 256.
Battle of Lexington Reenactment. The Minutemen versus the British, each April on Patriot's Day. See page 249.
Independence Day (Fourth of July). The Boston Pops performs a free evening concert at the Hatch Shell on the banks of the Charles River, culminating in a spectacular fireworks display. See page 250.
New England Spring Flower Show. The nation's oldest annual flower exhibition lasts for one week in March. See page 249.

St Patrick's Day Parade. Boston's Irish community hosts a big parade on the Sunday nearest to March 17. See page 249.
North End Festivals. A joyous series of saints' day feasts are held at weekends in July and August. Streets are closed to traffic and the aromas of fried dough and grilled sausage and peppers permeate the air. See page 117.
First Night. New Year's Eve arts and entertainment events are held throughout the city from mid-day to the wee hours of January 1. See page 250.
For a full list of events, see page 249.

ABOVE: Little Italy in Boston's North End during a street festival.
LEFT: at Franklin Park Zoo.

BEST MARKETS

Farmers' Markets. Held at Copley Square Plaza on Tuesdays and Fridays, 11am–6pm, and at City Hall Plaza on Mondays and Wednesdays, 11am–6pm, both from late May until late November.

Haymarket Square. This plaza in the North End becomes a bustling open-air farmers' market on Fridays and Saturdays.

Chinatown. A compact area near the Theater District, this is packed with gift and antiques shops, and food markets. See page 105.

Quincy Market. Packed with take-out eateries, souvenir vendors, and gift shops. See page 108.

Formaggio Kitchen. Offers hundreds of specialty cheeses, artisanal oils, hard-to-find spices and other delicacies, at 244 Huron Avenue, Cambridge (tel: 354-4750) and a smaller location at 268 Shawmut Avenue, South End (tel: 350-6996). See page 196.

Savenor's. A gourmet butcher and grocery in Beacon Hill offering exotic game, rare cheeses, fresh fish, and more. 160 Charles Street (tel: 723-6328). See page 90.

BEST WALKS

Freedom Trail. Sixteen locations that played a part in the city's Colonial and Revolutionary history are linked by a 2.5-mile (4km) red-brick and red-painted path. See page 40.

Beacon Hill. Narrow, gas-lit streets, row houses, and haunts of Boston's elite characterize this storied neighborhood bordering Boston Common. The Black Heritage Trail lies along the way. See page 75.

Back Bay. Amble along the Commonwealth Avenue's Mall, Newbury Street's fashionable shopping district, and quiet Marlborough Street, admiring Boston's finest residential architecture. See page 145.

Charles River Esplanade. Walkways along the banks of the Charles are popular with strollers, cyclists, and joggers, and offer splendid city views. See page 86.

Boston Common and the Public Garden. The 48-acre (19-hectare) Common is America's oldest public park (1634). Adjacent is the country's first public botanical garden, with rambling paths and formal flower beds. See pages 89 and 148.

Battle Road. Trace the route taken by the Minutemen and Redcoats on April 19, 1775, at the start of the American Revolution. See page 206.

ABOVE: joggers on the Charles River Esplanade.
ABOVE LEFT: Heymarket Square farmers' market.

BEST FREE ACTIVITIES

Arnold Arboretum. Part of Harvard University; free at all times. See page 174.

Art Galleries. Many galleries, including those along Newbury Street, are free to enter. See page 158.

Boston Public Library. Home to murals by John Singer Sargent and Puvis de Chavannes; free at all times. See page 152.

Campus Tours. Free guided tours are offered of both MIT and Harvard University. See page 186.

Church Concerts. King's Chapel: Numerous free musical events, including recitals featuring jazz, folk, and classical music. Emmanuel Church (Newbury Street): Sunday morning's 10am service, September to May, usually includes a cantata by J.S. Bach. See pages 95 and 150.

Trinity Church. Henry Hobson Richardson's Romanesque masterpiece in Back Bay contains interior decorations by John La Farge and William Morris. See page 151.

FREE MUSEUMS

Some museums are free at certain times:

USS *Constitution* and Museum. Free at all times. See page 139.

Museum of Fine Arts. Free on Wednesdays, 4–9.45pm. See page 162.

Institute of Contemporary Art. Free Thursdays, 5–9pm, and for families on the last Saturday of the month, except in December. See page 127.

Children's Museum. $1 on Fridays, 5–9pm, and free for active New England teachers (K-8). See page 126.

MIT List Visual Arts Center. Free at all times. See page 195.

Above: in the Boston Public Library.
Right: artworks at the MFA.

BEST BARS WITH LIVE MUSIC

Bee Hive. Popular South End bar and eatery with a bohemian vibe and live jazz and blues. 541 Tremont Street. See page 173.

Middle East. Local rock, indie, and folk bands on the rise. 472 Massachusetts Avenue, Cambridge. See page 254.

The Plough and Stars. A tiny Irish bar with a wide range of music. 912 Massachusetts Avenue, Cambridge. See page 254.

Regattabar. Upscale bar featuring top jazz performers. Charles Hotel, 1 Bennett Street, Cambridge. See page 254.

Ryles Jazz Club. Live jazz, blues, Brazilian, and Latin music. 212 Hampshire Street, Cambridge. See page 254.

Wally's Café. A hole-in-the-wall, long-running jazz and blues joint in the South End. 472 Massachusetts Avenue. See page 254.

BEST CHEAP EATS

Central and Harvard squares. Clusters here (and on Massachusetts Avenue) of many good-value eateries. See page 198.

Charlie's Sandwich Shoppe. South End diner with all-day breakfast and a signature turkey hash. 429 Columbus Ave. See page 173.

Chinatown. Many inexpensive places open late. See page 105.

Food Trucks. Inexpensive food trucks can be found at 20 public locations around Boston. See page 56.

North End. This predominantly Italian district has great pizzerias, sub shops, and coffee houses. Among the best deals are Pizzeria Regina (11.5 Thatcher Street), Dino's (141 Salem Street), and, for fresh seafood, the Daily Catch (323 Hanover Street). See page 118.

ABOVE LEFT: Alex Cuba performing at the Regattabar.
ABOVE: Chinatown eatery.

MONEY-SAVING TIPS

Go Boston Card. Tel: 866-628-9027; www.smartdestinations.com. Unlimited admission to 58 attractions and tours, good for one, two, three, five, or seven days. A one-day pass is $60 for adults and $40 for children. Passes can be purchased at Boston Common and The Prudential Center visitor information centers.

Boston CityPass. Tel: 888-330-5008; www.citypass.com. Nearly 50 percent savings on five famous attractions:

the Museum of Fine Arts, Museum of Science, New England Aquarium, Skywalk Observatory at Prudential Center, and either the Harvard Museum of Natural History or the Revolutionary Boston at The Old State House. The pass ($46 adults, $29 children) is good for nine consecutive days, and sold at all attractions included in the pass.

MBTA Visitor Pass. Tel: 888-844-0355; www.mbta.com. A one-day LinkPass ($11) or weekly LinkPass ($18) covers unlimited travel on the

subway (the T), local buses, the Inner Harbor Ferry, and Commuter Rail Zone 1A. Passes are sold at the Back Bay, Downtown Crossing, North Station, and South Station ticket offices. See website for more sales locations.

BosTix Ticket Booth. Tel: 262-8632; www.bostix.org. Tickets and information for over 100 entertainment and cultural attractions, including day-of, half-price theater tickets. Faneuil Hall and Copley Square, Tue–Sat 10am–6pm, Sun 11am–4pm.

THE HUB OF THE UNIVERSE

History, architecture, sports teams, museums, restaurants – Bostonians have much to be proud of, and proud they are.

'The Bostonian who leaves Boston ought to be condemned to perpetual exile.' This line in William Dean Howells's *The Rise of Silas Lapham* conveys a sense of the fierce loyalty and pride Bostonians feel for their city. Boston certainly gives its residents plenty to be proud of: historic landmarks on the Freedom Trail, foodie-beloved restaurants, diverse architecture, world-class art museums, a revitalized waterfront, 34 Harbor Islands, high-end boutiques, character-filled neighborhoods, Fenway Park and the Red Sox (and the Celtics, Bruins, and Patriots), and the list goes on.

Is Bostonian pride justifiable or closer to arrogance? Perhaps no other American city has provoked so many polarized opinions. Writers in particular have always flocked to Boston, drawn by its strong literary tradition, so the quality of both praise and invective is of an uncommonly high standard. In 1860, Harvard professor Oliver Wendell Holmes called it 'the thinking centre of the continent, and therefore of the planet.' Other 19th-century boosters went even further, extending Holmes's tongue-in-cheek description of the Massachusetts State House as the hub of the solar system to the city itself, calling Boston 'The Hub of the Universe'; today 'The Hub' is still a name locally synonymous with Boston. Spanish philosopher George Santayana called Boston 'a moral and intellectual nursery.' 'A museum piece,' thought architect Frank Lloyd Wright. 'A hole,' wrote the poet Robert Browning.

Most people find that neither the positive nor critical superlatives capture the whole of Boston. The city and the attitudes of its residents are diverse, and each visitor experiences for himself the city that Mark Twain (or arguably Ralph Waldo Emerson or Thomas Appleton) described simply as a 'state of mind.'

PRECEDING PAGES: Public Garden in the snow; sail boats on the Charles River. **LEFT:** Downtown. **ABOVE:** Boston Public Library.

THE BOSTON CHARACTER

Bostonians pride themselves on their cultural and intellectual achievements, and on their sense of uniqueness reflected in the contrast between old colonial heritage and modern commercial thrust.

Boston's self-proclaimed status as the Hub of the Universe, though it wasn't meant to be taken entirely seriously, was a red rag that has infuriated many literary bulls, who could not understand what the big fuss was about. 'Boston prides itself on virtue and ancient lineage – it doesn't impress me in either direction,' wrote the philosopher Bertrand Russell in 1914. 'It is musty, like the Faubourg St-Germain. I often want to ask them what constitutes the amazing virtue they are so conscious of.'

Russell is certainly not the only one to have been mystified by the diverse and dynamic characteristics of Boston. For more than two centuries, the Boston character has delighted and infuriated, almost in equal measure, and has defeated attempts to define it. Such attempts, some Bostonians will tell you, are in any case futile unless you had the good fortune to be born and brought up in the Hub of the Universe. And so the debate goes on.

Birth of the Brahmins

In the mid-19th century, the virtue on which Bostonians prided themselves was culture, as the New World, rapidly approaching adulthood, sought to convey its maturity to the Old. When Oliver Wendell Holmes described the wealthy and influential Boston merchant families as 'Boston Brahmins,' they readily approved. Not only was the alliteration attractive, but

the term also suggested an ancient lineage, a certain austerity, and unquestioned wisdom. No matter that the 19th-century businessmen who ran Boston were often closer in their intellectual interests to Donald Trump than to an Indian ascetic: 'Brahmin' was accepted. No Madison Avenue copywriter could have done a better job.

The tone had been conveyed in 1841 by British George Combe, a phrenologist who, having studied the heads of the city's inhabitants from 1838 to 1840, delivered the kind of prognosis that court physicians reserved for absolute monarchs: 'The cerebral organization of this people, taking them all in all, appears

---

LEFT: a student at Boston University, one of over 250,000 in the city's various higher education institutions. **RIGHT:** café culture on Newbury Street.

really to have been enlarged in the moral and intellectual regions by long cultivation, added to the influence of a favorable stock.' The city's establishment was undoubtedly pleased with the prognosis.

As Boston's richness in art and architecture increased and its intellectual community grew, the city became known as the 'Athens of America.' The Boston Brahmins were swelling with pride, but not everyone appreciated

BOSTON DRIVERS

Many visitors remark that the locals' driving behavior sets Boston apart from other American cities. The layout of the city's roads remains more faithful to 17th-century cow tracks than to anything resembling a grid, and encourages local drivers to be aggressive: they speed constantly, change lanes erratically, and tailgate alarmingly. Visitors from Europe are familiar with such behavior; visitors from other American cities think they're in a Hollywood movie. Given the jams, cabs aren't always helpful either; as the joke has it: 'Shall we walk or do we have time to take a cab?' Luckily, Boston is one of America's most walkable cities.

Boston's newfound culture to the same extent: 'In Boston,' wrote Charles Mackay in 1859, 'the onus lies upon every respectable person to prove that he has not written a sonnet, preached a sermon, or delivered a lecture.' The problem for many was that Boston, rather than creating its own distinctive culture, was slavishly imitating the discredited characteristics of its cast-off colonial parent. 'The Bostonians are really, as a race, far inferior in point of anything beyond mere talent to any other set upon the continent of North America,' wrote Edgar Allan Poe in 1849. 'They are decidedly the most servile imitators of the English it is possible to conceive.'

Even the Bostonians' speech patterns and accent came under fire as being slavish replicas of Oxford English. As an anonymous wit put it, if you hear an owl hoot 'To whom' instead of 'To who,' you can be sure it was born and educated in Boston. Such criticisms can now be laid to rest (especially given the pronounced South Boston accent). Today's Boston accepts a variety of influences of course, and is all the more interesting and complex for doing so, but ultimately it is a city that isn't trying to be anything but Boston.

The Boston intellect is no doubt influenced by the large number of higher education institutions in its vicinity, including Harvard, MIT, Boston College, Northeastern, Boston University, Brandeis, and Tufts.

Split personality

Walking in Boston is often a necessity due to the traffic chaos, but it is also often a pleasure, as walking enables one to savor the strange contradictions of this untypical town. The architecture expresses part of its split personality: the size, color, and design of the carefully preserved older buildings convey class, heritage, and a human scale, while the gleaming new skyscrapers and vast concrete bunkers radiate boldness, modernity, and commercial confidence but can sometimes seem soulless to the visitor. A spell of window-shopping on Newbury Street will quickly indicate that Boston is an expensive

FROM LEFT: motorcycle cop on patrol; the Public Garden, a popular meeting place; jazz busker on Newbury Street; part of the Museum of Fine Art's European art collection.

place to live; yet here also are working-class neighborhoods and dozens of bargain shops and inexpensive Irish pubs. The city is unquestionably one of America's medical hubs; yet in its very center sits the vast Christian Science complex, whose members reject many of the tenets of modern medicine.

Academics adore such paradoxes, and there are certainly plenty of academics to be found in Boston, what with Boston being a factory town whose product is college graduates. Each new generation adds its own pinch of quirkiness to the cocktail, sustaining the legend. Also, many find jobs and stay on in the area after graduating, adding fresh blood to the population and keeping urban sclerosis at bay.

No matter how many paradoxes exist in Boston, one unifying perspective remains: Bostonians love Boston. It's an attitude summed up by the old story of the Bostonian who dies and, with due dignity, approaches St Peter at the Pearly Gates in order to present his credentials and seek permission to enter. St Peter asks him where he is from, and on being told 'BOSTON', hesitates, then says, 'Well, your record is spotless, and you may come in, but I don't think you will like it here.'

DECISIVE DATES

1625
William Blackstone, 29, an Anglican clergyman and Boston's first European settler, builds a log cabin on what is now Boston Common.

1630
John Winthrop, recently elected governor of the Massachusetts Bay Company, leads the *Arbella* and 10 other Puritan ships into Boston Harbor after a three-month trip from England.

1631
Boston court officials create America's first police force by putting watchmen on duty from sunset to sunrise.

1635
The Boston Latin School, the nation's first public school, is founded.

1636
The Puritans show their commitment to education by founding a college at New Towne, later Cambridge. It was subsequently to be named after its English-born benefactor, John Harvard, a young Charlestown minister.

1640
Stephen Day, a locksmith and ironworker turned printer, publishes the first book produced in the colonies, *The Bay Psalm Book*.

1660
A Quaker, Mary Dyer, is hanged on the Boston Common. The Quakers are denounced by the Puritans as a 'cursed sect.'

1684
The Massachusetts Bay Colony Charter is revoked, bringing to an end Puritan independence from royal control.

1690
The first American newspaper, *Publick*

Occurences: Both Foreign and Domestick, is published in Boston.

1692
The Salem Witch Trials begin, leading to the arrest and imprisonment of over 150 people.

1716
The Boston Light, the oldest lighthouse in the nation, is erected in the harbor.

1761
Boston lawyer James Otis declares: 'Taxation without representation is tyranny.'

1764–1765
The Sugar Act (1764) and the Stamp Act (1765) arouse anti-royalist sentiments.

1770
British troops fire on a rock-throwing mob, killing five, an incident that becomes known as The Boston Massacre.

1773
Phillis Wheatley, a young slave living with a wealthy Boston family, becomes

Our Country is the World, our Countrymen are all Mankind.

the first published African-American poet. The Boston Tea Party, in which a shipment of tea is thrown into the harbor in protest against a new threepence tax on tea, takes place.

1775
Paul Revere's ride and battles of Lexington and Concord spark American Revolution. Battle of Bunker Hill. George Washington takes command of Continental Army at Cambridge.

1776
British troops evacuate Boston. The Declaration of Independence is read from the State House balcony.

1780
John Adams drafts the Massachusetts Constitution, including a Bill of Rights; John Hancock becomes the first governor of the Commonwealth of Massachusetts.

FROM LEFT: the *Mayflower*; John Winthrop, the first governor of the Massachusetts Bay Company; the trial of Martha Corey for witchcraft in Salem, 1692; masthead of William Lloyd Garrison's abolitionist newspaper, *The Liberator.*

1795
On Beacon Hill, Paul Revere and Samuel Adams lay the cornerstone for the new State House designed by Charles Bulfinch, America's first professional architect.

1812
The War of 1812 against the British paralyzes the city's commerce.

1814
The American Industrial Revolution begins at Robert Cabot Lowell's first mill on the Charles River in Waltham.

1815
The Handel and Haydn Society, now the nation's oldest continuously performing arts organization, gives its first concert.

1822
Boston is incorporated as a city.

1831
William Lloyd Garrison begins publishing an abolitionist journal, *The Liberator*. Mount Auburn Cemetery, the nation's first garden cemetery, opens in Cambridge.

1845
Henry David Thoreau begins his three-year spell at Walden Pond.

1846
The first operation under general anesthesia is performed at Massachusetts General Hospital.

1848
Boston Public Library, the first free city library supported by taxes, opens.

1857
The filling of Back Bay begins, cleaning up a foul-smelling public dump.

1861
The Massachusetts Institute of Technology is granted its charter.

1863
The 54th Massachusetts Voluntary Infantry, the first African-American regiment, is formed. The Oneida Club plays American-style football for the first time on Boston Common.

1868
Louisa May Alcott of Concord publishes her novel *Little Women*.

1872
The Great Fire of Boston destroys Downtown, killing 33 people and razing 776 buildings.

1876
The first words are spoken over a telephone by Alexander Graham Bell.

1877
Swan boats are launched at the Public Garden.

1879
Radcliffe College is founded for women.

1881
Boston Symphony Orchestra is founded. Frederick Law Olmsted, landscape architect, begins work on Emerald Necklace park system.

1886
Henry James publishes *The Bostonians*.

1892
The First Church of Christ, Scientist, is established in Boston by Mary Baker Eddy.

1897
First Boston Marathon. The first subway in America opens at Park Street.

1903
The Boston Pilgrims defeat the Pittsburgh Pirates in the first baseball World Series.

1909
Filene's Automatic Bargain Basement opens in Washington Street.

1919
Strike of 1,300 Boston police. Breaking it brings to national prominence

Massachusetts Governor Calvin Coolidge.

1920
The Red Sox controversially sell Babe Ruth to the New York Yankees for $125,000.

1927
Italian immigrants Nicola Sacco and Bartolomeo Vanzetti are executed in a Charlestown prison for alleged killings and holdups. The case became a model for social injustice in the 1920s.

1942
Fire in a Bay Village nightclub kills 492.

1944
The computer age dawns in Cambridge laboratories as a calculating machine, 50ft (15 meters) long, gets its sums right.

1945
James Michael Curley, although under indictment for fraud, wins a fourth term as mayor.

1946
John Fitzgerald Kennedy, 29, is elected to US

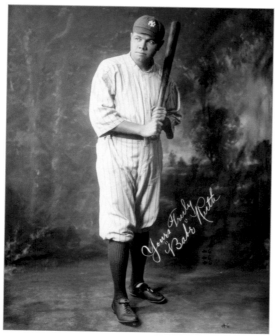

Congress from Charlestown and Cambridge.

1947
Polaroid founder Edwin Land demonstrates his first instant camera in Cambridge.

1950
A Brinks armored car is robbed in North End and the thieves net $2.7 million. Eight men are convicted six years later.

1953
The world's first kidney transplant is performed at Brigham Hospital.

1959
The Boston Redevelopment Authority begins razing the old West End, long a center for gambling dens, burlesque halls and brothels, but home to 7,000 people, and starts building Government Center and luxury apartments.

1962
The 'Boston Strangler' begins a 21-month rape and murder spree, killing 13 women.

1972
After 75 years as a men-only race, the Boston Marathon acknowledges the first women's winner.

FROM LEFT: sporting hero Babe Ruth played for the Boston Red Sox from 1914–19; the elegant swan boats in the Public Garden have been running since 1877; the Red Sox celebrate their World Series victory over the St Louis Cardinals.

1990
In the largest art heist in history, thieves remove 13 paintings worth $300 million from the Isabella Stewart Gardner Museum.

1993
The TV series *Cheers*, set in a fictional Boston bar, ends after 275 episodes.

1996
The Harbor Islands are designated a national park area.

2001
Two planes are hijacked after taking off from Logan Airport and are crashed into New York's World Trade Center, killing nearly 3,000 people.

2004
Massachusetts Senator John F. Kerry wages an unsuccessful presidential campaign. Boston Red Sox win first World Series in 86 years. Massachusetts legalizes same-sex marriage.

2005
The 14-year 'Big Dig,' replacing Downtown's elevated highway with an underground route and creating a third harbor tunnel, is completed.

2007
The Boston Red Sox win second World Series in four years.

2012
The Isabella Stewart Gardner Museum opens a new Renzo Piano-designed addition. Former Massachusetts Governor (2003–2007) Mitt Romney unsuccessfully runs for President.

THE MAKING OF BOSTON

Boston is the cradle of American independence, where Samuel Adams, Paul Revere, and John Hancock were transformed into players in a national mythology. Later, energy generated by waves of immigrants ensured that modernity wasn't suffocated by tradition.

Although a solitude-seeking clergyman named William Blackstone had settled in 1625 on a spot now occupied by Boston Common, the history of the city really dates to 1630, when John Winthrop and a group of Puritans determined to create a new society – a 'visible kingdom of God' – on the hilly Shawmut peninsula. While still aboard the *Arbella*, Winthrop laid out to his fellow colonists the terms of the covenant with the Almighty that would form the foundation of their new enterprise.

'We must be knit together, in this work, as one man,' he told them. 'We must entertain each other in brotherly affection... We must delight in each other; make others' conditions our own; rejoice together; mourn together; labor and suffer together... For we must consider that we shall be as a City upon a Hill. The eyes of all people are upon us.'

The great adventure

The Puritan colonists were Calvinist reformers, seeking to purify the English Church and develop a 'holy commonwealth.' Winthrop had joined several other middle-class Puritans in purchasing a charter issued by the king and entitling the group, known as the Massachusetts Bay Company, to occupy a strip of land between the Charles and Merrimack rivers. They also arranged to 'transfer the government of the plantation to those that shall inhabit there,' which effectively conferred independence on the company.

Winthrop set out from England on March 29, 1630, with a fleet of 11 ships and about 750 colonists. They headed to the future site of Charlestown to build a settlement. This first camp lacked reliable fresh water supplies, and several parties headed inland to where Watertown, Medford, Saugus, Dorchester, and Roxbury would arise. John Winthrop took up the invitation of an eccentric minister, William Blackstone, who sold the newcomers his land at Shawmut. Some 150 settlers moved to the site and named it Boston, after their hometown in Lincolnshire.

LEFT: British ships on the warpath in 1776.
RIGHT: eight-year-old Anne Pollard, the first white female to set foot in Boston (1630).

An age of intolerance

The town grew quickly. There were about 300 people in 1632, and 1,200 in 1640 – most living in wood houses huddled around Town Cove or in the marketplace near present-day North Square. Although democratic in structure, the government was basically a theocracy. Only male Church members could vote, and the ministers were consulted on all but administrative matters.

Settlers continued to pour into Boston – but many were more interested in the condition of their purses than the health of their souls. By the time John Winthrop died in 1649, Boston had become quite a different place, with an 'aristocracy of saints' still commanding most of the political power through the churches, and the remainder of the community devoting itself increasingly to Mammon. By the late 1630s, Boston ships were carrying loads of cod to England, Spain, and Portugal, and were returning with much-needed manufactured goods. New England ships carried West Indies

WHAT THE PURITANS BELIEVED

To the Puritans, people were naturally sinful and required unrelenting discipline. Work, frugality and humility were valued, while 'harmless' distractions such as dance, music, and stylish clothes were scorned as frivolities. Education was deemed essential, and within six years of their arrival the Puritans established a public school for children and a college for ministers (later Harvard University).

The cornerstone of Puritan theology was the Calvinist doctrine of predestination, a belief that God preordained who was saved and who was damned. The key to acceptance in Puritan society was to demonstrate clearly through pious demeanor that you were, in fact, one of God's chosen

people. Because a saint was thought to despise sin in others, much effort was put into reforming those who didn't quite measure up.

Making a public display of just how much they detested sin was also believed to be a good way of protecting the town from divine retribution, and wayward members of the community were often cruelly punished. Even minor offenses like cursing or gossiping could lead to whipping, branding, or being placed in the stocks. Ironically, the stockmaker, who gave the General Court an inflated bill, was the first to be locked in his contraption. A sailor just back from a long voyage was whipped for kissing his wife in public.

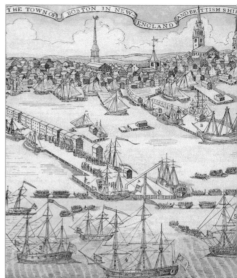

molasses to Boston distilleries, and brought slaves from Africa to the Caribbean.

Interference from England

In its first 30 years the Massachusetts Bay Colony enjoyed virtual autonomy. But when, after England's Civil War and the republican rule of Oliver Cromwell, the monarchy was restored under Charles II in 1660, this age of benign neglect came suddenly to an end. The new king quickly acted to rein in the New England colonies, which were governing themselves like a sovereign nation and bringing little revenue to the Crown. The Navigation Acts forced colonial merchants to do business exclusively with England. In order to hamstring the Puritan leadership, Charles ordered voting rights in Massachusetts be granted to all men of 'good estate' regardless of Church membership.

Although the Puritans made a fuss over the change in suffrage, most merchants simply

Puritans showed little tolerance for other beliefs. Quakers were whipped and exiled, and those brave enough to return, including Mary Dyer, were hanged from the Great Elm on the Common.

ignored the Navigation Acts. When Charles got wind of how widespread smuggling had become, he revoked the Massachusetts Bay Colony Charter in 1684, transforming New England into a single royal colony.

Charles's successor, his brother James II, continued where Charles had left off, appointing Sir Edmund Andros governor-general of the Dominion of New England in 1686. Bostonians chafed under Andros, who converted the Old South Meeting House into an Anglican church, limited town meetings to one a year, and forced all property-holders to make new payments on land titles.

The colonists were furious. When word reached them that the Catholic King James had been ousted during England's 'Glorious Revolution' of 1689, they staged an insurrection of their own, jailing Andros and shipping

FROM LEFT: the 1692 trial of George Jacobs for witchcraft; Native Americans welcome Puritans with a gift of fish on the Charles River, Massachusetts Bay Colony; British ships landing in Boston in 1776.

Paul Revere

A prominent 18th-century Bostonian craftsman and respected patriot, who also excelled as an artist, inventor, and politician.

It was a lucky day for the Bay Colony when Paul's father, Apollos Rivoire, left his home in the Channel Islands, between Britain and France, and set sail for Boston. Apollos was a talented craftsman who produced goldware and silverware of exquisite design. And on January

1, 1735, he and Mrs Rivoire welcomed an extraordinary Boston baby into the world: Paul Revere.

Paul inherited the family business, improved on his father's craftsmanship, and, from his shop in the North End, quickly won the reputation of being the best silversmith in colonial America. His career broadened to embrace enough sidelines, specialties, diversions, adventures, and excitements to satisfy a dozen men. He was an expert horseman, a skilled man-at-arms, and an authority on explosives. As a young man, he served as a worthy artillery lieutenant in the French and Indian Wars.

Through the years, Paul also excelled as an artist, inventor, merchant, mechanic, politician, engineer, orator, dispatch rider, bell-ringer, metallurgist, participant in the Boston Tea Party, printer, publisher, and propagandist. Meanwhile, he found time to marry and to sire eight children; when his first wife died, he re-married and fathered eight more.

History beckons

This, then, was the man the Committee of Safety summoned on the night of April 18, 1775. There was a critical message to be delivered. Somebody must mount up and ride post-haste to Buckman's Tavern in Lexington to warn John Hancock and Sam Adams that 800 Redcoats would be moving out from Boston to arrest them, and would then march on to Concord to destroy a store of rebel guns and ammunition.

Revere galloped to Medford, where he stopped at the home of Captain Isaac Hall, commanding officer of the local Minutemen as well as a well-known distiller of Medford rum and a most generous host. That might account for the unproven allegation that Revere hadn't bothered to wake up anybody between Charlestown and his stop-off at Isaac's.

At Buckman's Tavern, Revere joined with the alternate dispatch rider, William Dawes, who had made the run from Boston via another route. Neither Revere nor Dawes ever got to Concord that night. En route, they joined up with Dr Samuel Prescott of Concord, heading home from Lexington. The Redcoats ambushed all three horsemen, but Dawes and Prescott escaped, with Prescott managing to alert the colonial militia at Concord. The war was on.

As for Revere, the tireless old patriot was still handling enough tasks to keep 10 normal men busy when he died in 1818, aged 83. His much-visited grave is in the Old Granary Burying Ground.

LEFT: Paul Revere, a man of many talents.

him back to England. Boston's most prominent minister, Increase Mather, was sent to England to ask William and Mary, the new Protestant monarchs, to restore the original Massachusetts Bay Colony Charter. They offered a compromise: the colonists would be allowed to elect their own representatives, but suffrage would be extended to all property-holders, irrespective of religion, and the Crown would appoint the governor. Puritan ideals would remain an integral part of everyday Boston life, but the old theocratic order was broken.

The rise of the merchant class

With suffrage now open to all property-holders, a class of wealthy merchants emerged as an influential force in Boston's affairs. Shipbuilding, cod fishing, and the 'triangle trade' (shipping fish and crafted goods to Europe and picking up molasses and slaves in the West Indies) enriched entrepreneurs, who built handsome homes, and financed civic projects such as Faneuil Hall. But, although a handful of merchants were doing well, the rest of the city was not. There was competition from other colonial towns, especially

New York and Philadelphia, and the French and Indian Wars, which flared again in 1740 and 1754, had also hit the town hard – hundreds of men were killed, ships were destroyed, and the city was overburdened with the care of widows and orphans. By the time the French were defeated in 1763, Boston was in perilous economic condition. Just as it began to recover, the British renewed the old tug-of-war by trying to impose further taxes. In doing so, they lit the fuse of revolution.

FANEUIL HALL'S WEATHERVANE

The weathervane in the shape of a grasshopper atop Faneuil Hall – sometimes called 'Jiminy Cricket' – is said to have been placed there by none other than Peter Faneuil, who donated the building to the city in 1742. Faneuil, who had been a member of the Royal Exchange, remembered a similar ornament atop the Exchange's London HQ. Sir Thomas Gresham, the Exchange's founder, was said to have been an abandoned baby, found in a field in 1519 by children chasing grasshoppers. As a successful financier, he supposedly erected the Exchange weathervane in memory of his humble origins.

ABOVE: Harvard College buildings in 1743.

The road to rebellion

England's aim was to get as much money out of the colonies as possible. In 1763, King George III launched the effort with a battery of legislation that prohibited colonial currency and cracked down on the lucrative sugar trade between Boston and the West Indies. Before New Englanders could mount an effective protest, Parliament also passed the Stamp Act (1765) requiring colonists to pay taxes on legal documents.

To Bostonians, these restrictions were worse than the old Navigation Acts. The rallying cry went out, 'No taxation without representation,' as mobs took the protest into the streets. At the heart of the uproar was an organization called the Sons of Liberty, which included Paul Revere, John Hancock, Dr Joseph Warren, and their leader, Samuel Adams. While the Sons of Liberty were raising hell in Boston, the hastily formed Stamp Act Congress called for an American boycott against British goods. By March 1766, the boycott had caused so much damage to British commerce that King George III relented and lifted the tax.

King George didn't take defeat lightly. In 1767 his new chancellor of the exchequer,

Charles Townshend, lashed out with a new tax on imported items such as paper, lead, and tea. Again, the town reacted with predictable fervor. When the Massachusetts House of Representatives issued Sam Adams's 'circular letters' denouncing the Townshend Acts, the governor closed it down – and Bostonians hit the streets. Four thousand British soldiers were sent to quell the unruly mobs. An ugly game of brinkmanship finally erupted into all-out violence on March 5, 1770, when a group of Redcoats fired into a threatening crowd. This 'Boston Massacre' claimed the lives of five colonists. Ironically, the Townshend Acts were repealed in England on that very day. But a nominal tax on tea remained.

The Boston Tea Party

The tea tax won no friends in Boston, and when the first loads arrived in Boston Harbor, the Sons of Liberty were ready. On December 16, 1773, about 50 townsmen disguised as Indians boarded the cargo ships and dumped the tea into Boston Harbor while a crowd of thousands cheered from the wharves.

The Boston Tea Party was more than the British could tolerate. They unveiled the Coercive Acts, closing Boston Harbor, dissolving the government of Massachusetts, installing General Thomas Gage as military governor and providing for the use of private homes to quarter British troops. Thousands moved out of Boston, and business in the town ground to a halt.

In September 1774, the First Continental Congress met in Philadelphia and voted to form a colonial army. In and around Boston,

JOHN ADAMS

John Adams, who would emerge as one of the most important American revolutionary figures and who would serve as the second US president from 1797 to 1801, was a rising attorney in the years before the rebellion. One of his most unusual cases – and one which earned him the temporary enmity of many of his fellow patriots – was his defense of the soldiers involved in the 1770 Boston Massacre. Adams and fellow lawyer Josiah Quincy, both ardent foes of British oppression but equally supportive of the right to fair trial, won acquittal for seven of the nine Redcoats. The other two were branded on the hand for manslaughter.

citizens stockpiled guns and ammunition. When General Gage heard of a weapons cache in Concord, 20 miles (32km) west of Boston, he sent 800 Redcoats to capture it. But as his troops prepared to move out, on the night of April 18, 1775, Paul Revere was already paddling across the Charles River to warn the countryside of the British march. When he reached Charlestown he borrowed a horse and rode into the countryside, warning villagers that the British were coming.

By the time the British regulars reached Lexington Green en route to Concord, 70 local 'Minutemen' – armed civilians pledged to fight at a minute's notice – were assembled. The rebels were ordered to lay down their weapons, but refused. The British fired, the rebels scattered – and when the smoke finally cleared, eight Minutemen lay dead.

The British marched on to Concord, destroyed the few weapons they found there,

The Sons of Liberty were unlikely conspirators: Sam Adams was a failed businessman; John Hancock the wealthiest man in New England; Joseph Warren a physician; Paul Revere a working-class Renaissance man.

and tried to return the same way they came. But by then rebels were hidden along the road and peppered the Redcoats with musket fire all the way back to Charlestown. By the time the troops returned to Boston, 73 Redcoats had been killed and 200 wounded.

The Battle of Bunker Hill

As news of the confrontation at Lexington spread out from Boston, thousands of colonials poured into the area, forming an arching line of siege between Charlestown and Boston Neck. On June 17, 1775, more than 2,600 Redcoats tried to break the siege by storming a rebel position on Breed's Hill (adjacent to Bunker Hill). The colonials repelled two attacks and then, running out of ammunition, retreated on the third. It was a pyrrhic victory for the British, who sustained more

FROM LEFT: 19th-century illustration of Paul Revere riding to Lexington to warn the Minutemen of the British advance; patriots dressed as Indians destroying crates of tea at the so-called Boston Tea Party; the Battle of Bunker Hill.

than 1,100 casualties, and an enormous boost in American spirits.

Less than a month later, General George Washington arrived in Cambridge and took command of the colonial forces. The siege of Boston continued through the bitter winter of 1775–6, until Washington forced out the British with a clandestine placement of artillery on Dorchester Heights. On March 17, 1776, nearly 9,000 Redcoats and 1,000 Tories sailed away while American militiamen reoccupied the town. The Revolution raged for seven more years and, although Boston was spared further combat, the population was reduced from 20,000 to 6,000 residents.

Rise of the Brahmins

After the Revolution, Boston returned to business as usual. Wealthy merchants were still in control of local affairs, although their port city still largely resembled the colonial outpost of the century past. All that changed between 1795 and 1818, as the merchants' money, and the genius of a young architect named Charles Bulfinch (see page 61), transformed an 18th-century town of wooden houses and crooked lanes into a 19th-century city of cobblestone and brick. Bulfinch spearheaded the development of Beacon Hill, and crowned it with the magnificent State House.

Politically, the merchant princes ensconced in their new Beacon Hill mansions were Federalists, favoring government by men of property. The egalitarian Thomas Jefferson's election as President in 1800 was bad enough news for them, but worse yet was his foreign policy. In 1807, hostilities with England led to the Embargo Act, which nearly strangled the lucrative China trade. The War of 1812, fought to stop England forcibly checking US vessels at sea, only made a bad situation worse, and Boston ships languished in the harbor while merchants scrambled to reinvest their capital.

They found their answer in New England's rivers, which soon powered mills that produced a river of cloth. The Lowells, Appletons, and others later labeled 'Brahmins' by the doctor-poet Oliver Wendell Holmes showed impeccable timing. With European trade impaired by the war, Americans were clamoring for manufactured goods – and the old money was soon making new fortunes in the textile industry.

Reform and abolitionism

From the days of the Puritans, Boston's ruling class acknowledged its obligation to improve the conditions of the less fortunate, if not by actual material assistance, then by the power of example. But in the early years of the new century Brahmin paternalism took on a more ardent quality. The Unitarian Church grew popular. Unitarianism did away with the old Calvinist notions of predestination and original sin, stressing instead the benevolence of God and the potential for human perfectibility. The road to salvation, for Unitarians such as Ralph Waldo Emerson, was through the exercise of conscience, rationality, and tolerance.

Causes such as temperance, prison reform, and women's rights were all taken up in the new spirit of the age. But the most significant new movement was William Lloyd Garrison's crusade against slavery. In 1831, Garrison began publishing an antislavery newspaper,

FROM LEFT: section of a painting by John White Allen Scott (1815–1907) showing Broad Street as it was in 1853; streetcar on Washington Street, 1895; John F. 'Honey Fitz' Fitzgerald.

The Liberator, from a tiny office on Washington Street. Garrison's blistering diatribes naturally inflamed Southerners, but also unnerved Brahmins dependent on Southern cotton for their textile mills. Still, Boston became known as a hotbed of abolitionism, and even conservative Yankees joined the protest against slavery's expansion into western territories. When the Civil War began in 1861, Bostonians responded dutifully to Lincoln's call for volunteers.

Expansion and immigration

By the end of the Civil War, the balance of national economic power was shifting away from New England to New York City. Nevertheless, Boston was growing, and changing physically. The city's population had not only increased (to 314,000, by 1875), but landfill projects such as the Back Bay had swollen its dimensions from an original 780 acres (316 hectares) to 24,000 acres (9,700 hectares). Most important of all, Boston had undergone a huge increase in its immigrant population. Most newcomers were Irish, starved out of their homeland by the potato blight of 1845–50. Uneducated and desperately poor, they came by the thousands and huddled into tenements.

Shunned and vilified not only for their foreignness but also for their Catholicism, the Irish began to break out of the slums and into at least partial respectability only in the 1880s. To some extent that was due to modernization of the city. The installation of electric wires, the construction of the country's first subway, and the expansion of city bureaucracy created a demand for civil servants and utility workers. In 1884, Hugh O'Brien became the first Irish mayor of Boston.

As the Irish started to move up the economic ladder, a new wave of immigrants from Southern and Eastern Europe arrived at the bottom rung. By 1890, the Irish were sharing their neighborhoods with about 45,000 Italians, 4,000 East European Jews and a scattering of Poles, Portuguese, and Greeks. Bigotry reared its head again, but the tide could not be stemmed. By 1910, 30,000 Italians and 40,000 Jews were firmly entrenched in the North and West Ends.

Quintessential Boston Irish politicians like mayor John F. 'Honey Fitz' Fitzgerald, grandfather of President John F. Kennedy, dominated

city politics. Another celebrated example was James Michael Curley, who served at various times as mayor, governor, and congressman, and, in 1943, even won an election from a jail cell. A charming, witty, and ambitious man with poor immigrant parents and no formal education beyond grammar school, he devoured books on law, politics, literature, and the fine arts and had a remarkably photographic memory. By the time he was a public figure, he dressed impeccably and could impress voters by quoting passages from Shakespeare and Tennyson.

Curley thumbed his nose at both Republicans and Democrats and created a citywide patronage system, the 'Curley Machine.' He considered the bosses petty (the Democratic City Committee was a 'collection of chowder-heads') and the Brahmins 'gabbing spinsters and dog-raising matrons in federation assembled.' The day after his election he sent the Yankees into fits of apoplexy by proposing to sell the Public Garden for $10 million and put a water pumping station under the Common.

With a healthy cut of Franklin Roosevelt's New Deal and, after 1941, a piece of the war industry, Boston survived the Great Depression. But Curley's success at attracting federal projects helped lead to his downfall. With the US government supplying jobs and money, the patronage system was destroyed. Additionally, the Irish and the Brahmins were discovering the advantages of cooperation in financial and political affairs. Curley, always hated by the Brahmins and no longer needed by his old constituency, was eased out.

An era of urban renewal

Boston politics underwent a change after World War II. A younger electorate was more interested in economic progress than stale ethnic rivalries. Second- and third-generation immigrant families had now become part of the middle classes, and they wanted leaders who represented mainstream values and clean government. In 1946, Bostonians elected a congressman who seemed to epitomize those qualities. John F. Kennedy, grandson of 'Honey Fitz,' was handsome, charming, and idealistic, and he came to symbolize, both for Boston and for the nation as a whole, the hope of progressive politics.

At the local level, John Hynes, an unassuming, soft-spoken bureaucrat, handed Curley a

stunning defeat in 1949. 'Whispering Johnny' showed remarkable ambition as mayor, launching in 1957 the Boston Redevelopment Authority, which, over the next 15 years, would carry out urban renewal projects covering 11 percent of Boston's land. Public money went into a complex of government buildings, while private capital raised the Prudential Center, John Hancock Tower, and other landmark structures. By the 1970s, the thrust of the urban renewal campaign changed from mega-development to recycling. The star effort of the 1980s was Faneuil Hall Marketplace, a spectacular revival of the old Quincy Market along with adjacent Faneuil Hall.

But while resources were being lavished on the city center, trouble was brewing in the neglected outer neighborhoods. Since the war, middle-class families had been moving out to the suburbs, with the city losing nearly 250,000 residents between 1950 and 1980. The decline was exacerbated by conflicts between entrenched ethnic groups and a new influx of black and Hispanic residents. These conflicts were brought to a head during the school-bussing crisis of the 1970s, which began when a federal court ordered that racial balance in Boston public schools be remedied by bussing students out of their neighborhoods. The riots that surrounded the bussing crisis shocked the nation and stained the reputation of its 'cradle of liberty.'

The 'Massachusetts Miracle'

After years of economic stagnation, Boston in the 1980s became the hub of the 'Massachusetts Miracle,' based largely on the high-tech know-how cultivated in the region's universities. Boston's long investment-banking tradition helped get startup companies off the ground, and soon a thicket of new office towers radically transformed the skyline. Unfortunately, the end of the decade saw a marked reversal in the city's economic fortunes.

In less than 10 years' time, though, it was apparent that the 'roaring '80s' would have a successor in the dot-com '90s. Again, Boston was poised to ride the crest of the boom – and to ride out the inevitable bust. As the city celebrated its 375th anniversary in 2005, it had a lot more to boast about than mere survival

FROM LEFT: a canine supporter of Mayor James Michael Curley; John F. Kennedy applauds his brother Edward at a Democratic fundraising dinner in Boston.

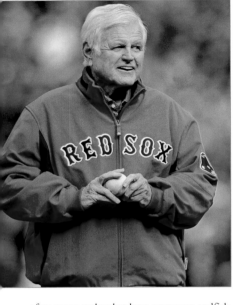

of so many cycles that have swung on codfish, rum, sailing ships, and computer chips. In 2004, the city hosted its first major-party political convention, sending local favorite Senator John Kerry into the presidential fray and generating more than $160 million in local revenues. In 2012, former Massachusetts governor Mitt Romney shone the political spotlight on Boston's convention center once again, when he based himself there for election night at the culmination of his unsuccessful bid for the US presidency. Meanwhile, at long last, the 'Big Dig' – America's most ambitious, expensive public works project – was completed, with a new tunnel under Boston Harbor and a despised elevated highway erased from the Downtown landscape. Derelict piers and tired industrial blocks in South Boston had been transformed by hotels and exhibition space. The challenges of housing and schools were met head-on, and *Forbes* magazine praised Boston as offering the best public education of any large US city.

Conflict and unity

Controversy and political contentiousness, no strangers to this city through all of its history,

continue to arrive in new packages, from old tussles between city and state, such as Boston fighting for what it considers to be its fair share of state largesse, to 'hot button' issues such as gay marriage – Massachusetts became the first US state to legalize same-sex marriage in 2004.

The same year proved to be a unifying one in another respect, however, as the Boston Red Sox baseball team finally won the World Series after an 86-year dry spell. Luckily, Boston didn't have to wait as long for its next victory – the team won the World Series again in 2007.

Not surprisingly, the city was united in approving the decision of the Red Sox owners to fix up century-old Fenway Park, and keep it right where it is. After ten years of renovations, costing $285 million, team president Larry Lucchino announced in 2011 that there are no plans for a new ballpark. There are some things you can't tamper with – especially when you are a 'City upon a Hill' and everyone's watching.

FROM LEFT: former Governor of Massachusetts, the late Ted Kennedy, prepares to throw a ceremonial first pitch; Senator John Kerry at a Democratic Convention in Boston.

The Big Dig

The most expensive highway project in America was designed to reroute traffic under the city.

Bostonians have long worked wonders with their physical surroundings, drastically expanding the size of the peninsula and linking it to surrounding communities with a lacework of bridges and tunnels. In a colossal planning fiasco, however, the traffic engineers of the 1950s isolated the North End from Downtown with the elevated Fitzgerald Expressway, or Central Artery.

The Central Artery cut an ugly swath through the city – and by the 1990s, it no longer moved traffic efficiently. Designed for 75,000 cars a day, it now carried 190,000 vehicles between points south and the Charles and Mystic river crossings of Interstate 93 and Route 1. Another problem was getting to and from Logan Airport from the south and west.

A radical solution

A radical solution was proposed: if you can't beat the cars, bury them. This remarkable project became known as the 'Big Dig,' a drastic makeover involving 15 years of hellish traffic snarls and a cacophony of excavators and pile drivers that drove people to distraction.

The elevated highway was replaced by a tunnel following the same route, a huge task that involved digging the new subterranean roadway – now the Thomas P. ('Tip') O'Neill Tunnel – while retaining the existing structure until traffic could be rerouted beneath it. Large sections of the granny knot of bridges and ramps crossing the Charles River were replaced with the dramatic Zakim-Bunker Hill Bridge, with its sleek tracery of cable stays.

Instead of the dreary green girders of the old Fitzgerald Expressway, the central city would now be bisected by a 27-acre (11-hectare) swath of parkland, officially

RIGHT: the sleep cables of the Bunker Hill Bridge.

named the Rose Kennedy Greenway. The North End, which spent two generations isolated by traffic and water on either side, could reclaim its position as a coveted place to live.

The Big Dig's other major component was a third tunnel beneath Boston Harbor. The new Ted Williams Tunnel, named for the Red Sox great (1918–2002), veers away from expressways south of the center and keeps airport traffic away from Downtown.

Escalating costs

The project was finally completed in 2005 at a cost of more than $14 billion in public funds. Contributing to such high costs was a deluge of problems. For example, it was discovered in 2011 that the tunnels' light fixtures were corroding. As of 2012, all 25,000 light fixtures were due to be replaced, at a predicted cost of $54 million.

Boston's Freedom Trail

Boston is both rich in history and small enough to navigate on foot. The Freedom Trail is a handy way for visitors to take in the most important sites.

The Freedom Trail is a 2.5-mile (4km) painted path linking 16 historic locations that all played a part in Boston's Colonial and Revolutionary history. It was born in 1951 and, in 1974, part of it became Boston's National Historical Park. Although its individual attractions are several centuries old, it was only in 1951 that newspaperman William Greenough Schofield suggested that the sites be linked in a numbered sequence. Until then, according to Schofield, 'Tourists were going berserk, bumbling around and frothing at the mouth because they couldn't find what they were looking for.'

A leisurely pace

It may be tempting to see the city by tour bus, sightseeing trolley, or the amphibious vehicles called duck boats. All provide quick introductions to some of the major sites, but only by walking can you

ABOVE: in Boston's Veterans' Day parade, groups dress as Revolutionary War-period soldiers and march with flags from Boston Common to City Hall.

LEFT: the Freedom Trail is marked by a red line of paint or brick running from Boston Common to the Bunker Hill Monument in Charlestown.

choose your own pace, decide when to eat, or explore that interesting-looking building around the corner that isn't on the tour guide's itinerary. Good walking shoes and a map are a necessity. (Free Freedom Trail maps are available at the National Park Visitor Center at 15 State Street next to the Old State House, or at the Visitor Center at the Boston Common at 148 Tremont Street, near Park Street, or download one in advance at www. thefreedomtrail.org.) The entire trail can be walked in one day, but it's probably wiser to do it more leisurely over two days.

These four pages give a broad overview of the Freedom Trail. The individual attractions are covered in detail in the various chapters of the Places section; cross-references are given.

LEFT: Charles Bulfinch designed the magnificent red-brick and domed State House ('the hub of the solar system') when he was only 24. Guided tours are available.

The Freedom Trail

ABOVE: a red-brick path guides walkers through the Downtown.

BELOW: Park Street Church (see page 77) dates from 1810 and is known for its architecture and its place in abolitionist history. The hymn *America* was first sung here on July 4, 1831.

ABOVE: the Freedom Trail is well-signposted.

LEFT: King's Chapel Burying Ground (see page 96) became the town's first cemetery in 1630. A chapel joined it in 1689. Many colonists are buried here, including John Winthrop, the colony's governor; Hezekiah Usher, its first printer; and Mary Chilton, the first woman to step off the *Mayflower* in 1620.

ABOVE: on the first Monday in June, the Ancient and Honorable Artillery Company gathers at Faneuil Hall (see page 108) and parades to Copley Square (see page 152).

BELOW: the Old State House (see page 100), now a history museum, was the center of political life and debate in colonial Boston. On July 18, 1776, citizens gathered in the street to hear the Declaration of Independence read from the building's balcony.

LEFT: Old North Church (see page 115) is Boston's oldest place of worship, dating from 1723. The interior high box pews and brass chandeliers are original.

BELOW: a statue of Colonel William Prescott, who led the troops at the Battle of Bunker Hill and was said to have given the legendary order 'Don't fire until you see the whites of their eyes,' stands in front of the 221ft (67-meter) Bunker Hill Monument (see page 141).

PAUL REVERE RIDES AGAIN

Boston misses few opportunities to relive its stirring history. On March 5, Boston Massacre Day, the Charlestown Militia leads a parade from the Old State House to City Hall Plaza. Patriots' Day, on the third Monday in April, is the year's biggest celebration. Paul Revere's and William Dawes's rides are reenacted the previous evening. On the day itself, after a parade in Back Bay, the first two battles of the Revolution are staged with gusto at Lexington Green and Concord. June sees the Ancient and Honorable Artillery Company parade and on the 17th, the Battle of Bunker Hill (see page 33) is re-enacted at the Monument, following a parade from Charlestown. On July 4, the Declaration of Independence is read from the balcony of the Old State House and on December 16, the Boston Tea Party of 1773 is re-enacted (see page 32).

ABOVE: Paul Revere's House (see page 114) is the oldest house in Downtown Boston. Its frame is mostly authentic, but the interior is a recreation of a colonial

ABOVE: the Paul Revere Statue in the North End's Paul Revere Mall.

BELOW: USS *Constitution* (see page 139), or 'Old Ironsides,' is the US Navy's oldest commissioned ship and the Freedom Trail's most popular sight.

TREASURE TROVES OF ART

The founding fathers had little time for frivolities such as painting and sculpture, but their descendants determined to turn Boston into the Athens of America.

Eighteenth-century Boston, like any self-respecting English provincial capital, delighted in status symbols and luxury goods – portraits, tombstone carvings, silver teapots, and coats of arms on carriage panels. There was no artistic past; even if there had been, nobody would have cared. Boston was a thoroughly modern town: everything was fashion and the latest style. The cult of the past would arrive only later.

Monumental sculpture and history painting, the touchstones of the visual arts on the Continent, would not be appreciated to any real degree – and then only in a limited manner – until the early 1800s and the Federal era. Landscape painting would not truly flourish before the coming of the Victorians. Genre painting appeared with the Edwardians and the 'Boston School' of 1900.

Copley and Revere

In artistic terms, however, great strides were made in the 18th century by Bostonians as gifted as John Singleton Copley and Paul Revere, and the general level of artistic achievement was unsurpassed, and quite probably unmatched, in the American colonies.

Generally considered the finest artist in colonial America, John Singleton Copley was in high demand as a portrait painter. His subjects included significant colonial figures such as Samuel Adams, and, of course, Paul Revere,

whose portrait was the result of a fortuitous meeting of artist and sitter, and worth careful study for what it tells of 18th-century Boston – practical, proud, and unafraid of a dignified opulence.

The message is writ large in Copley's great realist portraits of Boston's mercantile aristocracy, featuring elegant settings and expensive costumes. Keeping these faces in mind gives added meaning to a visit to King's Chapel, where it is easiest to find the 18th century in the modern city. The air is chill and sweet with an unmistakable New England tang. Copley's portraits are shown in the Museum of Fine Arts (MFA), which in 2010 opened an 'Art of the Americas' wing with 5,000 works on view.

PRECEDING PAGES: *West Church* by Maurice Prendergast. **LEFT:** *Mrs Fiske Warren and her Daughter* by John Singer Sargent. **RIGHT:** self-portrait by John Singleton Copley.

19th-Century Boston

The Revolution changed many of Boston's players, but the game remained the same as the city entered its 19th-century era of greatness. Even so, the arts remained more than a little suspect. John Adams, with a whiff of brimstone, still pondered whether the arts, those suspicious handmaidens of luxury and aristocracy, had any place in a democracy. 'Are we not,' he cautioned with fretful anxiety, 'in too great a hurry in our zeal for the fine arts?' Federal Boston, unlike earlier periods, remains very much in evidence, with Charles Bulfinch's gold dome of the State House – it was originally gray – dominating Beacon Hill. Esthetically, the city today is its own greatest asset, with the carefully preserved Federal townscape of the Hill blending seamlessly with the Victorian sweep of the Back Bay.

Nineteenth-century Boston took pride in its transformation of the 'howling wilderness' into

THE BOSTON SCHOOL

Painting would flourish once again around 1900 with the emergence of the 'Boston School.' Encouraged by the vital example of John Singer Sargent, who indulged the contemporary taste for mural painting in the Boston Public Library, MFA, and Harvard's Widener Library, the work of William Paxton and Edmund Tarbell clearly also grew out of the esthetic shock administered by Mrs Gardner's superb Vermeer at Fenway Court. (This Vermeer and several other treasures were stolen in 1990 during a $300-million art heist.)

The Boston School summarized everything that Boston had come to admire in the arts: technical skill, languid sentiment, and an often maddening refinement

brought to the study of a narrow, genteel world. Looks can be deceiving, because the style took root with the rude health of a roadside weed, and its practitioners are still numerous and popular. Their work, in fact, fuels the success of today's Newbury Street art market.

Newbury Street, long the center of the art market and the luxury trades in Boston, has always suffered because of its proximity to New York. Madison Avenue is too close for comfort, and collectors, no less than artists, regularly fall subject to its variety and charm. Nonetheless, artists both serious and admirable remain, and the graduates of the art schools and universities continually swell the ranks.

the 'American Athens' – no mean feat in a scant 200 years when the odds are stacked against you. Educational, charitable, and cultural institutions (with 'fair' Harvard generally given pride of place) were carefully nurtured as the proper sphere for a 'Brahmin' aristocracy, rich beyond the wildest dreams of their immigrant ancestors and heavy with intellectual pretension. Artists were admired and assimilated as the ornaments of that society. This high regard is sometimes said to account for the decorative rather than incisive character of much of this Brahmin culture, where the unpredictable tendency of artists to comment and to criticize was curbed with the flattery of dinner invitations and with kind words.

In a few notable cases – Copley and William Morris Hunt, for example – a handsomely dowered daughter tempered the force of artistic fury.

Private Collections

Most private collections formed in 19th-century Boston were smaller and generally less showy

FROM LEFT: *Boston Common at Twilight* by Childe Hassam; *The New Necklace* by William Paxton; *The Breezy Common* by Maurice Prendergast; *Rockport, Mass* by Maurice Prendergast.

than their counterparts in New York. They were, however, often more discerning, and ranged through the entire history of taste with a remarkable lack of prejudice. The MFA has been heir to quite a few of these collections, and its galleries on Huntington Avenue are unsurpassed in areas as diverse as Asian and classical art and 19th-century French painting.

In the 1850s, Boston showed a bold and unexpected interest in modern French art. Its earliest

THE ATHENAEUM

No cultural institution was as central to the arts in Federal Boston as the Boston Athenaeum. In a series of increasingly grand homes, it mounted the city's first public exhibitions of painting and sculpture and assembled its first generally accessible public collection of art. By 1850, it had taken up residence in the Italianate palazzo on Beacon Street, where it remains. Some of its collection also remains, and some has gone to enrich the holdings of the MFA, whose parent the Athenaeum became in 1870 when it divided its responsibilities between literature and the visual arts. The Athenaeum represents the penetrating taste that marked Federal America's neoclassicism.

champion was the painter William Morris Hunt, a New Englander who had studied in France with Couture and Millet, and who married so well that Bostonians paid more attention to his taste than they might otherwise have done. They patronized his French friends and acquired fine collections of French pictures into the bargain. Hunt is responsible for many of the Millets and Monets that found their way to the MFA.

In plastic arts, the MFA's Egyptian Old Kingdom collection, unrivaled except at the Cairo Museum, is the result of joint Harvard-MFA expeditions, which began in 1905 under the direction of Dr George A. Reisner. The glorious sculpture and the architectural pieces in the Indian Art section owe much to joint MFA-University of Pennsylvania expeditions.

A number of other institutions, mainly educational, have also assumed the role of the private collector. The Harvard Art Museum in Cambridge houses outstanding collections. Also noteworthy are the Rose Art Museum at Brandeis University in Waltham, with its remarkable contemporary American art, and Wellesley College's Davis Museum in Wellesley, with its distinguished historical collection. The progressive Institute of Contemporary

---

HOW ISABELLA STEWART GARDNER BUILT AN INSTITUTION

Isabella Stewart, born in New York in 1840, became a Bostonian when she married the financier John 'Jack' Lowell Gardner. The Brahmin and his vivacious wife, whose actions were often frowned upon by proper Bostonians, became enthusiastic art collectors and filled their Commonwealth Avenue home with treasures from Europe.

When Mr Gardner died in 1889, 'Mrs Jack' set about building the Venetian palazzo of her dreams and embellishing it with her collection of spectacular paintings, sculpture, furniture, and textiles. Fenway Court opened with a private party on New Year's Day, 1903. Mrs Gardner received her guests at the head of the double staircase

while 50 members of the Boston Symphony Orchestra entertained. Logs burned in each room as guests indulged in two of her delights: doughnuts and champagne.

Mrs Gardner lived on the top floor of Fenway Court until her death in 1924, and she still presides there in the shape of her controversial portrait painted by Sargent in 1888. It caused a Boston scandal because Mrs Gardner appeared in what was then considered to be a revealing low-cut gown. Fenway Court's surfeit of masterpieces has less to do with its glory than one might expect, for although masterpieces are not in short supply, some museums would consign a good part of the collection to the storeroom.

Art offers contemporary art of varied media, including visual art, music, film, video, and performance.

Collecting as a cultural pursuit began rather later than it did elsewhere in America, and the few early local collections of importance have long since been dispersed, as have those of early institutions such as the Athenaeum. Several important collections from the second half of the 19th century were embedded more or less intact in various local museums, but one – the finest of them all – has been preserved as it was created, a few hundred yards from the MFA. For many, the MFA, with all its masterpieces, takes emotional second place to the Isabella Stewart Gardner Museum, for where the MFA is great, the Gardner is unique.

The Gardner Museum

Although the collection built up by Isabella Stewart Gardner (see box and page 157) is uneven, its highlights are remarkable. They include Giotto, Degas and Sargent, and the Titian Room is stunning. But even Titian's masterpiece is not as impressive as the ensemble Mrs Gardner lovingly created. In an age when museums have decontextualized their works of art, Mrs Gardner's context makes her Titian sing with an added resonance. There is really nothing more wonderful, or more of a piece with Boston, than the Gardner. In 2012, the Gardner opened an airy steel-and-glass expansion designed by Renzo Piano, which houses special exhibitions and a four-story concert hall. One of the project's challenges was to avoid competing with Mrs Gardner's legacy –the house and its unique collection. And because Mrs Gardner's will required that no artwork leave the building, a connecting greenhouse corridor enables paintings to move from the original building to the special exhibition space and back again.

FROM LEFT: *The Green Parasol* by John Singer Sargent; Raphael's *Portrait of Fedra Inghirami,* on display at the Gardner Museum; *The Oyster Gatherers of Cancale* by John Singer Sargent.

LITERARY BOSTON

From Puritan times to the present, Boston authors have put the distinctive stamp of the New England character on American literature.

The Puritans who founded Massachusetts placed great value on literacy. The colony's first printing press arrived in 1640, and promptly turned out *The Bay Psalm Book*. Puritan authors soon began producing original material, much of it theological. Increase Mather, in *An Essay for the Recording of Illustrious Providences* (1684), chronicled the Devil's work in Massachusetts; his son, Cotton Mather, was author of more than 400 works, including *Memorable Providences, Relating to Witchcrafts and Possessions* (1689). Puritans also penned biographies and histories: Governor John Winthrop himself wrote a chronicle of the Massachusetts Bay Colony.

Remarkably, for such a patriarchal society, 17th-century Boston produced a competent female poet. Anne Bradstreet, who arrived with the first settlers, collected her early work in *The*

Several US literary firsts took place in Boston. Harvard had the first printing press (1638). The Boston News-Letter was the first newspaper in 1704. In 1848, the Boston Public Library became the country's first.

Tenth Muse Lately Sprung Up in America, By a Gentlewoman of Those Parts (1650), which was the first book written by a woman to be published in the United States.

LEFT: Oliver Wendell Holmes reading to the Boston Society for Medical Improvement.
RIGHT: Ralph Waldo Emerson.

Political polemic

Although early 18th-century New England writers still frequently mined a religious vein – this was the era of Jonathan Edwards and his 1741 sermon 'Sinners in the Hands of an Angry God' – the era marked the beginning of a secular turn of mind. In Boston, James Franklin (brother of Benjamin) launched one of New England's first successful newspapers, the *New England Courant*, in 1721, introducing America to the urbane style of Addison and Steele.

As tensions with Britain heightened, Boston was more concerned with politics than literature. The city retained a reputation for political polemic in the mid-19th century, when William

Longfellow, James Russell Lowell, Harriet Beecher Stowe, Henry David Thoreau, Mark Twain, and John Greenleaf Whittier.

The Fireside Poets

The post-Civil War 'Indian Summer' of New England literature was the era of William Dean Howells, who made Boston the setting of *A Modern Instance* (1882) and *The Rise of Silas Lapham* (1885), both about men on the make. Henry James set many of his short stories in Boston upper-class society, and satirized the city's radical and reformist circles in *The Bostonians* (1886).

On a gentler note, Boston and its environs nurtured the 'Fireside Poets' of the late 1800s.

Lloyd Garrison made it the base for his abolitionist newspaper, *The Liberator*. The true center of New England literary activity in those years was Concord (see box), while Boston itself was renowned as a publishing capital. Periodicals such as *The North American Review* and *The Atlantic Monthly*, and the downtown publishing firm of Ticknor and Fields, helped secure its reputation. Ticknor and Fields published a seriously impressive list of authors, including Horatio Alger, Charles Dickens, Ralph Waldo Emerson, Nathaniel Hawthorne, Oliver Wendell Holmes, Henry Wadsworth

CONCORD'S RENAISSANCE

In 1836, a Unitarian clergyman living in Concord published *Nature*, an essay emphasizing the unity of the individual soul with all creation and with the divine. Ralph Waldo Emerson became the outstanding voice not only of the Transcendentalist movement the essay helped inspire, but also of a famous coterie of Concord writers.

The 'Concord Renaissance' included Emerson's friend Henry David Thoreau. The two men became the focus of New England Transcendentalism, a literary movement that emphasized emotion, intuition and nature, and above all valued the individual above society. Striving for self-sufficiency, the 27-year-old Thoreau built his own home on the shores of Walden Pond, on land owned by Emer-

son. He lived there from 1845 to 1847, growing his own food, fishing, and meditating. He later documented these two years of solitude in 18 essays called *Walden; or, Life in the Woods* (1854). His most influential essay was *Civil Disobedience*, published in 1849.

Another prominent member of the circle was Bronson Alcott, father of Louisa May Alcott *(Little Women)*. A Concord school superintendent, Alcott was an educational reformer and philosopher. Nathaniel Hawthorne, of *The Scarlet Letter* (1850) and *The House of Seven Gables* (1851) fame, was also close to the Concord Transcendentalists. All of these authors lie in Concord's Sleepy Hollow Cemetery.

> The phrase 'One if by land, Two if by Sea' was coined by Henry Wadsworth Longfellow in his historically inaccurate poem 'Paul Revere's Ride,' first published in 1861.

Working in genres such as the pastoral (John Greenleaf Whittier's 1866 'Snow-Bound') and historical narrative (Henry Wadsworth Longfellow's 'Evangeline' and 'The Song of Hiawatha,' published respectively in 1847 and 1855), these poets were often read aloud. This genteel tradition was shared by writers such as poet and essayist Oliver Wendell Holmes, Sr (*The Autocrat of the Breakfast-Table*, 1858), and poet James Russell Lowell. (The poetic tradition ran strong in later generations of Boston's Lowell family. Amy Lowell was a leader of the early 20th-century Imagists, and Robert Lowell's *For the Union Dead* and *The Public Garden* take up Boston themes.)

Children's classics

Boston has also featured in what have become timeless children's literature classics, enjoyed by generations of youngsters. Robert McCloskey wrote and illustrated *Make Way for Ducklings* (1946), a children's book about a family of ducks living in the Boston Public Garden's Lagoon. E.B. White set part of *The Trumpet of the Swan* (1970) in the Public Garden, too. A slightly older audience reads Esther Forbes's *Johnny Tremain* (1943), a novel that retells events leading up to the American Revolution from the perspective of a young teenage boy.

Contemporary concerns

The critical view of Boston society resounded in John P. Marquand's skewering of the Brahmins in *The Late George Apley* (1937), and in George Santayana's *The Last Puritan* (1936). John Updike presented the quandaries of his characters in early novels and stories set in the Boston suburbs. Edwin O'Connor offered an insightful portrayal of a James Michael Curley-based Boston politician in *The Last Hurrah* (1956). In response to McCarthyism, Arthur Miller wrote *The Crucible*, a play about the events leading up to the Salem Witch Trials in 1692–3, during which over 150 people were prosecuted.

Boston lawyer George V. Higgins gave us the rough side of his city's life and language via *The Friends of Eddie Coyle* (1972). Archibald MacLeish, a onetime Boston lawyer, struck a remonstrative note in his 1976 poem 'Night Watch in the City of Boston,' written amid the school bussing crisis.

More recently, Jhumpa Lahiri's novel *The Namesake* (2003) was adapted to film in 2006; the book explores the cultural challenges faced by Indians who move from Calcutta to Cambridge. Lahiri's earlier collection of Pulitzer Prize-winning short stories, *Interpreter of Maladies* (2000), is also partially set in the Greater Boston area. Other contemporary novels set in the Boston region include Zadie Smith's *On Beauty* (2005), which follows a mixed-race British/American family, and Mathew Pearl's The Dante Club (2007).

Today, the Boston literary world comes together each October for the annual Boston Book Festival, which has been held in the Back Bay since 2009. A street festival on Copley Plaza hosts exhibits, live music, writing workshops and activities for kids, and presentations are given by authors such as Bill Bryson, Joyce Carol Oates, Ken Burns, and Orhan Pamuk.

FROM LEFT: William Dean Howells; the *Make Way for Ducklings* sculpture in the Public Garden; a scene from the 1996 film of Arthur Miller's *The Crucible*.

NEW ENGLAND CUISINE

Seafood remains one of the New England classics, but the influence of immigrants and new traditions are making their mark.

Stereotypically, Boston is considered the home of the baked bean, traditionally cooked with molasses, brown sugar, or maple syrup. Yet one will have to search scores of restaurant menus – offering everything from *crème de cailles au genièvre* to *pla rad pik* – before finding Boston brick-oven baked beans.

Not so with seafood, which figures strongly in Boston cuisine. Of course, some seafood

Food trucks are perfect for on-the-go snacks, serving everything from smoked-cod sliders (Go Fish!) to breakfast sandwiches (Clover) to cookie-dough cupcakes (Kickass Cupcakes). Visit www.cityofboston.gov/business/mobile/ for daily schedules and locations.

preferences have changed over time. The Pilgrims would have been confounded by today's mania for lobster. They considered the crustaceans fit only for pig food, or bait; well into the 19th century, boatloads of lobsters sold for pennies, and prisoners rioted at the prospect of yet another lobster dinner. Today, New England's lobster harvest rakes in millions of dollars. Creative preparations abound, but menus still feature traditional boiled lobsters and 'lobster rolls' – toasted hot dog buns filled with chunks of lobster meat, tossed with celery and mayonnaise.

Clam chowder

Boston's fabled clam chowder got its name from the Breton French settlers of Quebec, who simmered their soups in a *chaudière* (cauldron). Such long, slow cooking is needed to render the hard-shell quahogs (pronounced 'co-hogs') palatable. The small and medium-size versions – cherrystones and littlenecks – are delectable served raw, on the half-shell. Soft-shell, long-neck clams – commonly known as 'steamers' – are a favored food all along the coast, dipped first in brine (to wash off the grit), then in melted butter. Outside of the city, clam shacks fire up their fry-o-lators to prepare another favorite: clams batter-coated and fried.

Clambakes were once a New England tradition, especially on Cape Cod. The customary procedure was to lay out a stone pit on the beach, build a driftwood fire, cover the hot stones with seaweed, add clams and their

FROM LEFT: ingredients for a clambake; harvesting cranberries; Boston's most famous dish.

During the biannual Boston Restaurant Week in March and August, discounted lunches and set menus are offered at over 200 venues in Boston, Cambridge, the suburbs, and beyond.

accompaniments (typically lobsters, potatoes, and corn on the cob), and then top it all off with more seaweed, a sailcloth tarp, and plenty of sand, leaving it to bake for about an hour. Most coastal resort restaurants these days dispense with clambake per se, and just serve what's called a 'shore dinner' – steamed.

It was the abundant cod, however, that initially lured English fishermen, and eventually settlers, to the Boston area. Fillet of young cod, called scrod (from the Dutch *schrood*, for 'a piece cut off'), still graces traditional menus.

Exposure to European traditions has introduced two relatively new seafood treats. Mussels, long ignored by Boston restaurants, are now very nearly ubiquitous, usually served *marinière* (poached in white wine). Bay scallops are now available all year round, and adventurous fine restaurants serve them whole, whether on the half-shell or cooked.

Cranberries are one of the few fruits that are native to North America. Long before Vitamin C was recognized, whalers would set off to sea with a barrel of cranberries to prevent scurvy. Today, visitors can tour Massachusetts cranberry bogs and celebrate fall festivals from Plymouth to Nantucket.

INTERNATIONAL INFLUENCES

In Boston, flavors that would previously have been considered 'exotic' have entered the mainstream food vocabulary, in part due to the waves of immigration that have brought new culinary traditions to the city.

The Italian immigrants who settled in the city in the late 1800s and early 1900s left an indelible stamp on its food, and the many North End restaurants are always popular.

Boston also now has Chinese, Japanese, Thai, Vietnamese, Cambodian, Malaysian, Puerto Rican, Mexican, Haitian, and many other ethnic eateries, where clams in black bean sauce and lobster sautéed with ginger and scallions blend local ingredients into the classic cuisines of their home countries. The possibilities are endless.

This melting pot of flavors has also turned into more upscale fusion cuisine, where celebrity chefs are transforming Boston restaurant menus.

Adventurous eaters can indulge in salad of Maine rock crab with lobster knuckles and fried taro, crispy squash risotto cakes, pumpkin ravioli with mussels *marinière*, lightly fried lobster with lemongrass and Thai basil, ginger barbecued skate wing served over spicy jalapeño slaw with Boston baked beans, or seared scallops in cider sauce.

A PASSION FOR SPORT

Baseball, basketball, hockey, and football all have their fanatical followers. And few participatory activities can outpace the Boston Marathon.

On the morning after, the headline on the *Boston Globe* said it all: 'On Top of the World.' It was October 28, 2004, and for the first time in 86 years, the Red Sox were the champions of baseball. Who was on top of the world? The Sox, of course. But so were most Bostonians.

Bostonians are sports fanatics. The Red Sox, the New England Patriots (football), the Celtics (basketball), and the Bruins (ice hockey) all inspire desperate allegiance. To put it simply, Bostonians love their teams because they consider them to be their patrimony. How many times it must have been repeated during that ebullient autumn of 2004: 'If only my dad and my granddad were around to see this.'

The Sox

Before their 2004 redemption the Red Sox were considered to be not merely unlucky, but the victims of a curse – specifically, the 'Curse of the Bambino,' brought down on their heads when the team's owner sold Babe Ruth to the Yankees in 1920. It wasn't that the Sox were perennially awful. It was worse: they were often quite good, with a roster that at various times boasted all-stars like Ted Williams, Carl Yasztremski, and Roger Clemens. But they would either get into the Series and lose, as in 1946, '67, '75, and '86, or else collapse (usually at the hands of the Yankees) before season's end. Some philosophers even looked beyond the curse, portraying the team as a paradigm of Calvinist mortification in Puritanism's hometown. Still the faithful came, sinners in the hands of an angry God, to their Fenway Park shrine. And eventually their prayers were answered in 2004, and then again in 2007 with another World Series win.

The Celtics

The Boston Celtics followed a far different script, chalking up 17 NBA championships. Unlike the Sox, who began at the top and went into decline, the Celtics started disastrously when the 11-team NBA was founded in 1946. Then, coached by Arnold (Red) Auerbach and fielding such immortals as Bob Cousy, Dave Cowens, John Havlicek, Tom Heinsohn, K.C. Jones, Sam Jones, Bill Russell, and Larry Bird, they started winning until the rafters at Boston Garden (since replaced by the TD Garden, formerly the FleetCenter) had scarcely space for another banner. From the mid-1980s, the Celtics were largely eclipsed by powerhouses like the Chicago Bulls and LA Lakers,

FROM LEFT: Celtics game at the Fleet Center; the Boston Bruins take on the New York Rangers in the National Hockey League; the Patriots keep football's flag flying.

but in 2008, the Celtics won the championship again, for the first time since 1986.

The Bruins

Next to the Celtics, Boston's most successful team has been the Bruins of the National Hockey League (NHL). The Bruins logged a winning record for 23 years in a row – the longest of *any* professional team in any sport. Greatest of all Bruins was Bobby Orr, who joined the club when only 18 and who revolutionized hockey by showing that defensemen could attack and score goals. Other greats have included Eddie Shore, Phil Esposito, and Ray Borque. Scarcely a season passes when the Bruins fail to reach the playoffs. Like the rest of the North American professional hockey world, they languished in limbo throughout the 2004–5 season as a labor impasse kept NHL teams off the ice. In 2011, they won the Stanley Cup for the first time since 1972.

The Patriots

The National Football League (NFL) team now called the New England Patriots debuted in 1965. In 1971, they moved to suburban Foxboro and dropped 'Boston' from their name in favor of 'New England.' Like the Red Sox, the Pats for years never seemed more futile than when playing for the championship. Super Bowl appearances in both 1986 and 1996 ended in successive maulings by the Chicago Bears and Green Bay Packers. But, like the Sox, the Patriots made it to the promised land. Thanks to the coaching of tactician Bill Belichick, the arm of quarterback Tom Brady, and the accuracy of kicker Adam Vinatieri, the Pats won the Super Bowl for the 2001, 2002, and 2004 seasons. But for Boston fans, last year was last year. Let's see what the teams can do this season.

THE BOSTON MARATHON

It all began in 1897 when 15 runners lined up in Ashland and, when the gun was fired, started to run to Boston. Thus began the world's oldest annual marathon, held on Patriots' Day (the third Monday in April), and drawing its inspiration from the marathon at the first modern Olympics in 1896. Since 1907 the race has started at Hopkinton rather than Ashland and, since 1927, has been run over the official Olympic distance of 26 miles, 365 yards. The race passes through eight municipalities and is watched by over 500,000 spectators.

Apart from 10 years between 1973 and 1983 when the laurel wreath crowned an American entrant seven times, foreigners have dominated since World War II. The first wheelchair competitor raced unofficially in 1970, completing the course in about seven hours. Visually impaired runners also compete. Women first began to run in 1966, but official entries weren't accepted until 1972.

In the early 1980s the marathon ran into cash problems. The John Hancock financial company came up with a sponsorship deal, and prize money at Boston is now the same as that awarded at other major marathons. Today, about 20,000 runners who have met pre-entry time qualifications line up for the starter's gun, but thousands more manage to find their way to Hopkinton and then jog, walk, or limp across the finish line as unofficial entrants.

ARCHITECTURE

Boston is like a museum of architecture – but it's a living museum, still setting standards for the rest of the United States.

Boston has been called the 'most European city in America,' thanks primarily to its compact urban scale. Arguably, Chicago is its only rival as a living study of American architecture and urban planning, though due to the latter's relative youth and the catastrophic fire of 1871, Chicago can't claim a comparably rich legacy – something quite evident when one walks Boston's Beacon Hill, the North End, or Back Bay.

Utilitarian and Georgian artifacts

Like most East Coast cities, Boston has been too short on space to have preserved its earliest buildings. One exception – the Paul Revere House – survives more because of history than esthetics. Other 17th-century structures must have been similarly utilitarian, until expanding prosperity allowed grander statements.

The State House dome that dominates the skyline with its golden hue was originally covered in shingles. When they proved leaky, Paul Revere sheathed it in copper. Gold leaf was added in 1861.

British-inspired, early 18th-century Georgian architecture is best represented in Boston by the Old State House, step-gabled and gracefully steepled, at the head of State Street, and by a pair of churches – Old North, on Salem Street

LEFT: the Old State House, built in 1748. **RIGHT:** the ornate facade of the Tremont Temple Baptist Church.

CHARLES BULFINCH

Boston-born Charles Bulfinch (1763–1844), America's first professional architect, took much of his inspiration from the classical and neoclassical traditions of Europe. After graduating from Harvard University, he traveled widely in Europe, seeking the advice of Thomas Jefferson, who he met in Paris, and being strongly influenced in London by the style of Robert Adam. As head of Boston's local government for many years, he played a central role in upgrading the street system and improving Boston Common. In 1818 he became the fourth architect to take responsibility for designing the US Capitol in Washington, DC.

in the North End, and Old South Meeting House, on Washington Street. Elegantly simple, these churches have, like the Revere House, survived as much as historical icons as architectural artifacts.

The Federal period and Granite Age

Boston's Federal period of the late 18th and early 19th centuries belongs to Charles Bulfinch. Bulfinch brought the chaste, restrained Federal esthetic to the three Harrison Gray Otis houses on Beacon Hill and in the West End, and to smaller row houses on the Hill. His masterpiece is the 1795 State House, whose dome caps Beacon Hill as it once did the entire Boston skyline.

The Greek Revival 'Granite Age' survives in the three buildings of Quincy Market (1826), designed by Alexander Parris. Parris was also responsible for a Greek Revival successor to the Federal hegemony on Beacon Hill, the 1819 Somerset Club (originally the Sears mansion) at 42 Beacon Street. And Ammi Young's 1847 Custom House – the original part, beneath the 1915 tower – is a splendid coda to the Greek era in Boston.

French Empire and Renaissance Revival

Little more than two decades later, the weighty extravagances of the French Empire style arrived in the shape of Old City Hall (Bryant and Gilman, 1869). The period of Victorian eclecticism it helped usher in is best represented in the Back Bay, where historicism ran riot. The most inspired of the architects who mined the past in this era was Henry Hobson Richardson, whose 1877 Trinity Church in Copley Square is regarded as the masterwork of the man who gave his name to 'Richardsonian Romanesque.' McKim, Mead, and White finished the century of historical eclecticism with their Boston Public Library, exemplifying the Renaissance Revival.

The 20th century

Economic doldrums kept Boston architecture in an undistinguished state in the early 20th

THE JOHN HANCOCK TOWER

A photographer's favorite because of the mirrored images it provides of its more classical neighbors, New England's tallest building was designed by I.M. Pei & Partners for the John Hancock Mutual Life Insurance Co. and was completed in 1976. Its 60 stories of gray-tinted glass framed in black aluminum reach 740ft (226 meters) into the sky. Built over eight years, the tower was plagued with problems after its 10,000 panes of glass were installed. Unanticipated torquing of the structure caused some of the panes to pop out (remarkably, there were no casualties among passing pedestrians) until the building's core was stiffened.

century. But a number of non-native architectural titans soon left their mark, particularly in Cambridge. Walter Gropius, Eero Saarinen, Le Corbusier, and Alvar Aalto all designed notable structures for Harvard and MIT. On the Boston side of the Charles, I.M. Pei's work in the 1970s and '80s included the Christian Science Center and the West Wing of the Museum of Fine Arts. In 1995, the evocative Holocaust Memorial near Faneuil Hall was dedicated. It consists of six luminous 54ft (16.4 meter) glass towers, on which six million numbers are etched.

In 2006, the new home for the Institute of Contemporary Art opened. Designed by Diller Scofidio + Renfro, the dramatic, top-heavy building overlooks the waterfront. This was the first new museum to be built in Boston in over 100 years. Of course, old museums have added extensions, including the MFA's Art of the Americas wing (2010) and Isabella Stewart Gardner Museum's Renzo Piano-designed extension (2012). Also new in 2012 was Hostelling International's 450-bed downtown hostel, the first LEED-certified accommodations in the city.

Modern renewals

Boston's massive redevelopment projects of the 1960s frequently disregarded human scale. Government Center Plaza (1969) is a prime example, a stark inverted ziggurat. But in the 1970s, adaptive reuse became the byword, with

The design of the ICA (Institute of Contemporary Art; 100 Northern Avenue) balances the museum's objectives: interactive public areas are built 'from the ground up' and intimate private spaces for contemplation of art are built 'from the sky down.'

the Rouse Company's rejuvenation of Faneuil Hall Marketplace. Lewis and Mercantile wharves have been converted into condominiums. Graham Gund's Church Court condominium transforms the shell of a 19th-century Gothic Revival church into a structure that blends seamlessly with the surrounding Back Bay.

None of this is to say that original designs have been lacking. Goody, Clancy, & Associates created the splendid multi-use State Transportation Building close to the Theater District, and the landmark Tent City residential complex in the South End. Philip Johnson designed stylish high-rises at 500 Boylston and International Place. And Skidmore, Owings, & Merrill's Rowes Wharf and Boston Harbor Hotel finally gave Boston the majestic waterside portal it deserved.

FROM LEFT: Boston Public Library; the State House; Trinity Church in the shadow of the John Hancock Tower; the Financial District.

INTRODUCTION

A detailed guide to Boston and its surroundings,
with principal sites clearly cross-referenced by
number to the maps.

By American standards, Boston is old. There are cobbled streets still lit by gas-lamps and dozens of National Historic Landmarks. Yet, because of the hundreds of thousands of students who flock to the more than 50 colleges in metropolitan Boston alone (and the many who remain after graduation), Boston is also a continually renewed young city, well endowed with innovative restaurants, trendy bars, and a vibrant musical and theatrical life. It has superb museums covering art, history, and science, and outstanding modern architecture (which couldn't be further from the historic Victorian brownstones). This juxtaposition of old and new is central to Boston's character.

Boston is also a small city. Its population is around 617,000 and its area is 40 sq miles (105 sq km); and the central, most historic quarter is compact enough to be easily walkable. The broader Metropolitan Boston area, with over 100 towns, encompasses several million people.

The city proper officially consists of 21 tight little neighborhoods, each embracing its territorial imperative. Thus, those who reside in Dorchester, Charlestown, or South Boston (all part of the city) scarcely admit to being from Boston: rather, they belong to Dorchester, Charlestown, or South Boston. On the other hand, those who live in Newton or Quincy, separate cities within the metropolitan area, are perfectly content to be called Bostonians.

The harbor – always Boston's and Massachusetts's greatest natural asset – has been resurrected and the waterfront is now a joy. Then there is the river. Paris may have the Seine and Cairo the Nile, but locals exalt the glorious Charles River, which separates Boston and Cambridge. The latter, home of both Harvard University and the Massachusetts Institute of Technology, is not part of Boston but a city in its own right, with a population of about 106,000 and more than a dozen National Historic Landmarks.

Boston is also an excellent base for excursions. Head south to historic Plymouth, and the inviting beaches and dunelands of Cape Cod; to the north, discover the old seafaring towns that dot Cape Ann and points beyond. Westward lie Lexington and Concord, crucibles of the American Revolution.

PRECEDING PAGES: Copley Square's Trinity Church reflected in the John Hancock Tower; stained glass featuring state seals in the Great Hall of the Massachusetts State House. **LEFT:** cobblestoned Acorn Street in Beacon Hill. **ABOVE, FROM LEFT:** Boston Light on Little Brewster Island; Boston Children's Museum.

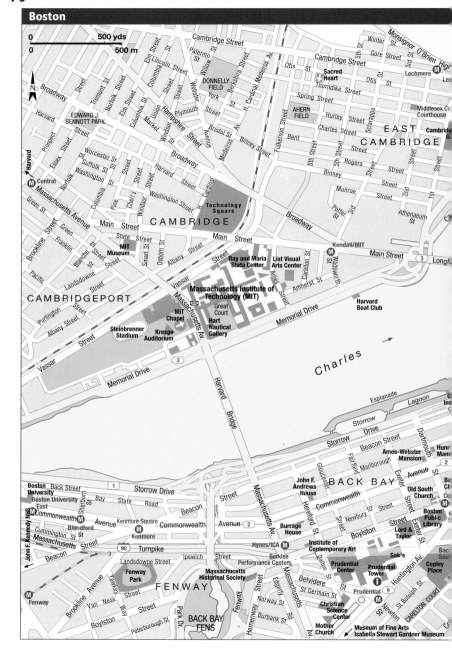

Boston

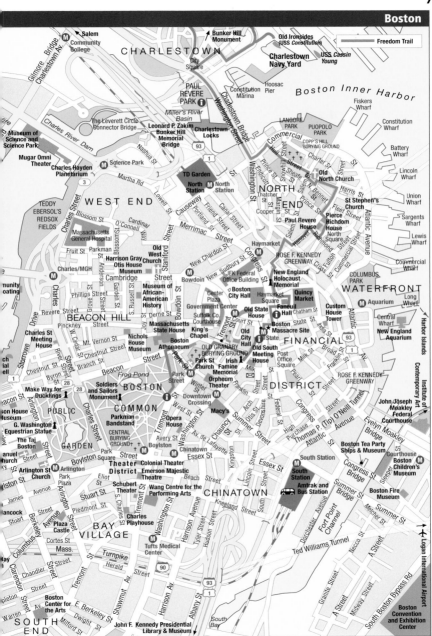

BEACON HILL AND BOSTON COMMON

The gold-domed State House overlooks the lively Common; the Freedom Trail and Black Heritage Trail meet; and architectural gems from Charles Bulfinch pepper quietly refined streets.

Back in the 1970s, when American television executives had been blindsided by the success of *Upstairs, Downstairs*, the British import depicting life among Edwardian nabobs and their servants, they did what television executives always do: they quickly cobbled together an imitation. Of course, they had to set their creation in an American neighborhood more ineradicably associated with old money, exclusivity, and propriety than any other. That neighborhood – and the name of the short-lived program – was Beacon Hill.

The Americanized *Upstairs, Downstairs* failed, no doubt in part because no one could believe that a rich Irish family could have inhabited these precincts in the 1920s, when the show was set. Beacon Hill was *ur*-Yankeedom, and it still is, at least in the cultural imagination. Today, an up-and-coming investment banker of any ethnicity can buy a million-dollar condominium on 'The Hill,' but its bricks and its gas lamps, its narrow side lanes and secret gardens, are forever associated with the elite, close-knit tribe that created them.

From 1800 to about 1870, Beacon Hill was the home of Boston's oldest, wealthiest, and most distinguished families – those whom Oliver Wendell Holmes called 'the Brahmin caste of New England, the harmless, inoffensive, untitled aristocracy.' Appleton, Cabot, Lodge, Lowell – the list includes several hundred, all of them related to early Boston settlers and many of them enriched by the china trade. It was a class, said social historian Cleveland Amory in *The Proper Bostonians*, that had

LEFT: the gleaming dome of the State House. **RIGHT:** a tour guide in period costume.

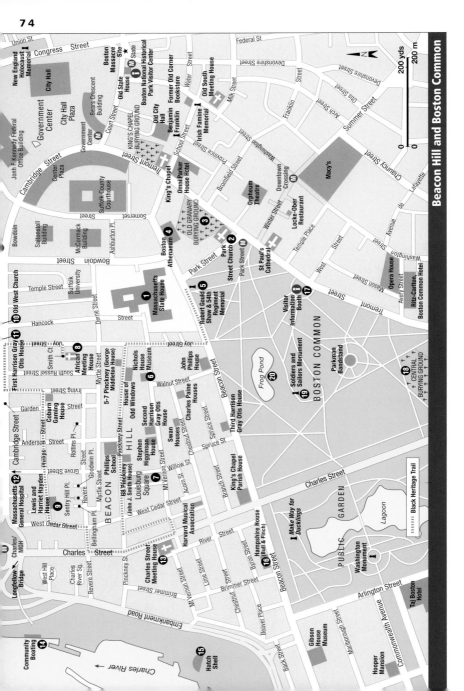

Beacon Hill and Boston Common

New England Holocaust Memorial

City Hall

Government Center

John F. Kennedy Federal Office Building

City Hall Plaza

Union St

Congress Street

Federal St

Boston Massacre Site ★ 16 State Street

Old State House 9

Boston National Historical Park Visitor Center

Former Old Corner Bookstore

Old South Meeting House

Devonshire Street

Devonshire Street

Otis Street

Sears Crescent Building

Court Street

KING'S CHAPEL BURYING GROUND

Benjamin Franklin

Irish Famine Memorial

School Street

Water Street

Milk Street

Cambridge Street

Suffolk County Courthouse

Saltonstall Building

McCormack Building

Ashburton Pl.

Somerset Street

Tremont Street

King's Chapel

Omni Parker House Hotel

Province Street

Bromfield Street

Washington Street

Franklin Street

Arch Street

Summer Street

Chauncy Street

Lafayette

Bowdoin Street

Suffolk University

Boston Athenaeum 4

OLD GRANARY BURYING GROUND 3

Park Street Church 10

Orpheum Theatre

Downtown Crossing 16

Macy's

Chauncy Street

Old West Church 10

First Harrison Gray Otis House 11

Temple Street

Massachusetts State House 1

Park Street 2

St Paul's Cathedral

Locke-Ober Restaurant

Winter Street

Temple Place

West Street

Mason Street

Avery Street

Washington Street

Tremont Street

Opera House

Ritz-Carlton Boston Common Hotel

Hancock Street

Derne Street

Robert Gould Shaw & 54th Regiment Memorial 5

Visitor Information Booth 17

BOSTON COMMON

Soldiers and Sailors Monument 19

Parkman Bandstand

CENTRAL BURYING GROUND 18

Massachusetts General Hospital 12

African Meeting House 8

Joy Street

Smith Ct.

South Russel Street

Nichols House Museum 6

5-7 Pinckney (George Middleton House)

House of Odd Windows

John Phillips House

Walnut Street

Joy Street

Beacon Street

Frog Pond 20

Charles/ MGH

Lewis and Harriet Hayden House 9

Coburn Gaming House

Phillips Street

Garden Street

Irving Street

Myrtle Street

BEACON HILL

Phillips School

68 Pinckney (John J. Smith House)

Stephen Higginson House 7

Pinckney Street

Second Harrison Gray Otis House

Chestnut Street

Charles Paine Houses

Third Harrison Gray Otis House

Anderson Street

Rollins Pl.

Goodwin Pl.

Louisburg Square

Swan Houses

Mt Vernon Street

Willow St

Spruce Street

Spruce St

Grove Street

Revere Street

Phillips Street

Bellingham Pl.

Sentry Hill Pl.

Harvard Musical Association

Mt Vernon Street

King's Chapel Parish House

West Cedar Street

Pinckney St.

West Cedar Street

Charles Street Meeting House 13

Charles Street

River Street

Branch Street

Acorn St

West Cedar Street

West Hill Place

Charles River Sq.

Brimmer Street

Hampshire House (Bull & Finch) 10

Byron Street

Beacon Street

Make Way for Ducklings

PUBLIC GARDEN

Lagoon

Charles Street

Longfellow Bridge

Community Boating 14

Hatch Shell 15

Charles River

Embankment Road

Mt Vernon Street

Lime Street

Chestnut Street

Brimmer Street

Beaver Place

Gibson House Museum

Hooper Mansion

Back Street

Marlborough Street

Washington Monument

Commonwealth Avenue

Arlington Street

Taj Boston Hotel

Black Heritage Trail

N

0   200 yds

0   200 m

'grandfather on the brain.' Beacon Hill isn't the oldest neighborhood in Boston, nor is it now the wealthiest or liveliest, but its importance to the city was permanently cemented by its 19th-century inhabitants, and what they came to represent.

In many ways, Beacon Hill and the adjacent Boston Common make an unlikely pair. Beacon Hill is a quiet and reserved residential neighborhood, and the Common is loud and lively, with all kinds of characters passing through. It's the nation's first public park and the democratic heart of Boston, a place where anyone with a soapbox is welcome to hold forth. Together, the two areas have a dynamic but balanced relationship, and it's safe to say that neither would be the same without the other.

A little world all its own

Beacon Hill rises from the northern border of the Common at Beacon Street, peaks at the crest of old Mt Vernon, and then slopes down to the Charles River and the West End. The streets are relatively long and narrow, and the tidy rows of Federal-style houses make this one of Boston's loveliest and most architecturally homogeneous quarters.

By accidents of history and geography, Beacon Hill is divided into three distinct sections. The **South Slope**, generally recognized as classic Beacon Hill, is bordered by Beacon, Pinckney, Bowdoin, and Charles streets. The less exclusive **North Slope** runs down the opposite side of the Hill from Pinckney to Cambridge Street. This is where, in the early 1800s, a community of free blacks gathered around Joy Street; many of its members were leaders in the anti-slavery movement preceding the Civil War. And the **Flat Side**, which is built entirely on landfill, occupies the broad area of level ground west of Charles Street and bordering the Charles River.

The first European resident of Beacon Hill was the Rev. William Blackstone, an English hermit who settled on the Shawmut peninsula several years before the Puritans. After selling most of his land to John Winthrop, Blackstone retired to a small, 6-acre (2.4-hectare) estate at the foot of the South Slope.

'A small, but pleasant Common, where the Gallants a little before Sun-set walk with their Marmalet-Madams… till the nine o'clock bell rings them home to their habitations [and] the Constables walk their rounds to see good order kept, and to take up loose people.'

John Josselyn, describing Boston Common in 1674

Famous Residents

Beacon Hill's roster of illustrious residents include Henry James, Louisa May Alcott, Charles Sumner, and Oliver Wendell Holmes, and there are plenty of stories in the annals about Charles Dickens hanging around with Henry Wadsworth Longfellow and publisher 'Jamie' Fields, and Edgar Allen Poe getting kicked out of parties for drunkenness.

In 1849, an upper-level Brahmin, George Parkman, was killed and dismembered by Dr John Webster, a Harvard Medical School professor who owed him money, and then shoved down the privy in his laboratory. Brahmin society, always mortified by excessive attention, was doubly mortified by the sordid nature of the crime.

BELOW: row houses on Beacon Hill.

WHERE

In the State House's Doric Hall hangs a portrait of Abraham Lincoln in a rare standing pose. The painting is sometimes called the 'Five Dollar Lincoln,' as the original American five-dollar bill borrowed the image.

At the time, the area was called Trimount after the three distinct peaks (Sentry Hill, Mt Vernon, and Cotton Hill) that rose above the Common. Between the 1790s and 1830s, all three summits were gradually flattened by as much as 60ft (18 meters) and the excess soil and rock were used to fill in the North Cove, between modern-day Beacon Hill and the North End, and tidal flats where Charles Street is today.

The relatively modest homes of Beacon Hill were perfectly suited to the Brahmins' peculiar blend of wealth and self-restraint. But, by about 1870, many of the old families began leaving Beacon Hill for more spacious homes in the Back Bay, which was then being developed. The Hill was considered quaint and a bit déclassé for some years, until its charms were rediscovered by a new generation of residents in the mid-1900s. Today, many single-family homes have been made into condos and apartments, but externally the Hill still represents a remarkably complete picture of early 19th-century architecture and urban planning.

A sense of separation

Of all the neighborhoods in Boston, Beacon Hill is the most insulated and self-contained. It's as if the architects designed it as an answer to the old Puritan dilemma – how to be in the world but not of it – because the area is both a part of, and apart from, the surrounding city.

The first thing you notice on entering Beacon Hill is exactly this sense of separation. It feels as if you've left modern Boston behind and stepped into a 19th-century village. Traffic thins out, the streets narrow, and city noises begin to fade to a serene hush. This is the Boston of another age, a town of red brick and cobblestone, walled gardens, and graceful bay windows. Trees shade the quiet sidewalks, and flower boxes brim with cheerful color. Aside from a few other tourists, there's almost no one on the street.

The effect is created by a number of factors, but the most important element is stylistic homogeneity. Except for the parked cars (resident stickers required), the modern world

RIGHT: Park Street Church.
BELOW: inside the Grand Hall in the State House.

intrudes little, and thanks to aggressive historic preservation, many of the original details survive. Above all, Beacon Hill owes its special ambience to its original developers and to the native talents of the untrained housewrights who designed and built most of the homes.

THE STATE HOUSE AND ITS ENVIRONS

Massachusetts State House ❶

Address: Beacon and Park streets, www.sec.state.ma.us/trs
Tel: 727-3676
Opening Hrs: Mon–Fri 8.45am–5pm, tours 10am–3.30pm, reservations requested
Entrance Fee: free
Transportation: Park Street

Begin a tour of Beacon Hill and Boston Common with the landmark that most dominates the skyline: the Massachusetts State House. This is the masterpiece of Charles Bulfinch, the most important American architect of his day (see page 61), and the building Oliver Wendell Holmes called 'the hub of the solar system,' thereby giving the city itself its nickname, 'The Hub.' (Of course, Holmes also wryly remarked that 'the axis of the earth sticks visibly through the center of each and every town or city.')

Today, the State House's appearance is the result of several significant changes. The original red-brick structure is now flanked on either side by marble wings and backed by an ungainly rear extension. Although clumsy, the side additions innocuously frame Bulfinch's dignified facade, whose grand two-story portico is surmounted by the famous gold dome. In Bulfinch's original design the dome was covered with white shingles. Paul Revere sheathed it in copper and later, in 1861, it was gilded with gold leaf. It was also changed during World War II, when

ABOVE: the Old Granary Burying Ground.

it was painted gray to keep it from shining as a beacon of the wrong sort in case of a nighttime air raid.

Visitors enter through the General Hooker entrance on Beacon Street, located to the right side of the building's grand facade. (Disabled access is on Bowdoin Street.) The Tours and Information Desk, where free guided tours begin, is on the second floor in Doric Hall.

The most impressive rooms are those that survived the building's alterations, including the Senate Chamber, the Reception Room, the House of Representatives (home of the beloved Sacred Cod, a carved wooden fish memorializing Massachusetts's original source of wealth), Nurses Hall, and Doric Hall, a vaulted, columned, marble chamber that rises beneath the dome.

Park Street Church ❷

Address: 1 Park Street, www.parkstreet.org
Tel: 523-3383
Opening Hrs: July–Aug Tue–Sat

ABOVE: gravestones in the Old Granary Burying Ground.

Entrance Fee: free
Transportation: Park Street

Although it's now surrounded by modern buildings, the **Old Granary Burying Ground** was originally a part of the Common and took its name from an old granary that once stood where the Park Street Church is now located. The first body was committed in 1660, making it one of the oldest cemeteries in Boston. Among the historic figures buried here are Samuel Adams, Peter Faneuil, Paul Revere, John Hancock, victims of the Boston Massacre, and Benjamin Franklin's parents. Unfortunately, the headstones have been moved so many times, they no longer correspond to the actual graves, some of which are four bodies deep. Believe it or not, the neat rows we see today are an accommodation to the lawnmower. Still, the icons and inscriptions carved into the stones tell much about the deceased and the era they lived in.

Boston Athenaeum ❹

Address: 10.5 Beacon Street, www.bostonathenaeum.org
Tel: 227-0270
Opening Hrs: Mon 9am–8pm, Tue–Fri 9am–5.30pm, Sat 9am–4pm
Entrance Fee: free
Transportation: Park Street

From the Old Granary Burying Ground, take the longer route back to the State House, walking down Tremont away from the Common and taking a left on Beacon Street. The **Boston Athenaeum**, a private library and Brahmin stronghold, has an unobtrusive entrance. Casual visitors are allowed only limited access to the first and second floors. Founded in 1807, the Athenaeum, whose barrel-vaulted fifth floor is nirvana for the book-lover, contains the library of George Washington and also houses a notable collection of American portrait paintings. (So impressive is the Athenaeum's superb Italian palazzo-inspired interior that Hollywood

9am–4pm for tours, Sun for services, Sept–June Sun for services and by appointment
Entrance Fee: free
Transportation: Park Street

From the State House, cross Beacon Street and stroll the short length of Park Street, which terminates below the sturdy Georgian steeple of the **Park Street Church,** designed by Peter Banner and completed in 1810. The renowned abolitionist William Lloyd Garrison launched his public crusade against slavery from the pulpit in 1829, and Henry James described the church as 'the most interesting mass of brick and mortar in America.' That may be true from a historian's point of view, but architecturally the interior is not especially interesting.

Old Granary Burying Ground ❸

Address: Park and Tremont streets
Tel: 635-4505
Opening Hrs: daily 9am–5pm

movie crews have used it to double for Harvard's libraries.) From here it is a very short walk up Beacon Street back to the State House.

Robert Gould Shaw Memorial ⑤

The **Robert Gould Shaw Memorial**, on Beacon Street directly across from the State House, is one of the most moving pieces of public art in America and, to many, the finest work of sculptor Augustus Saint-Gaudens. The bronze bas-relief honors the Massachusetts 54th Regiment, the first black regiment recruited in the North during the Civil War, and Shaw, a young white Bostonian who volunteered for its command. He and many members of the company were killed during the assault on Fort Wagner, South Carolina, an event recreated in the 1989 movie *Glory*. Although the bas-relief is only a few inches front to back, Saint-Gaudens created a sense of great visual depth, and gave the face of each of the marchers tremendous dignity and individuality. The memorial was celebrated by Robert Lowell in his poem 'For the Union Dead.'

THE SOUTH SLOPE

The Mt Vernon Proprietors

At about the same time that the State House was being completed, Charles Bulfinch became involved in another large-scale project on Beacon Hill. Together with other enterprising townsmen (including Harrison Gray Otis, Joseph Woodward, Jonathan Mason, and William Scollay), Bulfinch became a member of the Mt Vernon Proprietors, which bought about 19 acres (8 hectares) of pasture on the South Slope. Plans were drawn to level the summit, lay out streets, and subdivide house lots.

The Proprietors originally intended to build freestanding homes surrounded by gardens, but the economics of development soon dictated a more efficient plan – joining homes at a common wall. At first, two or three houses were built together, and then, as the pace of development quickened, entire streets were lined with single unbroken rows. Although Bulfinch designed several of Beacon Hill's grandest estates – and a few more modest row houses – most of the buildings were erected

TIP

One way to explore Beacon Hill history is by following the Black Heritage Trail, a sort of 'second Freedom Trail' overseen by the National Park Service. Meet at the Robert Gould Shaw Memorial for guided tours (tel: 742-5415; Memorial Day–Labor Day daily 10am, noon, and 2pm; Labor Day–Memorial Day, Mon–Sat 2pm; reservations needed for groups of 5 or more).

BELOW: the Robert Gould Shaw Memorial honors some of the first African American soldiers to fight in the American Civil War.

ABOVE: one of the Mt Vernon properties.
RIGHT: the African Meeting House.

by untrained artisans. Their instincts for proportion, sturdiness, and modest ornamentation still define the neighborhood's essential character.

A tour of the old Mt Vernon properties is limited entirely to the South Slope. The best place to start is on the northeast corner of the Common, directly in front of the State House. From here, proceed straight down Beacon Street toward Charles Street.

Beacon Street to Chestnut Street

Fronting the Common along its northern border, Beacon Street is the Hill's public face. This is Oliver Wendell Holmes's 'sunny street that holds the sifted few.' The buildings here are among the oldest on Beacon Hill, and boast a level of grandeur and ornamentation largely unmatched by the rest of the neighborhood.

In 1737, Beacon Hill got its first building of any true substance and Boston got its finest 'mansion-house.'

The house was built by Thomas Hancock, a wealthy merchant and the uncle of revolutionary figure and Massachusetts governor John Hancock, who inherited both house and fortune after his uncle's death. The landmark stood on Beacon Street overlooking the northeast portion of the Common until 1863. The site is marked by a plaque on the fence to the left of the State House.

As you stroll down the hill, note the **John Phillips House** (1 Walnut Street, on the corner of Beacon and Walnut streets) and the **Third Harrison Gray Otis House** (45 Beacon Street), both designed by Bulfinch between 1804 and 1808. At **King's Chapel Parish House** (63–4 Beacon Street), look for the unusually colored window panes – the tint is caused by a chemical defect. Installed in the early 1800s, these 'purple panes' have become a part of Beacon Hill folklore.

Turn right from Beacon Street onto Charles Street, and right again into **Chestnut Street**, one of many narrow, intimate streets that lead up the slope. The combination of simple structures, modest scale, and artful detailing make this one of the most pleasing streets on the Hill. The buildings are especially notable for the delicate use of ornamentation, including wrought-iron balconies, bootscrapers, Greek Revival porticoes, and fan lights, all of which tend to vary and lighten the plain brick facades. Pass the **Harvard Musical Association**, the country's oldest music library, at No. 57A.

There are far too many distinguished homes along Chestnut Street to list them all, but highlights include No. 29, the **Swan Houses** (13, 15, and 17), and the **Charles Paine Houses** (6–8 Chestnut Street), all attributed to Bulfinch.

Nichols House Museum ➏

Address: 55 Mt Vernon Street, www.nicholshousemuseum.org
Tel: 227-6993
Opening Hrs: tours on the half-hour Apr–Oct Tue–Sat 11am–4pm, Nov–Mar Thur–Sat 11am–4pm
Entrance Fee: charge
Transportation: Park Street

Turn left on Walnut Street to reach **Mt Vernon Street**, where you'll immediately see another Bulfinch creation, the 1804 **Nichols House Museum.** Like the Back Bay's Gibson House (see page 149), the lifelong home of the philanthropist Rose Standish Nichols is a true period piece; few of its furnishings are more recent than the mid-Victorian era.

Mt Vernon Street

Walk down Mt Vernon Street, where the houses are larger and the street wider; and the original families were more distinguished. In one of his more snobbish moments, Henry James called it 'the only respectable

street in America.' Pass an impressive series of freestanding mansions. The **Stephen Higginson House** (No. 87) and its much-altered neighbor (No. 89), and the **Second Harrison Gray Otis House** (No. 85), are all Bulfinch designs.

At Willow Street, turn left for a brief detour. Many of the smaller houses on Willow, Acorn, and West Cedar streets were originally servants' quarters and kitchens that serviced the wealthier households. Today, these slender byways are among the most private locations on the Hill. On the right you'll find the top of **Acorn Street**, a steep cobbled alley lined with gas lamps and flower boxes.

Louisburg Square ➐

Return to Mt Vernon Street to explore its main highlight, and the crown of Beacon Hill: **Louisburg Square**, a lovely little rectangle of grass and tall trees surrounded by a cobblestone border and stately homes built in the 1840s. The gently rippling bowfront houses on the west side of the square (numbers 8 to 22) have been called the finest

ABOVE: period décor at the Nichols House Museum.
BELOW: spiral staircase inside the Nichols House Museum.

ABOVE: fine houses grace Louisburg Square.

TIP

Forget street parking in Beacon Hill – residents' stickers are required and towing is a reality. Instead, take the 'T' to Park Street. If you must drive, there are garages on the hill's perimeter, including Center Plaza Garage (1 Center Plaza; tel: 742-7807) and Central Parking (15-17 Beacon Street; tel: 542-1549; Zero Charles Street; tel: 954-2098).

row houses in Boston, and possibly in the United States. Louisa May Alcott lived at No. 10; William Dean Howells at Nos. 4 and 16; and, at No. 20, the singer Jenny Lind married her accompanist Otto Goldschmidt.

The little park at the center of the square, graced by the statues of Christopher Columbus and Aristides the Just, is owned collectively by the square's householders – although perhaps condominium holders might be a more apt description today. One of the remaining single-family homes is owned by Massachusetts Senator John Kerry, the 2004 presidential candidate, and his wife Teresa Heinz Kerry.

Pinckney Street

Cross to the opposite end of Louisburg Square and turn right onto **Pinckney Street,** which runs along the crest of Beacon Hill, separating the South Slope from the less affluent North Slope. At **68 Pinckney** is a fine house that belonged to John J. Smith, a distinguished black statesman who

migrated to Boston from Virginia in 1848. Stationed in Washington during the Civil War, he was a recruiting officer for the all-black Fifth Cavalry. Later, he was appointed three times to the Massachusetts House of Representatives, and to the Boston Common Council. At the corner of Pinckney and Anderson streets is the **Phillips School**, which opened to blacks in 1855, becoming the city's first interracial school. At No. 24 is the '**House of Odd Windows**,' featuring an eccentric window design. Dating from 1791, the clapboard house at **Nos. 5–7 Pinckney** is the oldest existing home on the Hill built by a black person. The lot was bought by G. Middleton, a black equestrian, and Lewis Glapion, a mixed-race barber. Middleton, a colonel in the Revolutionary War, led the all-black company 'Bucks of America.'

THE NORTH SLOPE

Beyond Pinckney, the North Slope pitches toward Cambridge Street and the West End. Until not so long ago, this was the bohemian half of Beacon Hill, one of the few places where artists, writers, and students could find tiny yet affordable apartments. From the very beginning, it was considered the 'bad side' of the Hill, but that would be a relative term indeed given today's rental costs.

Still, the North Slope retains a different feel than 'classic' Beacon Hill. It doesn't share the same architectural pedigree, and even has a number of buildings built frankly as apartment houses. There are neighborhood businesses here – corner groceries, cafés, pizzerias, and barber shops. Students bustling up and down Temple Street near **Suffolk University** further animate the district, and you are far more likely, as you get down near Cambridge Street, to hear music blasting from an apartment window or car horns honking. That sort of thing simply wouldn't do on Mt Vernon.

African Meeting House ❽

Address: 46 Joy Street, www.afroam museum.org
Tel: 720-2991
Opening Hrs: Mon–Sat 10am–4pm
Entrance Fee: charge
Transportation: Park Street, Bowdoin
From Pinckney Street, turn left on Joy Street and walk two blocks to tiny **Smith Court**, where, at one time, all the houses were occupied by blacks. When Massachusetts declared slavery illegal in 1783, the migration of runaway slaves to Boston grew enormously. Free blacks settled in the North End but later moved to the North Slope of Beacon Hill.

Facing these houses is the **African Meeting House**, the oldest black church in the nation still standing. Dedicated in 1806, it was called 'the haven from the loft' because of the practice in Old North Church of relegating black worshippers to its loft. It was also known as 'Black Faneuil Hall' because of its fiery anti-slave

meetings. These culminated in 1832 when William Lloyd Garrison founded the New England Anti-Slavery Society here.

Next door, at the corner of Joy Street, stood the Abiel Smith School, dedicated in 1834 to the education of the city's black children. Although the black community had fought hard for this school, some were opposed, arguing that it would crystallize segregation. Led by William C. Neill, who lived in Smith Court and who was the first published black historian, they formed the Equal Schools Association, which called for the school to be boycotted.

In 1850 the state's highest court ruled that the school provided an education equal to that of other public schools in the city and so blacks need not be admitted to the public system. However, in 1855 the State Legislature outlawed segregation and the Smith School was closed.

North side cul-de-sacs and Phillips Street

From the African Meeting House, retrace your steps on Joy one block and

ABOVE: one of Beacon Hill's most typical streets.
BELOW: tailor's shop window.

BELOW: enjoying an autumn Saturday in the Public Garden.

turn right onto Myrtle. Make a right on Garden and left on Revere Street, and poke into the four quiet, charming cul-de-sacs that run off Revere Street. On **Rollins Place**, the classical two-story portico at the end is a mere facade – behind it is a 20ft (6-meter) cliff dropping down to Phillips Street. The other alleyways – **Goodwin Place, Sentry Hill Place,** and **Bellingham Place** – are equally enchanting, each paved with red brick and lined with compact row houses. Turn right at West Cedar Street, and right again onto Phillips Street. Branching off from opposite sides of Phillips Street (near the corner of West Cedar) are **Primus Avenue** and a very narrow passage known as **Flower Lane**, two other alleyways worth investigating.

At No. 66 Phillips Street is the **Lewis and Harriet Hayden House** ❾. This was one of the most important of the many 'underground railway' stops on the Hill that sheltered fugitive slaves on their way to freedom in Canada. In 1853 the Haydens were visited by Harriet Beecher Stowe, who was researching for her book *A Key to Uncle Tom's Cabin*. She

was astonished that the house was a haven for 13 slaves. It is said that Hayden kept two kegs of gunpowder in the basement so that the house could be blown up if searched.

Old West Church ❿

Address: 131 Cambridge Street, www.oldwestchurch.org
Tel: 227-5088
Opening Hrs: Tue–Fri 9am–3pm
Entrance Fee: free
Transportation: Bowdoin

The north side of the Hill ends in wide, busy **Cambridge Street**, on whose far side are several interesting buildings. At the west end of this street is **Old West Church**, a handsome red-brick Federal-style building from 1806. The original church was razed in 1775 when the British thought that the Americans were using it as a steeple from which to signal to their compatriots in Cambridge. The current building, primarily a Methodist church, is an oblong meeting house fronted by a rectangular block rising in several stages to a square cupola. The large, airy interior has a balcony, supported by delicate columns with

The Unsavory Slope

Soon after its founding around 1725, the North Slope Village began to take on an unsavory character. Its proximity to the river and its detachment from town made it a perfect spot for sailors looking for taverns and bordellos. North Slope entrepreneurs were only too glad to oblige them, and within a few years Boston had its first red-light district. Among sailors, the village became known as Mt Whoredom, and for nearly 100 years it rankled the morals of God-fearing citizens. In the early 1820s, though, a crackdown forced the last of Mt Whoredom's bawdy houses to shut down, and the area began to change as the city's black population moved in.

attenuated acanthus-leaf capitals, running around three sides.

First Harrison Gray Otis House ⑪

Address: 141 Cambridge Street, www.historicnewengland.org/historic-properties/homes/otis
Tel: 227-3956
Opening Hrs: tours every half-hour Wed–Sun 11am–4.30pm
Entrance Fee: charge
Transportation: Bowdoin

Next door to the Old West Church is the house Bulfinch designed in 1796 for Harrison Gray Otis, a Boston mayor, congressman, and real estate developer, whose later Bulfinch houses are on the South Slope of the Hill. This, the most distinguished old mansion still standing in Boston, is a completely symmetrical three-story rectangular block of red brick, with each story defined by a brownstone string course. The interior has been meticulously restored with furniture and portraits, bright replica wallpapers and carpets, and mirror-panelled doors that would reflect candlelight.

The basement contains an architectural museum.

Massachusetts General Hospital ⑫

Address: 55 Fruit Street, www.massgeneral.org
Tel: 726-2000
Entrance Fee: free
Transportation: Charles/MGH

On the other end of Cambridge Street, near the Charles River, is the sprawling **Massachusetts General Hospital**, possibly America's greatest hospital. Its very first building, the Bulfinch Pavilion and Ether Dome, was designed by Bulfinch just before he departed for Washington to work on the United States Capitol. Ask at the hospital's main entrance for directions to this building, a historic landmark twice over: once because of its architecture and once because here ether was used as an anesthetic for the first time (see page 88). The Federal-style building stands on a high podium, and the main entrance is approached by two stairways that lead to the sides of a portico formed by 10 unfluted Ionic columns.

LEFT: Third Harrison Gray Otis House.
BELOW: the glass-fronted Charles/MGH 'T' station.

BELOW: Lewis and Harriet Hayden House.

THE FLAT SIDE

Charles Street

The remaining part of Beacon Hill, a broad area of level ground built entirely on landfill, is known as the **Flat Side**. Most people come to the Flat Side to shop on Charles Street, Beacon Hill's only commercial street, which tends to be less hectic than Downtown and more casual than the boutiques on Newbury Street. Antiques are a local specialty and there are several good restaurants and cafés where one can buy Italian pastries, *gelati*, and a stiff cup of espresso.

The Flat Side's most distinguished building is the **Charles Street Meeting House** , on the corner of Mt Vernon Street. The Charles Street Meeting House was built in 1807 for the Third Baptist Church. In the mid-1830s the Church's segregationist traditions were challenged by Timothy Gilbert, who invited black friends to his pew. He was expelled and, with other white abolitionist Baptists, founded the First Baptist Free Church. It became Tremont Temple, 'the first integrated church in America.' In 1876 the Meeting House was bought by the African Methodist Episcopalian Church and, in 1939, was the last black institution to leave the Hill.

Relative to the other two sections of Beacon Hill, the Flat Side occupies a neutral position. It has few of the grand associations boasted by the South Slope and almost none of the negative ones once tagged on the North. As a result, people tend to overlook the residential areas, although here, as elsewhere on the Hill, the overall effect is of a quaint 19th-century town located in the middle of a modern city.

The finest homes tend to be gathered on Brimmer, Lime, and Mt Vernon streets between Charles Street and the river. There are also two very interesting courtyards in the northern end of the neighborbood, tucked into the block immediately off Embankment Road. **Charles River Square** is a hidden enclave of tidy row houses surrounding a rectangular plaza.

The Charles River and its Esplanade

Just downstream from Charles River Square is the **Longfellow Bridge**, completed in 1900 and the oldest and most ornate bridge across the river. Its four readily recognizable towers have led to the nickname Salt and Pepper Bridge. Originally called the Cambridge Bridge, it was renamed in honor of the poet Henry Wadsworth Longfellow (1807–82).

Tucked into the southwest corner of the bridge is the clubhouse of **Community Boating** , which organizes what is believed to be the world's oldest and largest public sailing program. Many an Olympic and America's Cup sailor first put to sea here on the embankment of the Charles River.

However, not all the scudding white sails of traditional centerboards and psychedelic sails of windsurfers

have set off from the Community Boating quay. Some belong to the Massachusetts Institute of Technology Sailing Club, whose clubhouse is somewhat upriver and across from the Community Boating one. Others belong to the Emerson College Sailing Club, whose headquarters building is just a few yards upstream from the Community Boating quay.

Immediately beyond this is the boathouse of the Union Boat Club, founded in 1851 by gentlemen interested in rowing who were also admirers of Daniel Webster's Union Forever speeches. In order to maintain the integrity of the riparian banks, they built their clubhouse not on the river, but diagonally across Embankment Road, at the foot of Chestnut Street.

Along the Esplanade just beyond the end of Chestnut Street is the **Hatch Shell** ⑮, an outdoor concert venue that is home to the Boston Pops and other performers during summer (the annual Fourth of July concert, followed by fireworks, is a

favorite tradition). It's accessible by a pedestrian bridge across Storrow Drive, at the corner of Beacon and Arlington streets.

Near the Shell is a large **bust of Arthur Fiedler** (1894–1979), who founded the Boston Sinfonietta in 1924 and went on to conduct its successor, the Pops, for 49 years from 1930 until his death. The atmosphere is informal: many concertgoers come equipped with blanket and picnic basket.

Stately homes and a famous saloon

Although the architecture of the Flat Side isn't as old or interesting as the rest of the Hill, there is an exceptionally handsome row of granite houses on Beacon Street directly across from the Public Garden. When they were built in 1828, most of the Flat Side was still under water. The houses actually stood on the Mill Dam, which started at the edge of the Common and arched across the Back

LEFT: restored salon in the First Harrison Gray Otis House.
ABOVE: Old West Church.

Medical Trailblazers

Just as Boston is top in education, so it is America's leader in medicine, with 17 major hospitals and three medical schools.

In 1846, Dr John Collins Warren delivered his verdict to those who had observed Mr Gilbert Abbot undergoing surgery at the Massachusetts General Hospital: 'Gentlemen, this is no humbug.' Mr Abbot, who was operated on for a tumor, had just told the entranced gathering that he had 'suffered no pain.' This was because here in Boston, for the first time in the world, ether had been used to anesthetize the patient. Today, at the hospital (usually known as the MGH, Mass General, 'Man's Greatest Hospital' or, to medical students, the 'massive genital'), the visitor can see the Ether Dome, the work of Bulfinch, and the operating theater where ether was first used. (Tours offered on request; call for reservations.)

In the past 50 years more than a score of doctors and scientists working at Boston's hospitals and medical schools have won Nobel prizes in physiology and/or medicine.

Among these is John Enders who, with Frederick Robbins and Thomas Weller, won this award in 1954 for his work in developing the poliomyelitis vaccine, which effectively eliminated this scourge. Almost 150 years before this, Dr Benjamin Waterhouse of Harvard Medical School (HMS) had been the first to introduce smallpox vaccination in the country.

Frontline surgery

A more recent Nobel laureate in medicine (1990) is Joseph Murray who, in 1954, at the Peter Bent Brigham Hospital, was part of a team that successfully performed the first human kidney transplant. And open-heart surgery was first performed at the Boston Children's Hospital by Professor Robert Gross in 1967. Then there was 12-year-old Danny Everett who, in 1962, while hitching a ride home on a train after pitching in a Little League baseball game, had his arm shorn off. Dr Ronald Malt and his emergency room team at the MGH performed the first successful replantation of a human limb.

The list of firsts is long: abdominal surgery (1886); creation of the Drinker respirator (iron lung) in 1928; artificial kidney (1945); clinical reports on efficacy of birth control pills (1959); techniques for freezing and thawing blood (1964); abdominal electrocardiography for monitoring the fetus during labor (1973); and creating artificial skin for burn victims (1981).

Less dramatic, but just as important, Boston national medical firsts include Linda Richards, the first trained nurse; the first medical school to admit women (Boston University); the first city to establish a municipal water supply; and the first Board of Health. On an international level, the much respected, oft-quoted *New England Journal of Medicine*, founded in 1812 by Dr John Collins Warren and James Jackson, is the oldest continuously published medical journal in the world.

LEFT: the imposing facade of the Massachusetts State House.

Bay. The dam later became the extension of Beacon Street that proceeds through the Back Bay.

Probably the most popular attraction on the Flat Side is still the **Hampshire House** ⓰ restaurant, with its street-level Cheers pub (formerly the Bull & Finch). In the early 1980s, this cozy watering hole on the corner of Beacon and Brimmer streets was scouted by television producers looking for inspiration for a situation comedy revolving around the characters frequenting a Boston bar. The show became *Cheers*, and its subsequent popularity transformed the place into a major tourist attraction (see page 91).

BOSTON COMMON

Boston Common is such an integral part of Beacon Hill that it's impossible to talk about one without mentioning the other. Although the two areas represent different aspects of Boston, they are linked by history and should be thought of as elements of a larger whole.

The Common, a pentagon covering about 50 acres (20 hectares), is bounded by Beacon, Boylston, Charles, Park, and Tremont streets. It is both a geographical and social crossroads: the people one sees on the Common represent a broad sampling of the city. Families picnic, office workers enjoy a sunny lunch, Chinese women practice t'ai chi, and kids splash in the water fountains on hot summer days.

For those unfamiliar with the city, the Common is probably the best place to start a visit. There is a **Visitor Information Booth** ⓱ (tel: 536-4100) just south of the Park Street subway station (corner of Park and Tremont streets), where maps are available and the Freedom Trail begins (see page 40). Most activity occurs on the fringe of the Common, near Park Street station. Here, vendors sell ice cream, fried food, hot dogs, T-shirts, and other souvenirs. Opened in 1897, 'Park Street Under' was the first subway station in the nation and is now a Historic Landmark.

From sheep to skaters

Most people don't realize that the Common is probably the oldest and least changed section of Boston. It was established more than 350 years ago, when John Winthrop and his neighbors bought the site from the Rev. William Blackstone. In 1640, the townsmen agreed to preserve the land as a 'Comon Field' *(sic)* on which sheep and cattle were to be grazed, and it soon became a popular spot for sermons, promenades, and, in the years before the Revolution, political protest. Militias used the land as a mustering ground, and public hangings were conducted at the Great Elm, which stood on the Common until 1876. Among the heretics who met a cruel end here was Mary Dyer, the Quaker who insisted on the right to worship freely. A statue in her memory, and another commemorating exiled religious dissenter Anne Hutchinson, stand near one of John F. Kennedy on the grounds of the State House.

ABOVE: bust of conductor Arthur Fiedler near the Hatch Shell.
BELOW: an aerial view of Back Bay, Charles River, and Longfellow Bridge.

ABOVE: a shady spot on Boston Common

During the American Revolution, the Common was transformed into a British military center. As many as 2,000 Redcoats were quartered here during the occupation of Boston, and several dozen British soldiers killed at the Battle of Bunker Hill were interred at the **Central Burying Ground** ⑰ in the southeast corner. It is the fourth-oldest cemetery in Boston, but few of note are buried here. One exception is Gilbert Stuart, the painter who gave us the classic portrait of George Washington.

Today, the west part of the common is devoted to athletic endeavor – baseball, tennis, volleyball, and frisbee are all popular – and to large public meetings. Elsewhere on the Common are several works of public art. Outstanding is the 70ft (21-meter) **Soldiers and Sailors Monument** ⑲, atop Telegraph Hill on the western side of the park. It is dedicated to the Union forces killed in the Civil War. Close by is the **Frog Pond** ⑳. In colonial times sheep and cows slaked their thirst at the pond. Later, proper Bostonians fished in it for minnows in the summer and ice-skated on it in the winter, and here they celebrated the first arrival of piped-in municipal water from a suburban reservoir in 1848. There are no minnows, nor frogs, in the pond today. It is lined with concrete and serves as a children's water park in summer and an ice rink in winter.

SHOPPING

The prime place for shopping on Beacon Hill is Charles Street, a go-to spot for gifts, antiques, women's clothing, and specialty foods.

Antiques

Devonia Antiques
15 Charles St
Tel: 523-8313
www.devonia-antiques.com
Full sets of fine china, glassware, and tableware, as well as distinctive individual pieces of glassware and porcelain.

Twentieth Century Ltd Goods
73 Charles St
Tel: 742-1031
www.bostonvintagejewelry.com
Vintage costume jewelry at its very best, from pearls to portrait pendants, along with purses, hats, and cufflinks galore.

Food

Beacon Hill Chocolates
91 Charles St
Tel: 725-1900
www.beaconhillchocolates.com
This artisan chocolate shop stocks gourmet treats from New England and around the world, from decadent truffles to dark chocolate-covered cranberries.

Savenor's
160 Charles St
Tel: 723-6328
www.savenorsmarket.com
Boston's premier gourmet butcher and grocery carries a fine assortment of exotic game, including caribou, quail, and alligator tail, along with other prime meats, cheeses, fresh fish, smoked salmon, and hard-to-find delicacies.

Gifts

The Flat of the Hill
60 Charles St
Tel: 619-9977
This girl-focused shop is heaven for hostess-gift hunters. Choose from books, body products, designer handbags, picnic baskets, jewelry, and hand-painted coasters.

Good
133 Charles St
Tel: 722-9200
www.shopatgood.com
Owner Paul Niski offers an exquisite selection of handsome, modern home accessories, jewelry, vintage items, and gifts.

Women's Clothing

Crush
131 Charles St
Tel: 720-0010
www.shopcrushboutique.com
Shop for sophisticated dresses and flirty blouses, denim from J Brand and Paige, and outfit-making accessories.

Wish
49 Charles St
Tel: 227-4441
Enjoy a well-edited selection – think Milly, Alice + Olivia, AG and Splendid – of casual and date-worthy dresses, premium denim, and a smattering of jewelry.

RESTAURANTS, BARS AND CAFES

Restaurants

American

75 Chestnut
75 Chestnut St
Tel: 227-2175
www.75chestnut.com
D daily, Br Sept–June Sat–Sun
$$$ ❶ [p268, C1]
This romantic hideaway offers good American comfort food – steak sandwiches, char-grilled salmon with crispy polenta, pasta caprese, roast chicken, filet mignon, and, for dessert, chocolate brownies with toasted marshmallow ice cream.

French

Beacon Hill Bistro
Beacon Hill Hotel,
25 Charles St
Tel: 723-7575
www.beaconhillhotel.com
B, L, & D daily, Br Sat–Sun **$$$**
❷ [p268, C1]
Executive Chef Joshua Lewin delivers inspired contemporary French bistro cuisine with a local, organic focus. The long, narrow room is cozy and stylish. Weekend brunch is popular.

No. 9 Park
9 Park St
Tel: 742-9991
www.no9park.com
D Mon–Sat **$$$$** ❸
[p272, D3]
Award-winning chef Barbara Lynch has created a fine-dining heavyweight in this elegant Bulfinch-designed townhouse overlooking the Common. Regionally inspired French and Italian dishes are offered on a three-course prix-fixe menu, an

à la carte menu, and a seven-course chef's tasting menu ($112, wine pairing $74).

Italian

Bin 26 Enoteca
26 Charles St
Tel: 723-5939
www.bin26.com
L & D daily **$$$** ❹
[p268, C1]
This convivial spot offers small plates for snacking and sharing as well as entrées, but the main decision will be what beverage to pair with your food – the wine list is over 200-strong, with more than 70 wines available by the glass.

Figs
42 Charles St
Tel: 742-3447
www.toddenglish.com
L & D daily **$$** ❺ [p268, C1]
Todd English, Boston's one-man restaurant consortium, offers tasty thin-crust pizzas, panini, and handmade pasta in this casual bistro.

Scampo
Liberty Hotel, 215 Charles St
Tel: 536-2100
www.scampoboston.com
L & D daily **$$$–$$$$** ❻
[p266, C4]
Created by award-winning chef Lydia Shire, Scampo serves up contemporary Italian food with Middle Eastern influences. The lively, open space features a house-made mozzarella bar, outdoor patio, and 38-seat private dining room.

Toscano
47 Charles St
Tel: 723-4090

www.toscanoboston.com
L & D daily **$$–$$$** ❼
[p268, C1]
Delicious Tuscan classics, including house-made pastas, slow-cooked meats, and fresh seafood, served in a warm, elegant setting of old walnut hardwood floors, painted chandeliers, and stone walls.

Upper Crust
20 Charles St
Tel: 723-9600
(also at 286 Harvard St, Brookline. Tel: 739-8518)
www.theuppercrustpizzeria.com
L & D daily **$** ❽ [p268, C1]
An open kitchen, pizza tins on the ceiling and flat-screen TVs all contribute to this popular pizzeria's atmosphere. Neapolitan-style pizzas are available by the slice, with toppings ranging from prosciutto to seafood to vegetables.

Mediterranean

Avila
1 Charles St
Tel: 267-4810
www.avilarestaurant.com
L & D Mon–Sat **$$–$$$** ❾
[p268, C2]
This chic spot offers small plates such as baked moussaka, Serrano ham, or crispy squid, and mains like hand-rolled potato gnocchi, rack of lamb souvlaki, and paella.

Persian

Lala Rokh
97 Mt. Vernon St
Tel: 720-5511
www.lalarokh.com
L Mon–Fri, D daily **$$** ❿

Prices for a three-course dinner per person, with tax and tip:

$ = under $25
$$ = $25–50
$$$ = $50–75
$$$$ = over $75

[p268, C1]
Sophisticated Persian cuisine with Indian, Turkish, and Armenian influences, in a romantic townhouse.

Bars

21st Amendment
150 Bowdoin St
Tel: 227-7100
❶ [p272, D3]
The neighborly 21st Amendment, a historic tavern near the State House, is named for the amendment repealing prohibition and draws an eclectic crowd.

Alibi
215 Charles St
Tel: 224-4004
❷ [p266, C4]
The Liberty Hotel's Alibi bar, whose name is inspired by the hotel's past life as a jail, is a lively scene.

Cheers
84 Beacon St
Tel: 227-9605
❸ [p268, C1]
At Cheers, tourists gawk and guzzle at the inspiration for the TV series.

Harvard Gardens
316 Cambridge St
Tel: 523-2727
❹ [p266, C4]
A happening place for singles on the Hill, Harvard Gardens also serves upscale pub grub.

DOWNTOWN

Old City Hall, Old South Meeting House, Old State House – everything seems ancient. But then there's Quincy Market and Chinatown.

To walk the streets of Downtown Boston today is to walk with the ghosts of colonial settlers upon ground now shadowed by modern skyscrapers. As the centuries have passed, many street names have changed. But the streets themselves follow much the same design as they did back in the 1630s, when Anne Hutchinson, the feminist leader of her day, was ousted from her home on what is now School Street, or in October 1746, when the Rev. Thomas Prince of Old South Meeting House "prayed up" a hurricane that wrecked an invading force of French warships.

Downtown commerce

There's nowhere more appropriate for starting such a walk than at **Downtown Crossing ❶**, where Summer and Washington streets intersect. At this spot, you are standing at the very center of Downtown Boston – a huge bronze disc embedded in the sidewalk assures you of the fact. What the plaque doesn't tell you is that South Boston is east of Downtown Boston, that East Boston is north of where you stand, and that the North End just north of Downtown Boston is south of

East Boston. Also, as you stand at the center of Downtown Boston, if you move your feet a few paces to the west, Summer Street becomes Winter Street without changing its face or its direction.

Downtown Crossing's Washington Street is a hub of the Downtown shopping opportunities. Among other chains, here is **Macy's ❷** (450 Washington Street; www.macys.com; tel: 357-3000; daily 10am–9pm). This outpost was formerly the flagship store of the Jordan Marsh chain, an

Main Attractions
DOWNTOWN CROSSING
KING'S CHAPEL
OLD STATE HOUSE
FANUEIL HALL AND QUINCY
   MARKET
UNION OYSTER HOUSE
HOLOCAUST MEMORIAL
CHINATOWN

Maps and Listings

LEFT: Faneuil Hall, built in 1742 with money from Peter Faneuil, a wealthy merchant.
RIGHT: outdoor stalls at Brattle Book Shop.

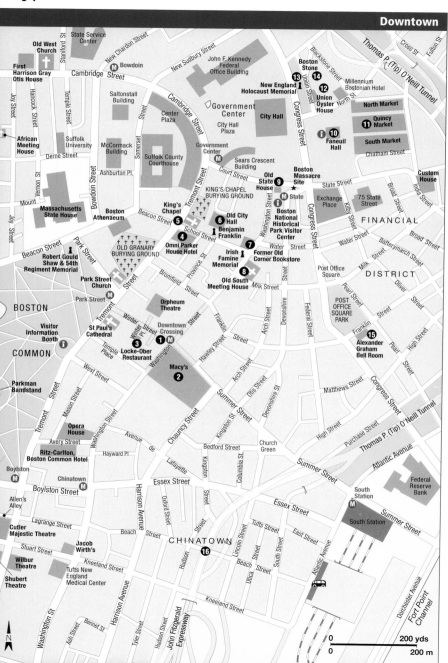

Old West Church
First Harrison Gray Otis House
State Service Center
New Chardon Street
Stanifond St
M Bowdoin
Cambridge Street
Joy Street
Hancock Street
Temple Street
Derne Street
African Meeting House
Suffolk University
McCormack Building
Ashburton Pl.
Somerset Street
Center Plaza
Saltonstall Building
Cambridge Street
New Sudbury Street
John F. Kennedy Federal Office Building
Government Center
City Hall
City Hall Plaza
Congress Street
New England Holocaust Memorial
Boston Stone
Union Street
Blackstone Street
13
12 Union Oyster House
North Street
Millennium Bostonian Hotel
Thomas P. (Tip) O'Neill Tunnel
Cross St
Fulton St
North Market
14
11 Quincy Market
South Market
Chatham Street

Mount Vernon St
Joy Street
Beacon Street
Massachusetts State House
Boston Athenaeum
Suffolk County Courthouse
Government Center M
Sears Crescent Building
Court Street
King's Chapel **5**
6 Old City Hall
4 Old Granary Burying Ground
Old State House **9**
Boston Massacre Site ★
State Street M State
Boston National Historical Park Visitor Center
i
10 Faneuil Hall
i
Custom House
Exchange Place
75 State Street
FINANCIAL
Broad Street
India Street
Bowdoin Street

KING'S CHAPEL BURYING GROUND
School Street
Benjamin Franklin
7
Irish Famine Memorial
8
Former Old Corner Bookstore
Old South Meeting House
Water Street
Washington Street
Congress Street
Devonshire Street
Federal Street
Milk Street
Post Office Square
Water Street
Kilby Street
Batterymarch Street
Broad Street
DISTRICT

BOSTON
Beacon Street
Robert Gould Shaw & 54th Regiment Memorial
Park Street
Park Street Church M
Park Street M
Tremont Street
Bromfield Street
Province Street
Orpheum Theatre
Winter Street
Winter Pl.
1 Downtown Crossing M
Franklin Street
Hawley Street
Arch Street
POST OFFICE SQUARE PARK
Pearl Street
Franklin Street
15 Alexander Graham Bell Room
High Street
Pearl Street
Oliver Street
Congress Street

Visitor Information Booth
i
COMMON
St Paul's Cathedral
Temple Place
Locke-Ober Restaurant **3**
Washington Street
Macy's **2**
Summer Street
Chauncy Street
Kingston Street
Otis Street
Devonshire Street
Summer Street
Church Green
High Street
Matthews Street
Purchase Street
Thomas P. (Tip) O'Neill Tunnel
Atlantic Avenue

Parkman Bandstand
West Street
Mason Street
Tremont Street
Avery Street
Opera House
Washington Street
Avenue de Lafayette
Hayward Pl.
Bedford Street
Columbia St
Kingston Street
Federal Reserve Bank

Ritz-Carlton, Boston Common Hotel
Boylston M
Chinatown M
Boylston Street
Allen's Alley
Lagrange Street
Cutler Majestic Theatre
Stuart Street
Wilbur Theatre
Shubert Theatre
Washington St
Bennet St
Ash Street
Harrison Avenue
Oxford Street
Essex Street
Beach Street
Jacob Wirth's
Kneeland Street
Tufts New England Medical Center
Hudson Street
CHINATOWN **16**
Tyler Street
John Fitzgerald Expressway
Kneeland Street
Lincoln Street
Tufts Street
Utica Street
Beach Street
South Street
East Street
Essex Street
Atlantic Avenue
Summer Street
South Station M
South Station

Dorchester Avenue
Fort Point Channel

0   200 yds
0   200 m

N

outfit that began on a frosty morning in 1851 when young Eben Dyer Jordan made his first sale in his newly opened shop – one yard of red silk ribbon, sold to a little girl for two cents. This was a big deal for a man who had sailed down from Maine five years earlier with just $1.25 in his pocket.

In contrast to the humble beginnings of the Jordan Marsh enterprise, Boston's financiers today handle transactions of mega-millions. Although not nearly as important as New York in general financial transactions, Boston has carved out for itself some special niches. Mutual funds began here in 1925 and, nearly a century earlier, the concept of venture capital was introduced in Boston.

Financial success here, as elsewhere, invariably translates into bricks and mortar. Two generations ago, the gold dome of the Massachusetts State House was surpassed on the skyline only by the similarly gilded summit of the United Shoe Machinery Building and the Custom House Tower (see panel, page 100). Today, all three of those edifices are lost in the vertical tumult of Downtown Boston's architecture. The 1970s, '80s, and '90s were a frenzied period of construction, with architects proceeding from the sleek but bland International style to various excesses of postmodernism.

Traditional institutions

Brown-bagging drones aside, much business in Boston is still conducted over lunch or dinner. From Downtown Crossing, head along Winter Street toward Boston Common. Just off Winter Street lies Winter Place, a narrow alley leading to the elegant and perennially popular **Locke-Ober** restaurant ❸, traditionally a stronghold of lamb chops, scrod and lobster (see page 106). Its menu has been updated by the celebrated chef Lydia Shire, but time

cannot improve on a bowl of oyster stew in the downstairs bar.

At the end of Winter Street, turn right onto Tremont Street and walk along Boston Common, passing Park Street Church and the Old Granary Burying Ground (see page 78) to arrive at School Street. At the corner of School and Tremont streets is the venerable **Omni Parker House Hotel** ❹ (see review, page 242). This is the oldest continuously operating hotel in the US, although the present building is not the original. Charles Dickens conducted literary seminars at an earlier Parker House, and here Ho Chi Minh waited on tables and Malcolm X toiled in the kitchen.

King's Chapel ❺

Address: 64 Beacon Street, www.kings-chapel.org
Tel: 227-2155
Opening Hrs: June–Aug Mon and Thur–Sat 10am–5pm, Tue–Wed 10–11.15am and 1.30–4pm, Sun 1.30–4pm, Sept–May Mon, Thur–Sat 10am–4pm, Tue–Wed 10am–11.30am, Sun 1.30–4pm; services Wed 12.15pm and Sun 11am

ABOVE: Irish Famine Memorial.
BELOW: silver service at Locke Ober.

ABOVE: Omni Parker House Hotel.
RIGHT: King's Chapel.

Paul Revere's largest bell is housed in King's Chapel. He called it "the sweetest bell we ever made." Another interesting feature of the Chapel is the pulpit staircase. The banister rails include one piece spiraling in the wrong direction, intended to symbolize human imperfection.

Entrance Fee: free
Transportation: Park Street, Government Center, State

Across School Street from the Omni Parker House is **King's Chapel**, an early stop on Boston's Freedom Trail. The Chapel had its origins in the 1680s, when Britain's King James II made a colossal political blunder by sending to Boston a clergyman whose job was to install in the town the very thing the Puritans had hated and fled: a branch of the Church of England.

The Rev. Robert Ratcliffe's arrival in Boston was greeted with a roar of protest. This bothered him not one whit, and since he had no church in which to hold services he teamed with the royal colonial governor, Sir Edmund Andros, to usurp a church the Puritan-Congregationalists were using, the Old South Meeting House. Finally in 1688, Andros seized a piece of land belonging to a Sir Isaac Johnson, and there the

original King's Chapel, a wooden structure, was built in 1689. This was replaced in 1754 by the present structure, built of granite blocks ferried from Quincy, 8 miles (13km) to the south. The dedication was attended by hundreds of Crown-hating locals who hurled garbage, manure and dead animals at the presiding Anglicans.

Next to the Chapel, on Tremont Street, is Boston's first cemetery, **King's Chapel Burying Ground**. In use from 1630 to 1796, it long pre-dates the Anglican edifice whose name it later assumed. The Bay Colony's first governor, John Winthrop, was buried here in 1649. The monument at the corner of the burying ground honors a French naval adjutant, the Chevalier de St Sauveur, killed by a Boston mob in September 1778 during an altercation over bread. The French, who had come to help the colonials, were baking bread using their own stores of wheat; Bostonians, who were enduring a severe shortage of flour, were incensed when told that they could not buy the French

Navy's bread. The Chevalier's funeral service is said to have been the first Catholic Mass said in Boston.

Old City Hall ❻

Old City Hall rises in the immediate background here, a massive pile of Second Empire granite architecture. The city government operated here from 1865 until 1969, when the new City Hall was built; the old mansarded structure now features a Ruth's Chris Steak House restaurant and office space. In its forecourt is a bronze statue of Benjamin Franklin, with pedestal tablets chronicling the important events of his life.

A plaque on the sidewalk to the left of the City Hall commemorates the site of America's first school. This was the original **Boston Latin School**, which opened in 1635, and accounts for the naming of School Street when it was laid out in 1640. (Boston Latin still exists, in a different part of town; although part of the

municipal school system, it accepts only students who pass an entrance exam.) Among the Boston Latin School's early pupils were Cotton Mather, Samuel Adams, Benjamin Franklin, and John Hancock.

A few more yards down the slope is the intersection of School and Washington streets, where stand two sets of bronze figures that constitute the **Irish Famine Memorial** commemorating The Great Hunger of the 1840s that resulted in many Irish emigrating to Boston.

Old Corner Bookstore ❼

Also on the corner of School and Washington streets is one of Downtown Boston's most loved and best-preserved colonial structures, the former site of the **Old Corner Bookstore**. Until 2004, the Boston Globe Company kept it going as a souvenir store selling such items as replica front pages with accounts of historic events. But they found it

ABOVE: Boston's Old City Hall is now home to offices and a restaurant.

TIP

At King's Chapel Burying Ground, look for the 1704 grave of Elizabeth Pain, said to have been the model for Hester Prynne in Nathaniel Hawthorne's classic novel *The Scarlet Letter*.

more profitable to move that business online, and the building has since been a jeweler's store, crafts showroom, and most recently, a Chipotle restaurant.

Originally on this site stood the home of the celebrated and courageous Anne Hutchinson. She lived here from 1634 to 1638, when she was banished from town by colonials who objected to her principles of free speech. In exile, she was killed during an Indian attack in what is now the Bronx, New York.

The big Boston fire of October 3, 1711, destroyed Anne's cottage. It was replaced in 1712 by the present structure, which over the years has served as an apothecary's shop, a dry goods store, and private residence; in 1828 it became the home of a bookstore and the eminent Ticknor and Fields publishing firm. In the Golden Age of American literature, this was a popular browsing and meeting place for John Greenleaf Whittier, Ralph Waldo Emerson, Harriet Beecher Stowe, and other distinguished writers. Charles Dickens, Henry Wadsworth Longfellow, Oliver Wendell Holmes, Nathaniel Hawthorne, and Henry David Thoreau were also published by Ticknor and Fields.

RIGHT: the Old South Meeting House.
BELOW: one of the bronze figures on the Irish Famine Memorial.

Old South Meeting House ❽

Address: 310 Washington Street, www.oldsouthmeetinghouse.org
Tel: 482-6439
Opening Hrs: daily Apr–Oct 9.30am–5pm, Nov–Mar 10am–4pm
Entrance Fee: charge
Transportation: Downtown Crossing, Government Center, State

Cross Washington Street to the juncture of Spring Lane and turn right. Walk just a few yards to reach one of the most important forum locations in the growth of American independence, the **Old South Meeting House**. The land on which Old South was built was originally a sloping cornfield and potato patch, owned and tilled by Governor Winthrop. When he died,

it was taken over by a preacher, John Norton, whose widow Mary offered it to her neighbors in 1663 as a church site. The grateful parishioners quickly built themselves a Meeting House of oak and cedar board, which served them for more than 60 years.

In March, 1727, the old wooden structure was replaced by a beautiful new church of bricks and mortar, styled after the graceful London churches of Sir Christopher Wren. "New" Old South, dedicated on April 26, 1730, figured in American annals as the most important Meeting House in American colonial history. It was the scene of scores of protest meetings denouncing British taxation, the Stamp Act, the presence of British troops, and the Townshend Acts. Ultimately, on December 16, 1773, it was the launching pad for a band of Bostonians who, inflamed by the oratory of Samuel Adams – then more famous for patriotism than beer – converged on Griffin's Wharf to stage the Boston Tea Party. Early in the Revolution, the Redcoats turned Old South into a stable and

riding school for the horses of the Queen's Light Dragoons. George Washington corrected that situation in March 1776.

When new Old South was new no more, it was replaced by the 1877 structure now known as New Old South, in the Back Bay (see page 153). The proposed demolition of the 1727 church was the occasion of perhaps the first successful Boston campaign to save a historic structure.

One of the more important events that took place at Old South occurred on a bitterly cold and blizzardy midwinter morning. This was the baptism of a squawking baby named Benjamin Franklin, who was born just around the corner at No.1 Milk Street. As a parish pastor later described it: "This little quivering mass of flesh, hardly a day old, was carried across the wintry street to be baptized on January 6, 1706, the parents evidently thinking that the midwinter climate here was less to be dreaded than the climate in the other world." Unfazed by the cold – or by much else in this world – Franklin lived until 1790.

The firm of Ticknor and Fields, once located in the Old Corner Bookstore, was founded in 1832 by George Ticknor, who partnered with James Fields in 1854. In addition to releasing works by many of the greatest literary lights of 19th-century New England, the firm published The Atlantic Monthly, one of America's most respected periodicals.

BELOW: the Old State House clock.

The Boston Massacre

Just outside the Old State House on the night of March 5, 1770, a group of citizens got into a hostile shouting match with British soldiers. Rocks and snowballs filled the air, bayonets clanged, then somebody fired a shot. Five colonists were killed. The only one widely remembered was the first to die, Crispus Attucks, a black sailor and former slave, aged around 47. His body lay in state for three days in Faneuil Hall. Samuel Adams, the leading advocate for independence from Britain, turned the incident, the most serious of a number of such brawls, into effective propaganda, presenting it as a battle for American liberty. From that moment, revolution became inevitable.

ABOVE: Faneuil Hall.

fire of 1711 burned the place flat, but within two years the colonists rebuilt with the present brick structure at the head of State Street. Then, on December 9, 1747, another great fire gutted the building and destroyed valuable town records but left the brick walls standing, as they are today. The walls even survived the horrendous conflagration of 1872, which leveled most of Downtown Boston's center.

Bostonians are very fond of this old building. It still displays the Lion and Unicorn symbols of British dominion (replicas, as the originals were cheerfully burned during the Revolution), and still features the white balcony where the Declaration of Independence was first read to the citizens of Boston. Inside is a small museum run by the Bostonian Society, formed in 1879 for the purpose of keeping the structure from being removed to Chicago. The museum contains items relating to maritime, military, and business history; also paintings and prints. It's recommended mainly for those with a deep interest

Old State House ❾

Address: 206 Washington Street, www.bostonhistory.org
Tel: 720-1713
Opening Hrs: daily Jul–Aug 9am–6pm, Sept–Dec and Feb–Jun 9am–5pm, Jan 9am–4pm
Entrance Fee: charge
Transportation: State

Turning back now on Washington Street, pass Spring Lane and Water Street on the right and arrive at the intersection with State Street. There stands the **Old State House**, the seat of colonial government.

Since 1632, in the Pudding Lane–King Street–Crooked Lane area (now Congress Street) there had been stocks and pillory, a whipping post, and a thatched-roof church of sorts. And here, in 1658, the Bostonians built their first official Town House, headquarters for royal rulings and demonstrations both for and against hanging Captain Kidd for piracy. The great

Vanished Glories

In the early 1900s, the architectural symbol of the Financial District was the new 495ft (151-meter) Custom House Tower. Some style-conscious financiers applauded the obelisk-like tower, some loathed it. The original Custom House, at its base, had been a thing of true beauty, a superlative example of Greek Revival architecture. But then, in 1913–15, the old Greek temple was encumbered with an extra 30 floors of office (now hotel) space, crowned by decorations that included winged beasts, scrolls, and a huge clock face. The top of the tower is now a nesting place for peregrine falcons, which swoop over the deep canyons between the counting houses.

in the city itself, and not simply its place in American history.

The area beneath the balcony was the site of the famed Boston Massacre on March 5, 1770, when a handful of British soldiers fired into a crowd that was jeering them and pelting them with snowballs; five men were killed. A circle of paving stones marks the spot of the Massacre.

Faneuil Hall ⓾

Address: Congress and North streets, www.faneuilhallmarketplace.com
Tel: 242-5642
Opening Hours: Mon–Sat 10am–9pm, Sun 11am–6pm; extended summer and restaurant hours
Entrance Fee: free
Transportation: State, Government Center, Aquarium, Faneuil Hall

From the Massacre site marker, head north on Congress Street and turn right to reach the Faneuil Hall–Quincy Market complex. Here, fronted by a statue of Sam Adams, stands **Faneuil Hall**, designated by patriot orator James Otis as "The Cradle of Liberty."

Faneuil Hall, built for the commercial benefit of Boston's merchants, was personally financed by Peter Faneuil, who John Hancock labeled "the topmost merchant in all the town." Designed by the Scottish-born portrait painter John Smibert, it was dedicated on September 10, 1742, and served as a forum for the raw opinions of rebels and patriots. In 1806 the hall was expanded by Charles Bulfinch. It is still in demand as a forum for oratory and opinion.

The historic Faneuil Hall sits on the western end of the "festival marketplace" variously known as Faneuil Hall Marketplace or simply **Quincy Market ⓫** (see page 108). This is a vibrant, contemporary urban spot resonant with history. Quincy Market was constructed by order of Mayor Josiah Quincy in 1826, and served for almost 150 years as a retail and wholesale distribution center for meat and produce. By the early 1970s the market and its surroundings, though still housing a number of old-fashioned food shops, had become extremely seedy and plans were afoot

Although born a Bostonian, Benjamin Franklin made his name in Philadelphia. He ran off to the Pennsylvania city at the age of 17 after a quarrel with his brother, a printer, to whom he had been apprenticed. The tale of the penniless youth's migration is engagingly told in his autobiography.

BELOW: Quincy Market.

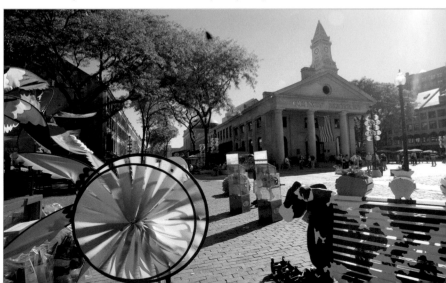

"I hope that visitors to the Memorial take away with them the ungraspable nature of the Holocaust, the completely overwhelming, inexplicable dimension of dimension. And coupled with that, a sense of hope that survival and the building of this memorial make possible."

Stanley Saitowitz, architect

for its demolition. Fortunately, "adaptive reuse" was just then coming into vogue, and Quincy Market became the template for renovated urban spaces throughout the nation.

Today, the market consists of three long Greek Revival buildings, chock-full of restaurants and shops. A lively flower market adds further color, as do wooden pushcarts in the tree-lined malls between the buildings, from which peddlers sell tourist-targeted wares. Entertainers perform regularly, too. Little wonder that Faneuil Hall Marketplace is now one of the major tourist attractions in the country.

A new **Boston National Historical Park Visitor Center** (tel: 242-5642; www.nps.gov/bost; daily 9am–6pm) opened in 2012 on the first floor of Faneuil Hall. Staffed by park rangers and volunteers, here you'll find maps, brochures, and free ranger-guided tours.

Union Oyster House ⑫

North from here, on Union Street, stands the **Union Oyster House** (see page 106). The building was

specifically mentioned in a plan of 1708, and has housed the restaurant since 1826; this would secure it a tie with Durgin Park (see page 106) for honors as Boston's oldest eatery. Oysters have long been its forte. Legend has it that the place sometimes served up 35 barrels of Cape Cod oysters a day, with Daniel Webster regularly downing six of the bivalves per glass of brandy – and he drank several of the latter.

The building housed the *Massachusetts Spy* newspaper from 1771 to 1775. It then became the headquarters for Ebenezer Hancock, brother of John Hancock and paymaster for the Continental Army, who lived in a neighboring house just a few steps along and to the right, on Salt Lane. The city's oldest brick house, it dates to 1660, when it was owned by Boston's first Town Crier, William Courser.

Later, the Oyster House building was briefly home to Louis-Philippe, later ruler of France (1830–48). He eked out his exile in Boston by teaching French to students in his second-floor bedroom.

BELOW: the New England Holocaust Memorial.

Scollay Square

Where City Hall now stands used to be Scollay Square. Here was the Old Howard burlesque theater, the stage-home of such showstoppers as Ann Corio, Jimmy Durante, and Sliding Billy Watson, and the Crawford House, in which dancer Sally Keith nightly twirled her two top tassels in opposite directions, openly defying the laws of physics. Here were tattoo parlors, fortune-tellers, gypsy palmists, cheap gin mills, snap-photo joints, hash houses – just about anything a lad on leave from the Charlestown Navy Yard could desire. The nostalgia surrounding Scollay Square is such that it is fondly remembered even by people too young to have yielded to its temptations.

New England Holocaust Memorial ⓭

Nearby is a slender line of six luminous glass-and-steel towers that form the **New England Holocaust Memorial**. The glass towers are etched with 6 million numbers, representing the 6 million Jewish victims killed in the Holocaust, and suggestive of the tattoos inflicted on many prisoners. The solemnity and severe design of the Memorial are juxtaposed by two nearby life-size bronzes – one seated, one standing – of former mayor James Michael Curley. The shine on the seated statue's knee suggests that many visitors like to perch there.

The Boston Stone

Behind the Oyster House, Marsh Lane, Salt Lane, and Creek Square meet at the Blackstone Block, where three centuries of architecture can be found. And here, at Salt Lane corner, sits the **Boston Stone ⓮**, a huge stone ball and a stone trough, shipped from England in 1700 to serve as a paint mill. Some say – and others dispute – that the stone was used as a surveying landmark, as the point from which all distances from Boston were measured.

Government Center

Return to Congress Street and climb the many stairs leading up to the new **City Hall** (1969), a charmless inverted ziggurat once described in the Boston press as "the ugliest pigeon coop in the world."

This area was Scollay Square, a slightly disreputable entertainments area. Then, in 1960, along came urban renewal in the form of the new Boston Redevelopment Authority. In rumbled the bulldozers to level not only Scollay Square but the entire West End, a tenement quarter that has been replaced by the luxury apartments of Charles River Park. Scollay Square suddenly

ABOVE: the famed Union Oyster House.

became the new squeaky-clean **Government Center**, as the planners wiped out almost every physical vestige of the past. They created an emptiness fanning out from Court Street and called it **City Hall Plaza** – a delightful place for those who like acres of dull bricks unrelieved by shrubbery or trees.

Financial District

Boston's Financial District is roughly bordered by Atlantic Avenue, State Street, and Devonshire Street. This part of Downtown, especially State Street, is a superb architectural sampler, encompassing a wide variety of styles. Step into Exchange Place or 75 State Street to gawk at their glorious marble halls.

Head to Franklin Street to visit the **Alexander Graham Bell Room** **⑮** at No. 185 (open during regular business hours) to view the reassembled attic from nearby Court Street, where, on June 3, 1875, the inventor sent speech sounds over a wire electrically. The telephone was born. On display are the world's first telephone switchboard – it connected six lines

ABOVE: find quirky items at Quincy Market.
RIGHT: Custom House tower.

in 1877 – and the world's first commercial telephone.

Downtown changes

Elsewhere, much of Downtown Boston has changed or disappeared during the past half-century. The famed Boston Wool District, liaison between Australia and New England's voracious textile mills, now exists in name only. The same is true of the Leather District, crippled by the disappearance of the New England shoe industry but recently revived by chic stores and eateries.

Returning to Downtown Crossing, and walking south along Washington Street toward Kneeland, soon you will pass on the right the site of the old Adams House, once a terminal stop on the early Boston–Hartford–New York stagecoach route. This section of the city has been in limbo for years. On Washington are the remains of what were once the movie palaces of the 1930s and 1940s. Little remains

SHOPPING

Downtown shopping is dominated by department stores (Macy's), chains (H&M), and tourist-targeting shops on Washington Street and in Faneuil Hall Marketplace. Washington Street is also home to fine jewelry shops.

Arts and Crafts

Windsor Button
35 Temple Place
Tel: 482-4969
www.windsorbutton.com
An excellent yarn selection for knitters and crocheters is found at this 1936 sewing standby, along with scores of buttons and sewing supplies.

Bargains

DSW Shoe Warehouse
385 Washington St
Tel: 556-0052
Top-quality, well-known brands sold for up to 50 percent off retail.

Books

Brattle Book Shop
9 West St
Tel: 542-0210
www.brattlebookshop.com
Established in 1825, the three-story antiquarian shop has more than 250,000 books, maps, prints, postcards, and ephemera.

of what was once the Combat Zone, one of the sleaziest and most notorious enclaves of commercial vice on the East Coast. Thanks to prolonged public outrage and the demands of civic leaders, it has been politically garroted to extinction. The topless bars and sex pockets have been virtually wiped out.

With Emerson College's purchase of many buildings on Tremont Street in the 1990s, this area began to transform itself. Pride of place on Emerson's urban campus goes to the College's glorious 800-seat **Cutler Majestic Theatre** in Boston's Theater District.

Nearby is **Allen's Alley**, honoring Boston's wry comedian Fred Allen, who left his imprint on most aspects of show business, from burlesque to musical revue, and from New York radio to Hollywood television. Allen loved his Boston. As he once remarked: "California is a great place to live – if you're an orange."

Chinatown ⑯

Alongside the former Combat Zone (and gradually absorbing its streets and alleys) is Boston's colorful **Chinatown**, guarded at its eastern gateway, diagonally across Atlantic Avenue from South Station, by a looping arch and an ornate pair of stone dragon dogs. Chinatown, whose main drag is Beach Street, is not very large but is packed with Asian restaurants and exotic stores that draw thousands of tourists and regulars nightly from the nearby Theater District on Tremont Street and the hotels to the west. It's great fun to visit.

On leaving Chinatown and turning right on Kneeland, look for **Jacob Wirth,** an old-time German restaurant on the right (see page 107). Since 1868, generations of newsmen, theater people, and students from Tufts University's nearby Medical Center have relished the dark brew and bratwurst (plated, oddly enough, not only with sauerkraut but with a stewed tomato), served by white-aproned waiters. It's a place that never changes.

Just up Stuart on Tremont Street are the **Wilbur** and **Shubert** theaters, where for years many Broadway-bound productions have had their first performances.

BEOW: a mural by Lisa Hoang in Chinatown.

RESTAURANTS, BARS, AND CAFES

Restaurants

American

Durgin Park
340 Faneuil Hall Marketplace
Tel: 227-2038
www.durgin-park.com
L & D daily $$–$$$
[p273, F2]
Yankee cooking attracts flocks of tourists to this legendary old dining hall (established 1826), famed for communal tables (smaller tables available on request) and huge portions.

KO Prime
Nine Zero Hotel, 90 Tremont St
Tel: 772-0202
www.koprimeboston.com
B & D daily $$$
[p273, D3]
A sophisticated carnivore's den, KO Prime has a lively atmosphere and steakhouse cuisine, including à la carte steaks, Kobe beef tartare

and bone marrow with a blood-orange salad.

Milk Street Café
50 Milk St
Tel: 542-3663
www.milkstreetcafe.com
B & L Mon–Fri $ [p273, E3]
Kosher cafeteria with a vegetarian slant, with dishes such as roasted salmon, and a good selection of nutritious, homemade soups.

North 26
Millennium Bostonian Hotel,
26 North St
Tel: 557-3640
www.millenniumhotels.com
B, L, & D daily $$$
[p273, E2]
Expect New England cuisine with creative flourishes: shellfish stew, chicken with sunflower pesto and farmstand ratatouille, oysters on the half-shell, specialty s'mores, and Boston cream whoopie pie.

South Street Diner
178 Kneeland St
Tel: 350-0028
www.southstreetdiner.com
B, L, & D daily $ [p268, D2]
Classic diner fare and funky atmosphere, right down to the jukebox and all-day breakfasts. Open 24/7.

Union Oyster House
41 Union St
Tel: 227-2750
www.unionoysterhouse.com
L & D daily $$–$$$
[p273, E2]
Steaks and seafood are served in atmospheric rooms with creaky floors, low ceilings, and wooden booths. Oysters, clam chowder, and the history – it's the oldest restaurant in the country (open since 1826) and Daniel Webster dined here – are the main draws.

Chinese

Chau Chow City
83 Essex St
Tel: 338-8158
http://chauchowcity.com
L & D daily $–$$
[p273, E4]
One of Chinatown's best destinations for dim sum, the glitzy three-story neon palace serves Hong Kong-style fare until 4am.

East Ocean City
27 Beach St
Tel: 542-2504
www.eastoceancity.com
L & D daily $ [p268, D2]
Marble floors, tablecloths, and exotic seafood raise this Chinatown restaurant a notch above the competition.

Empire Garden
690 Washington St
Tel: 482-8898
http://empiregardenboston.com
L & D daily $ [p268, D2]
Waitresses circle this large room with carts filled with dim sum – snack-size treats such as steamed dumplings and barbecue pork buns. Diners are charged by the number of plates stacked up at the end of the meal.

Gourmet Dumpling House
52 Beach St
Tel: 338-6223
www.gourmetdumpling.com
L & D daily $ [p268, D2]
Simple and crowded, but delicious dumplings and the assorted mains offer plenty of distraction. Service is efficient but brusque; don't plan on lingering long after the last bite.

Taiwan Café
34 Oxford St
Tel: 426-8181
http://taiwancafeboston.com
L & D daily $ [p268, D2]
Fresh, fast, tiny, and tasty. The long menu is varied: from eggplant with basil, to *ma po* tofu, to salt and pepper calamari and shredded pork with dried bean curd.

European

Locke-Ober
3 Winter Place
Tel: 542-1340
www.lockeober.com
D Mon–Sat $$$–$$$$
[p273, D3]

LEFT: there are several eateries at Faneuil Hall Marketplace.

One of Boston's oldest restaurants, Locke-Ober is more a destination for the experience rather than the food. Traditional favorites, such as JFK's lobster stew, remain and the mahogany bar is just as beautiful. Once a power-dining spot, the dress code has now vanished.

French

Café Fleuri
Langham Hotel,
250 Franklin St
Tel: 451-1900
www.langhamhotels.com
B & L daily, D Tue–Sat $$$ ㉓
[p273, F3]
Sunday jazz brunch and the Saturday all-you-can-eat chocolate buffet (served Sept–June 11am–3pm) are major draws at this upscale hotel café.

Pigalle
75 South Charles St
Tel: 423-4944
www.pigalleboston.com
D Tue–Sun $$$–$$$$ ㉔
[p268, C2]
Mark Orfaly delivers sophisticated Parisian-inspired fare in the heart of the Theater District.

Radius
8 High St
Tel: 426-1234
www.radiusrestaurant.com
L Mon–Fri, D Mon–Sat $$$ ㉕
[p273, E4]
Expect modern French cuisine, a round dining room with a warm ambience, and wonderfully refined service. The creative menu focuses on seasonal ingredients: ginger oil-poached duck with grilled scallion compote and spicy coconut caramel; a slow-roasted

RIGHT: beautifully presented sushi.

salmon with cockles, bouillabaisse consommé and uni-saffron emulsion; and a goat's cheese and huckleberry cheesecake.

Les Zygomates
129 South St
Tel: 542-5108
www.winebar.com
L Mon–Fri, D Mon–Sat $$$ ㉖
[p268, D2]
The name roughly translates to mean "the muscles in the face that make you smile," and patrons here are all smiles after enjoying bistro classics and fine wine in the casual, convivial atmosphere.

German

Jacob Wirth
31 Stuart St
Tel: 338-8586
www.jacobwirth.com
L & D daily $$ ㉗ [p268, C2]
This time warp in the Theater District has served wurst, sauerkraut, and beer since 1868. Also on the menu now are American standards,

including nachos, burgers, BLTs, and root-beer floats.

Italian

Marliave
10 Bosworth St
Tel: 422-0004
www.marliave.com
L & D daily $$–$$$ ㉘
[p273, E3]
A Downtown Italian-American institution that oozes ambience and red sauce in large portions. Delightful outdoor patio.

Seafood

McCormick and Schmick's
North Market Building, Faneuil Hall Marketplace
Tel: 720-5522
www.mccormickandschmicks.com
L & D daily $$–$$$ ㉙
[p273, E2]
This chain, decorated like an upscale steakhouse, serves 40 varieties of seafood. Offerings might include wild king salmon, Dungeness crab, lobster,

Prices for a three-course dinner per person, with tax and tip:

$ = under $25
$$ = $25–50
$$$ = $50–75
$$$$ = over $75

and Massachusetts scrod. The outdoor patio is a great spot for people-watching.

Bars

The Good Life
28 Kington St
Tel: 451-2622
❺ [p273, E4]
The Good Life delivers a decent burger and martini, and its downstairs AfterLife lounge offers DJ and live music and over 150 vodkas.

Posh BLU
4 Avery St
Tel: 375-8550
❻ [p273, D4]
Posh BLU features an upscale menu – think smoked mozzarella with basil pesto, and polenta fries with truffle fondutta.

FANEUIL HALL MARKETPLACE

Located on a well-traveled portion of the historic Freedom Trail, this vibrant bazaar attracts millions of visitors each year.

Faneuil Hall was built in 1742 as a gift from Peter Faneuil, a wealthy Boston merchant. First-floor stalls sold vegetables, meat, and dairy, while the second floor served as the Boston Town Hall. It was at town meetings here that patriots such as Samuel Adams and James Otis gave inspirational speeches, sparking revolutionary aspirations among colonists. Such activities, along with on-site protests of the Sugar Act, Stamp Act, and Townshend Acts, helped ignite the American Revolution and led Faneuil Hall to be christened 'The Cradle of Liberty'.

Today, the commercial first floor, with its festival-like atmosphere, takes center stage. Over 150 shops and eateries are spread among Faneuil Hall and the three long, granite buildings behind it – Quincy Market, North Market, and South Market, which contain major retailers such as Urban Outfitters, Ann Taylor, and Victoria's Secret, alongside independent shops, as well as restaurants. Quincy Market in particular attracts hungry shoppers with the diverse to-go options of its Food Colonnade. Between the halls, local artisans sell clothing, crafts, and souvenirs from 44 wooden pushcarts, collectively known as the Bull Market.

ABOVE: established in the 1980s, the Bull Market is said to be the world's first 'fleet' of wooden retail pushcarts, offering everything from beaded necklaces to Boston-themed socks and hand-roasted nuts.

BELOW: centrally located in the heart of Downtown Boston, Faneuil Hall and the plaza that fronts it bustle day and night with shoppers and tourists.

The Essentials

Address: Congress and North streets, www.faneuilhallmarketplace.com
Tel: 242-5642
Opening Hrs: Mon–Sat 10am–9pm, Sun 11am–6pm; restaurants daily until late
Transportation: State, Government Center, Aquarium, Faneuil Hall

ABOVE: the Faneuil Hall marketplace includes both indoor and outdoor space for varied retailers and restaurants, so inclement weather need not spoil your visit.

ABOVE: just by Faneuil Hall, the Haymarket farmers' market is one of the best places to find fresh produce – with some of the lowest prices for fruit and vegetables.

LEFT: seasonal scarecrows celebrate fall in front of the colorful Faneuil Hall Flower Market.

THE CHANGING FACES OF FANEUIL HALL

Faneuil Hall has endured numerous renovations. First, the building was gutted by a fire in 1761 and rebuilt two years later. Then, in 1806, noted American architect Charles Bulfinch expanded the hall in a Greek Revival style, doubling the height and width, adding a third floor, installing new interiors, and moving the cupola. In 1898–9, the structure was renovated to make it safe from fires, and further renovations occurred in both 1979 and 1992. Despite all these changes, one piece of the original structure remains: the grasshopper weathervane created by silversmith Shem Drowne in 1742, which sits atop the cupola. The gilded copper creature is 4ft (1.2 meters) long and weighs a hefty 80lbs (36kg). It is thought to have been inspired by the London Royal Exchange's grasshopper vane, which in turn was based on the family crest of the Royal Exchange's founder, Sir Thomas Gresham.

ABOVE: Faneuil Hall's cupola was originally centered atop the building, but was moved to the east end during Bulfinch's renovation of the hall in the early 1800s.

BELOW: by the 1920s, Faneuil Hall had already hosted an impressive list of orators, including Samuel Adams, Daniel Webster, Susan B. Anthony, and Oliver Wendell Holmes.

THE NORTH END

Paul Revere lived here, and so did successive waves of European immigrants. Old North, Boston's oldest church, is a major stop on the Freedom Trail.

In Boston's North End, there is a white marble bas-relief of Dante Alighieri in the central courtyard of the little branch library on Parmenter Street. Perhaps this doesn't seem so unusual – after all, great literary figures are often so commemorated, and in fact, the names of dozens of such luminaries are inscribed in the exterior walls of Boston's central library in Copley Square. However, the wise visage of Dante has a special meaning on Parmenter Street. Dante is the national poet of Italy, the first writer to create great art out of the nascent Italian language. And it is here, in the North End, that Italian was first commonly spoken on the streets of Boston.

An ethnic progression

Much of the North End looks and sounds like an Italian *quartiere*. Many streets are narrow and crooked, laundry flaps on outdoor clotheslines, and produce is sold at open-air stands. Children play in the street, young couples chat over espresso in cafés, devout Catholics head to Mass at St Leonard's Church, and young men argue about soccer in the middle of Hanover Street. But the Mediterranean cast of

these old streets, somewhat faded now but still apparent to even the casual visitor, is only the most recent face of what is, aside from Charlestown, the oldest neighborhood in Boston.

Three hundred years ago, the North End was known as the 'island of North Boston.' On colonial maps it looks like an irregular thumb jutting into the Atlantic Ocean with a canal, called the Mill Stream, cutting it off from the larger Shawmut peninsula. Until recently the Fitzgerald Expressway (also known as the Central Artery)

Main Attractions

PAUL REVERE'S HOUSE
HANOVER STREET
ST STEPHEN'S CHURCH
PAUL REVERE MALL
OLD NORTH CHURCH
COPP'S HILL BURYING GROUND

Maps and Listings

MAP, PAGE 112
SHOPPING, PAGE 117
RESTAURANTS, PAGE 118
ACCOMMODATIONS, PAGE 242

LEFT: North End streets decorated for a festa. **RIGHT:** flower-seller on Hanover Street.

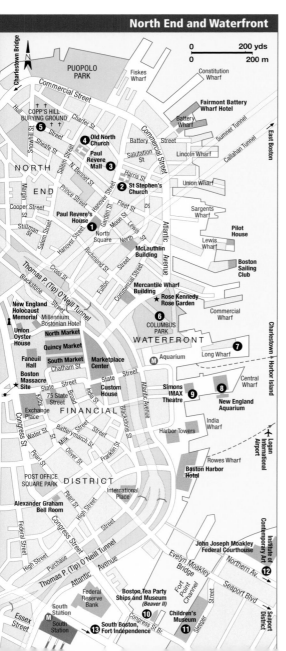

North End and Waterfront

followed the same course as the old canal, and cut off the neighborhood even more abruptly. While water no longer surrounds the North End, and the expressway has been rerouted underground, the neighborhood is still set apart from the rest of the city that grew out of and away from it.

When the Puritans arrived in 1630, the North End was a marshy finger of land with few apparent virtues. But by the late colonial period, the small cluster of wooden houses had become one of Boston's most fashionable quarters, with several fine brick homes and some of the richest families in town.

Unfortunately, many of the prominent residents were Tories who, when the British evacuated in 1776, hightailed it to Canada and took their money with them. Rich Yankees pulled out too, preferring the more genteel atmosphere of Beacon Hill, then being developed. Artisans, sailors, and tradesmen filled the empty houses, and throughout the 19th century the North End was a workingman's quarter dominated by the shipping industry.

Irish domination

In the mid-1800s, the North End was overrun by European immigrants, and the neighborhood became a slum notorious for its bordellos, street crime, and squalid conditions. The Irish were the first to settle in any great numbers. They poured into the neighborhood after the Irish Potato Famine of the 1840s and soon were dominating the area politically. A latter-day reminder of the old Irish days was the 1995 funeral of Rose Fitzgerald Kennedy, mother of President John F. Kennedy, which was conducted at St Stephen's Church on Hanover Street. Rose Kennedy had been born in that neighborhood 105 years earlier.

East European Jews followed the Irish, and by 1890 had established a thriving residential and business district along Salem Street. The Italians – mostly from Sicily and the southern provinces of the mainland – were the last group to arrive in substantial numbers; but by the 1920s they had established an overwhelming majority and have dominated the neighborhood ever since.

Good food, colorful history

Most people come to the North End for one of two reasons. During the day they visit historic sites, and at night they come to eat. Both activities are certainly worthwhile, but there's much more here than the Freedom Trail and veal scallopini.

By and large, the North End isn't much to look at. Unlike Beacon Hill or the Back Bay, it isn't a planned community. There isn't a uniform architectural style or much interest in large-scale historical preservation: in fact, quite the opposite. The North End has an improvisational quality, as if the neighborhood was built piecemeal without the benefit of an overall plan. What evolved is a hodgepodge of buildings, some quite

ABOVE: North End apartments.

attractive, others downright ugly. Many were built in the late 1800s as tenement houses for European immigrants. The concern at that time wasn't how pretty a building looked but how many people could be crammed inside.

The archaic street plan makes things even more confusing. It's easy to get lost, but it's also not necessarily a bad thing if you do. With alleyways and side streets running off in every direction, all kinds of unconventional spaces – from vegetable gardens to colonial graveyards – can be discovered in the neighborhood's less traveled areas. When you tire of walking around the neighborhood, you can always head for one of the cafés on Hanover Street and watch the neighborhood walk around you.

From Hanover Street, turn right on Richmond Street and then left to enter North Square, where the Paul Revere and Pierce-Hichborn houses stand side by side.

The Gentrifiers Arrive

In recent years, the North End's well-earned reputation for neighborliness has made it a prime target for gentrification, especially along the waterfront. Rents have skyrocketed, condo conversions have run rampant, and some old-time residents are getting priced right out of their homes. With the old guard aging and the new generation moving out, some dyed-in-the-wool North Enders worry that the old neighborhood is slipping away. But, although it's true that the Italian population isn't as large as it used to be, the spirit of the community persists. And more than a few of the clubs and cafés are patronized by suburban Italians who enjoy coming back to the streets where they grew up.

The speed of tenement building can be gauged by the fact that, between 1850 and 1855, the number of Irish in Boston soared from 35,000 to 50,000. Most of them settled in the North End.

Not long after Paul Revere bought his North Square House in 1770, he built an adjacent barn – only to learn that the new structure stood partly upon a neighbor's land. The neighbor, Manasseh Marston, graciously let the oversight stand.

Paul Revere's House ❶

Address: 19 North Square, www.paul reverehouse.org
Tel: 523-2338
Opening Hrs: daily mid-Apr–Oct 9.30am–5.15pm, Nov–mid-Apr 9.30am–4.15pm, closed Mon Jan–Mar
Entrance Fee: charge
Transportation: Haymarket

Paul Revere's House is a two-story dwelling with an overhanging second floor. It was built in 1676 and is the oldest house in this part of Boston. When the 35-year-old Revere (see page 30), then a silver-smith, purchased the house in 1770, the third floor had been added, but in the early 20th century this was removed to 'restore' the building to its original appearance. It is fur-nished today much as it was when it was home to Paul and the first Mrs Revere, who bore him eight children, and then, when she died, to the second Mrs Revere, who pro-duced a similar brood.

One of the upstairs rooms is cov-ered with wallpaper that is a repro-duction of paper made in Boston toward the end of the 18th century. The room also contains several pieces of furniture that belonged to the Reveres. A cabinet displays attractive silver, some made by Revere. Outside, in the courtyard, is a 931lb (422kg) bronze bell cast by Revere, generally acknowledged to have been the best bell-maker of his time.

Nowadays, when historic preser-vation is much more of a research-informed science than it was when the Revere House was rescued from near-dereliction, architectural histori-ans argue with some of the restoration work done back then. But this struc-ture provides as good a look as you are going to get anywhere in Boston at what domestic arrangements were like in the pre-revolutionary town.

Next door is the **Pierce-Hichborn House** (guided tours only, con-tact Paul Revere House, above, for hours), which belonged to Nathaniel Hichborn, Revere's cousin. This asym-metrical, three-story brick building was constructed between 1711 and 1715 in the new English Renaissance style, a radical departure from the Tudor-style wooden dwellings built

BELOW: the wooden facade of Paul Revere's House.

Hanover Street

The best place for people-watching in the North End is lively Hanover Street, the neighborhood's central thor-oughfare and the heart of its business district. Restaurants and cafés stretch from one end to the other, and a steady stream of tourists walking the Freedom Trail (see page 40) pass through. If you're looking for a place to eat, you can't go far wrong here, or for that mat-ter, anywhere else in the neighborhood. Whether you're hankering after sea-food, traditional pasta-and-tomato-based southern Italian fare, or the imaginative offerings of the trendsetter chefs that have been colonizing the district, there's a wide choice of eater-ies to try.

Church. Built in 1933, this generous brick courtyard is a sort of Americanized piazza where kids run around and footsore tourists take a breather from the Freedom Trail. In addition to the traditional Italian fountain, the Prado features a magnificent equestrian statue of Paul Revere, modeled in 1885 by Cyrus Dallin and cast in 1940. On the south (left) wall, bronze panels recall the history of Boston and its people.

At the far end of the Prado, cross Unity Street and enter the small gate which opens to the rear of Christ Church, more often known as Old North.

The four 18th-century Belgian Baroque cherubim with trumpets that stand in front of the organ in Old North Church were booty captured by a privateer owned by members of the congregation. They were probably destined for a French church in Canada.

in the previous century. It was restored in 1949.

St Stephen's Church ❷

Address: 401 Hanover Street
Tel: 523-1230
Opening Hrs: call for information
Entrance Fee: free
Transportation: Haymarket

Return to Hanover Street via Fleet Street and, after 150yds/meters, reach **St Stephen's Church**, with its white steeple. Built in 1804 as a Congregationalist Meeting House, this simple, dignified structure is the only one of five Boston churches designed by Charles Bulfinch that still stands. It has had a checkered history. In 1813 it became a Unitarian church and in 1862 it was acquired by the Roman Catholic archbishopric. Eight years later, when Hanover Street had to be widened to accommodate traffic, the church was moved back 12ft (4 meters) and raised 6ft (2 meters); then, in 1965, it was restored to its original level and to its Bulfinch stark simplicity.

Paul Revere Mall ❸

The **Paul Revere Mall**, known locally as the Prado, faces St Stephen's

Old North Church ❹

Address: 193 Salem Street, www.old-north.com
Tel: 523-6676
Opening Hrs: June–Oct daily 9am–6pm, Nov–Dec daily 10am–5pm, Jan–Feb Tue–Sun 10am–4pm, Mar–May daily 9am–5pm
Entrance Fee: free
Transportation: Haymarket

Boston's oldest church is one of its most treasured historical monuments.

LEFT: a reminder of local heritage.
BELOW: Old North Church.

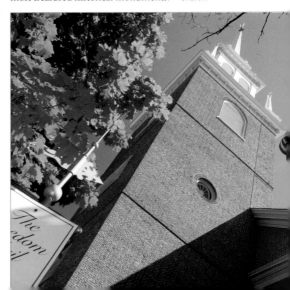

EAT

The North End Market Tour (tel: 800-979-3370; www.bostonfood tours.com) offers a tasting-filled three-hour exploration of vibrant, authentic North End markets. You might pop by fresh produce stands, *pasticcerie*, a *salumeria* stuffed with olive oil and prosciutto, or an *enoteca* for *aperitivi*... the colors, aromas, and tastes are all tantalizing.

BELOW: the Paul Revere statue on Paul Revere Mall.

Built in 1723 to house the town's second Anglican parish, the Old North is most famous for its part in Paul Revere's ride to Lexington. On April 18, 1775, sexton Robert Newman snuck out of his home and placed two lanterns in the belfry as a signal to Revere – 'one if by land, and two if by sea' – that the British Army was advancing to Concord. Ironically, British General Thomas Gage is said to have watched the Battle of Bunker Hill from the very same belfry only a few months later.

Old North's steeple, 191ft (58 meters) high, has always been Boston's tallest and a major landmark. Twice, in 1804 and again in 1954, it was blown over by hurricanes and subsequently restored. America's first peal of eight bells hangs in the belfry; it was first rung in 1745 and has tolled for every departed President of the nation since George Washington died in 1799. Paul Revere, at age 15, formed a bell-ringers' guild with some other young men, and helped ring Old North's bells.

Enter the church, whose interior has been painted white since 1912. The high pew boxes are still intact, with the names of the family owners engraved on bronze plates. These boxes were designed to keep in the warmth of braziers filled with hot coal or bricks, which were placed on the floor on wintry days. The clock at the rear of the church and the four Baroque Belgian cherubs that surround it date back to the opening of the church. So does the organ case, although the actual instrument dates only from 1759. The chandeliers are brass, made in Holland in 1700. The bust of George Washington, in a niche to the left of the apse, was the first public memorial to the great man and was said by General Lafayette in 1824 to be 'more like him than any other portrait.' Another historical artifact is the 'third' steeple lantern, lit by President Gerald Ford during the American bicentennial observance at the church in 1975. The church has 37 crypts, containing, it is claimed, 1,100 bodies.

Immediately to the north of the church is a small garden with markers recounting historic events and distinguished persons of the parish.

A Peal of Eight Bells

The bells of Old North Church were cast in 1744 by Abell Rudhall in Gloucester, England, and range in weight from 620 to 1,545lbs (281–701kg). They are a 'maiden peal,' because each bell has a perfect tone without having been filed down or machined. Reputed to be the sweetest in the nation, the bells bear unique inscriptions – some historical in nature ('We are the first ring of bells cast for the British Empire in North America'), and others more poetic ('Since generosity has opened our mouths, our tongues shall ring aloud its praise'). Today, the bells are generally rung Saturday mornings, and a copy of the Paul Revere-signed charter for local bell-ringers hangs in the room.

Copp's Hill Burying Ground ➎

Address: Hull Street, between Salem and Snowhill streets
Opening Hrs: June–Sept daily 9am–5pm, other months until 3pm
Entrance Fee: free
Transportation: Haymarket, North Station

From Old North, walk up Hull Street for 150yds/meters. On the right is **Copp's Hill Burying Ground**, Boston's second-oldest cemetery (after King's Chapel) and the North End's quietest corner. Its name comes from that of William Copp, who farmed on the hill's southeast slope in the mid-17th century. In the colonial period, the base of the hill was occupied by the city's first black community, and about 1,000 black people are buried in the cemetery's northwest corner.

A tall black monument commemorates Prince Hall, who helped found Boston's first school for black children. However, his main claim to fame is that he was the founder, in 1784, of the African Grand Lodge of Massachusetts, the world's first black Masonic Lodge.

Near here is the tombstone of 'Capt. Daniel Malcolm, Mercht,' who is remembered for smuggling 60 casks of wine into port without paying the duty. He asked to be buried 'in a Stone Grave 10 feet deep,' secure from desecration. His body may have been safe, but his tombstone was not: on it are scars made by the Redcoats who singled out this patriot's grave-marker for their target practice.

In the southeast corner of the cemetery is the Mathers' family tomb, where the Puritan divines Increase, Cotton, and Samuel Mather may be buried. Another Copp's Hill grave was left deliberately unmarked, and no one knows where it is. It holds the remains of Dr John Webster, murderer of George Parkman, who was hanged for his 1849 crime and promptly interred here.

Weekend processions

In summer, local feasts or *festas* celebrate saints' days. They are held almost every weekend in July and August, with Sunday being by far the more exciting day, and usually involve processions in which saints' statues are carried. Other highlights of the festivities include street fairs, brass bands, singers, raffles, and food stalls selling sausage and peppers, and *zeppole* (fried dough).

During the feast of the Madonna del Soccorso (Our Lady of Succor), celebrated in mid-August, the star of the show is the famous flying angel. The angel is the messenger of the Madonna, protector of the fishing fleet and patron saint of Sicilian immigrants. Portrayed by a little girl on a pulley, she floats above North Street, her arms outstretched to the crowd, and is lowered to the statue and the procession below.

'*Viva la Madonna!*' shout the men bearing the statue, and the throng echoes, '*Viva la Madonna!*' It is the language of Dante, and today still the nostalgic language of Boston's North End.

ABOVE: taking part in a Little Italy street festival.

SHOPPING

The North End is spare on boutiques, but a few women's clothing shops are worthy of a pit stop.

Women's Clothing and Accessories

In-Jean-ius
441 Hanover St
Tel: 523-5326
www.injeanius.com
Denim heaven, with over 30 premium brands, including Antik, Loomstate, Chip & Pepper, and Meli-Melo.

Shake the Tree
67 Salem St
Tel: 742-0484

www.shakethetreeboston.com
This gem of a shop features contemporary clothing from Ella Moss, Velvet, Sanctuary, and Splendid, bags from Orly Kiely and Latico, and jewelry from local artisans. Also stocks sweet-smelling soaps and candles, and other unique giftworthy items.

Twilight
12 Fleet St
Tel: 523-8008
www.twilightboutique.com
Find sophisticated feminine wear from the likes of Nicole Miller, Cosabella, and Autumn Cashmere. Jewelry and handbags are stocked too.

RESTAURANTS, BARS, AND CAFES

Restaurants

Fusion

Taranta
210 Hanover St
Tel: 720-0052
www.tarantarist.com
D daily $$$ **30** [p272, E2]
An imaginative blend of southern Italian and Peruvian cuisine yields great results at this eco-friendly eatery. More traditional antipasti and pasta dishes share the menu with offerings such as pork chop with a rocoto pepper and sugarcane glaze, yucca *piatella*, and sautéed Peruvian corn, and an Atlantic salmon with herbed risotto, Peruvian asparagus, and Pisco-Sicilian blood-orange sauce.

Italian

Antico Forno
93 Salem St

Tel: 723-6733
www.anticofornoboston.com
L Mon–Sat, D daily $$–$$$ **31** [p272, E2]
A large, beehive-shaped, wood-burning brick oven sets the mood for this cozy spot decorated to resemble a rustic Neapolitan trattoria. Just about everything – pizzas, gnocchi, roast chicken – is cooked in the oven.

Bacco
107 Salem St
Tel: 624-0454
www.bacconorthend.com
D daily $$ **32** [p272, E1]
Have a drink in the handsome first-floor bar, with French doors opening onto Salem Street, then head upstairs to an upscale Italian menu. Hearty entrées include potato gnocchi with braised Bolognese ragu and veal saltimbocca

with roasted red peppers, *prosciutto di parma*, potato gratin, and a sage marsala reduction. The wine is moderately priced.

Bricco
241 Hanover St
Tel: 248-6800
www.bricco.com
D daily $$$ **33** [p272, F2]
Restaurateur Frank De Pasquale's chic, upscale boutique restaurant offers treats such as pumpkin tortelli with amaretti and truffle honey, homemade gnocchi baked with buffalo mozzarella, and veal stuffed with prosciutto and fontina. More draws: an extensive, all-Italian wine list, $20 valet parking, gluten-free pasta options, and a late-night lounge serving pizza until 2am Tue–Sun.

Caffé Paradiso
255 Hanover St
Tel: 742-1768
www.caffeparadiso.com
7am–2am daily $$ **34** [p272, F2]
Though pricey, this is a prime North End choice for espresso and Italian desserts – cannoli, tiramisu, homemade *gelato* – and chitchat. The TV beams in European soccer games via satellite.

Cantina Italiana
346 Hanover St
Tel: 723-4577
www.cantinaitaliana.com
L Mon–Sat & D daily $$ **35** [p272, F1]
That large neon sign of a bottle pouring wine

directs diners to one of the North End's oldest (established 1931) and most traditional restaurants. The spacious booths are black and red, the wine of choice is Chianti, the house antipasto is a classic, and the pastas are homemade.

Dino's Café
141 Salem St
Tel: 227-1991
L & D daily $ **36** [p272, E1]
'No frills, fast feasts' is the promise of this tiny, efficient spot whose specialty 16-inch (40cm) hot and cold subs are one of the area's greatest bargains. Homemade pastas in a variety of permutations are also on the menu.

Giacomo's
355 Hanover St
Tel: 523-9026
D daily $$ **37** [p272, F1]
The warm and cozy atmosphere and deliciously simple pastas and fish are well worth waiting in the line that wraps around the corner of this North End institution. No reservations.

Lucca
226 Hanover St
Tel: 742-9200
www.luccaboston.com
Br & L Sat–Sun, D daily $$$ **38** [p272, E2]
Elegant, quiet, and dimly lit, Lucca has a sophisticated ambience that resonates in the menu – think rustic duck torta, homemade rigatoni with wild boar, a splendid flourless chocolate

LEFT: the colorful interior of Caffé Paradiso.

cake, and an extensive wine list.

Marco
253 Hanover St
Tel: 742-1276
www.marcoboston.com
D Tue–Sat $$–$$$ 39
[p272, F2]
Acclaimed chef Marc Orfaly serves up the cuisine of Rome at this charming trattoria, with its simple rustic decor of exposed brick walls and antique wood beams. A family-style chef's menu is served on Sunday.

Nebo
90 N. Washington St
Tel: 723-6321
www.neborestaurant.com
D Mon–Sat $$–$$$ 40
[p272, E1]
With modern decor (including sleek dark-wood tables and a marble bar), stylish Nebo attracts locals with over 20 kinds of Neapolitan-style pizzas, imported Italian meats, and rustic house-made bread. You can even choose an entirely gluten-free meal here.

Pizzeria Regina
11.5 Thatcher St
Tel: 227-0765
www.pizzeriaregina.com
L & D daily $ 41
[p272, F1]
Since 1926, this classic North End pizzeria has been the place to go for thin-crust Neapolitan pie. Waits for booths can be long. There are numerous branches throughout the area, but the original is still best.

Trattoria di Monica
67 Prince St
Tel: 720-5472
www.trattoriadimonica.com
D daily $$ 42 [p272, F1]
The Mendoza family know their pasta and pizza. Hence the sometimes long lines in front of this tiny, cheerful, and casual spot off the tourist track. On the menu: plenty of pizzas, and pasta dishes such as spinach and ricotta gnocchi, pappardelle Bolognese, and homemade black fettuccine with shrimp. The family also operates the more upscale Monica's at 143 Richmond Street. No reservations on weekends; cash only.

Seafood

The Daily Catch
323 Hanover St
Tel: 523-8567
www.dailycatch.com
L & D daily $$ 43 [p272, F2]
It's calamari all the way at this tiny, hole-in-the-wall institution, which specializes in Sicilian seafood. If you're not in the mood for heaping platters of fried calamari, calamari meatballs, or calamari scampi, other choices might include black pasta puttanesca, caramelized monkfish, or mussels marinara. No reservations or credit cards accepted.

Neptune Oyster
63 Salem St
Tel: 742-3474
L & D Mon–Sat $$$ 44
[p272, E2]
As the name suggests, this small seafood bistro has an excellent raw bar. The crudo specials are also tasty, but the joint is famous for its hot buttered lobster roll, which

Prices for a three-course dinner per person, with tax and tip:

$ = under $25
$$ = $25–50
$$$ = $50–75
$$$$ = over $75

has legions of loyal devotees.

Bars

Boston Beer Works
112 Canal St
Tel: 896-2337
7 [p272, E1]
This two-story, 16,000-sq-ft (1,500-sq-meter) brewery-restaurant features 15 televisions, 15 billiards tables, and at least 15 microbrews on tap at any time.

Goody Glover's
50 Salem St
Tel: 367-6444
8 [p272, E2]
Goody Glover's is a popular tavern that adds a touch of Irish blarney to the heart of the Italian North End.

ABOVE: tomato and burrata salad at Lucca. **RIGHT:** burger and beer at Boston Beer Works.

THE WATERFRONT

The handsomely renovated wharf district conjures up memories of the glory days of maritime trade and the colonial Boston Tea Party protest. Here are a world-class aquarium, engaging museums, and access to the fascinating Harbor Islands.

From its earliest days, Boston was a busy seaport. Until the second half of the 19th century, it was the busiest port in the nation, reaching its apogee in the 1850s when, it was said, 15 vessels entered and left the harbor every day of the year. Then, warehouses and counting houses occupied a dozen wharves at which clippers, 'the highest creation of artistic genius in the Commonwealth,' unloaded and loaded their cargoes.

In the second half of the 19th century the port went into decline, a process hastened when, in 1878, the construction of Atlantic Avenue severed the finger-like piers from the rest of the city. With the building in the 1950s of the Fitzgerald Expressway, which, mile for mile, was then the most expensive stretch of road ever built in the country (and which has since been relocated underground as part of a new superlative in highway spending), Boston finally turned its back on its patrimony.

In the 1970s, with the restoration of Quincy Market and Faneuil Hall, the resurrection began. Abandoned warehouses on dilapidated, rickety wharves were transformed into condominiums. Berths once occupied by barques and brigantines became home to elegant cabin cruisers and sleek sloops, many belonging to the condo dwellers. Offices, hotels, restaurants, and museums were also built, and the population of long-shoremen, truckers, and Irish laborers was replaced with an upscale collection of realtors and lawyers, as well as tourists. The waterfront has since regained its prominence, if not its old rough bustle.

Main Attractions
HARBORWALK
NEW ENGLAND AQUARIUM
BOSTON TEA PARTY SHIP AND MUSEUM
CHILDREN'S MUSEUM
INSTITUTE OF CONTEMPORARY ART (ICA)
FORT INDEPENDENCE

Maps and Listings
MAP, PAGE 112
RESTAURANTS, PAGE 129
ACCOMMODATIONS, PAGE 242

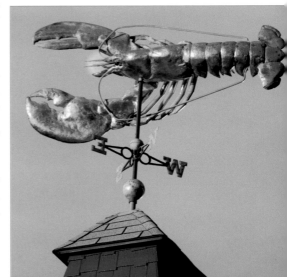

LEFT: Boston harbor at night.
RIGHT: a lobster-shaped weather vane pays tribute to the local catch.

COLUMBUS PARK AND THE WHARVES

If you leave the Quincy-Faneuil carnival and head toward the water, crossing busy Atlantic Avenue, you will immediately encounter **Columbus Park** , a small grassy expanse with the Rose Kennedy Rose Garden and a children's playground. Wisteria-covered trellises canopy a walkway that leads to the waterfront, which is romantically landscaped here with cobblestones, bollards, and anchor chains. This is a great place to begin exploring the Boston **HarborWalk**, an inviting public walkway along the waterfront, dotted with parks, interpretive signage, exhibit areas, public art, cafés, seating areas, and other amenities.

On the left stretches **Commercial Wharf,** where a massive granite warehouse, in which the second set of sails for the USS *Constitution* (see page 139) was made, has been recycled into a condominium complex. But the best example of a recycled warehouse stands inland (remember, the contours of the waterfront have been altered many times), behind you on the far side of Atlantic Avenue.

The **Mercantile Wharf Building**, originally twice its present length, is constructed of rough Quincy granite ashlar blocks and is the masterpiece of what has been called Boston's 'Granite Age,' part of the early 19th-century Greek Revival. Those interested in architecture will wish to continue along Richmond Street, at the north side of this building, and then turn right onto Fulton Street to see the **McLauthlin Building**, the first cast-iron building in New England. This five-story 19th-century jewel has delicate, rounded arched windows separated by subtle pilasters, and each level is separated by a string course. Its perfect, repetitive rhythm is marred only by the uppermost level.

From here, a right turn on Lewis leads back to Atlantic Avenue, which – if you turn to the left – soon becomes Commercial Street. Proceed northward past Lewis and Union wharves, the former of which is home to the Boston Sailing Club and the historic Pilot House. Granite is replaced by red brick on **Lincoln Wharf**, where a massive red building with magnificent rounded, arched windows

BELOW: Columbus Park.

covering five stories has been recycled into apartments.

The north side of Lincoln Wharf is bounded by **Battery Street**, whose name gives the clue to the fact that here, in 1646, the North Battery was built in order to command the entrance to the inner harbor and the Charles River. It was from here that, in 1775, British troops were ferried to Charlestown to take up their positions in the Battle of Bunker Hill. Immediately beyond this once stood Hartt's Naval Yard, where the USS *Constitution* was built and launched in 1797.

Battery Wharf is home to the Fairmont Battery Wharf hotel. This section of the HarborWalk features interpretive signage and telescopes, and a small maritime museum at the far end of the Fairmont hotel complex, including a second-floor observation deck.

Puopolo Park, just beyond, awaits those who are hot and tired with a playground and swimming pool. Others might wish to proceed on an immaculate waterfront esplanade to the Charlestown Bridge, which, after about a mile, leads to Charlestown and the USS *Constitution* and Bunker Hill Monument. But to go on exploring the waterfront, return to Columbus Park.

Long Wharf ⑦

Immediately to the south of Columbus Park is **Long Wharf**. When built in 1710, it was, if not one of the wonders of the world, at least the wonder of the region. The wharf, which had roots near where the Custom House now stands, stretched out into the harbor for almost 2,000ft (600 meters). It was here, in 1790, that the *Columbia Rediviva*, the first American ship to sail around the world and the first to participate in the China trade, berthed after a 35-month, almost 50,000-mile (80,000km) voyage. From here, in 1819, the first missionaries for Hawaii departed and, in 1895, Joshua

ABOVE: Mercantile Wharf building.

WHERE

At Long Wharf, you can still fantasize that you are on a clipper setting sail for the East Indies or China, even if you're only taking brief passage on one of the boats for Provincetown, the Charlestown Navy Yard, or the Harbor Islands (see page 131). All of these depart from Long Wharf. There is a ticketing area for the Harbor Islands Ferry next to the Long Wharf Marriott.

ABOVE: coral at the New England Aquarium.

In addition to being incensed over the tax on tea, colonial Bostonians were also upset that Britain had awarded the East India Company a monopoly on sales of the popular commodity in America. To add to the insult, the British had cut out local retailers by assigning 'consignees' sole right to sell the tea.

Slocum set off aboard the *Spray* on the first one-man voyage around the world – an adventure that lasted more than three years.

Gaze out from the beautiful esplanade at the end of the wharf to East Boston and to the planes taking off from **Logan Airport**. These are the successors to the swift clippers that Donald McKay built on land now occupied by the airport. McKay's clippers, epitomized by the *Flying Cloud*, were the fastest and most beautiful sailing ships ever to fly the stars and stripes. 'The *Flying Cloud* was our Rheims, the *Sovereign of the Seas* our Parthenon, the *Lightning* our Amiens,' wrote maritime historian Samuel Eliot Morison, 'but they were monuments made of snow. For a brief moment of time they flashed their splendor around the world, then disappeared with the sudden completeness of the wild pigeon.' Mountains of sail gave the clippers remarkable speed, which made them

ideal for tea, silks, and other high-value cargoes; but they were all too soon eclipsed by steamships that could carry far more than the clippers' narrow holds would allow.

New England Aquarium ⑧

Address: 1 Central Wharf,
www.neaq.org
Tel: 973-5200
Opening Hrs: July–Labor Day Sun–Thur 9am–6pm, Fri–Sat 9am–7pm; Labor Day–Jun Mon–Fri 9am–5pm, Sat–Sun 9am–6pm; exceptions most holidays
Entrance Fee: charge
Transportation: Aquarium

Long Wharf on its south side joins with the vestigial remains of **Central Wharf**, built according to Charles Bulfinch's plans in order to accommodate the overflow of the China trade. The wharf is now home to one of Boston's most fascinating attractions, the **New England Aquarium**, which attracts 1.3 million visitors each year.

There are 30,000 animals and 50 exhibits, representing unique habitats from all over the globe. Before entering, check out the outdoor harbor seals exhibit to the left of the front doors. Inside, the Aquarium's penguin exhibit covers most of the first floor, and holds more than 70 penguins belonging to three species. The African penguins are also known as jackass penguins, because their loud calls resemble a donkey braying. The rockhopper penguins feature a funky bright-yellow hairdo, and the little blue penguins are the smallest penguin species in the world. No one has told the rockhoppers that the cold-water section is their territory and that the warmer water is for the jackass penguins – and so they swim from island to island and the groups freely intermingle.

Another attraction is the giant 200,000-gallon (900,000-liter) ocean tank, the world's largest cylindrical saltwater habitat, in which giant turtles, sharks, moray eels, and a multitude of other fish swim in and out of a spectacular man-made coral reef. At set times, a diver enters to feed the tank's occupants. A ramp gradually winds around the tank, ascending for four stories and providing a view of more than 70 small tanks containing thousands of fish from all over the world. A hands-on tidal pool enables small fry to become acquainted with the marine realm.

The *Voyager III* – a high-speed catamaran – makes whale-watching cruises (see page 134) from the Aquarium with a naturalist aboard who also lectures on the harbor and its islands; rain checks are given if whales are not seen.

Just across the plaza from the Aquarium is the six-story-high **Simons IMAX Theatre ❾**, which shows spectacular IMAX and IMAX 3D films of the natural world's wonders (tel: 866-815-4629 for program information and tickets).

New at the aquarium is the New Balance Foundation Marine Mammal Center, where Northern fur seals, Atlantic harbor seals and California sea lions play. During special presentations (check the website for the daily schedule) trainers interact with the seals, who wave, roll, and stretch.

ABOVE: in the New England Aquarium. **BELOW:** commuter boats at Rowes Wharf.

ABOVE: a Tea Party reconstruction.
BELOW: monumental arch at Rowes Wharf.

India and Rowes wharfs

Immediately south of the Aquarium, on the stump of **India Wharf**, two bland 40-story towers, designed by I.M. Pei and built in 1971, soar skyward. These are the **Harbor Towers**, originally comprising rental units but now converted to some of the choicest waterfront condominiums in Boston.

Next comes **Rowes Wharf**, entered through a monumental gold-and-russet postmodern six-story arch penetrating the **Boston Harbor Hotel**. The lavish hotel stands on the site of the South Battery, built in 1666. The wharf, no longer busy with clippers and barques, is now the terminal for sleek commuter craft that serve the South Shore and Logan Airport. Some harbor cruises also depart from here.

FORT POINT CHANNEL

Boston Tea Party Ships and Museum

Fort Point Channel now intersects the waterfront. This area was the bustling transfer point for many New England industries during the latter years of the 19th century. On a short wharf in the Channel at Congress Street Bridge stands the **Boston Tea Party Ships and Museum** (www.bostonteapartyship. com), which, after an 11-year hiatus and a $28 million renovation, reopened in 2012. Focusing on the Tea Party and its aftermath and continuing to the start of the American Revolution, it displays replicas of the three ships involved in the historic rebellion: the *Eleanor* (due to open in 2014), the *Dartmouth*, and *Beaver II*. Exploring these vessels should give visitors a reasonably authentic feel for life on board 18th-century sailing ships, and the new interpretive facility – with reenactments, film, and one of the two surviving crates from the actual Tea Party – illuminate the event in depth.

The three tea ships were moored at Griffins Wharf on a December evening in 1773 when patriots disguised as Mohawk Indians boarded the ships and threw all their tea – 340 chests of it – into the harbor. This was the most flamboyant act of defiance against the British Parliament for its manipulation of taxes, such as that on tea, to favor British interests. It was later described by politician John Adams as 'the spark that ignited the American Revolution.'

Children's Museum

Address: 308 Congress Street, www.bostonkids.org
Tel: 426-6500
Opening Hrs: Mon–Thur, Sat–Sun 10am–5pm, Fri 10am–9pm
Entrance Fee: charge
Transportation: South Station

On leaving the Boston Tea Party Ships and Museum, turn left and make for a giant, 40ft (12-meter) milk bottle, a vintage lunch stand from the 1930s. It marks the entrance to the **Children's Museum**. Reaching its 100th birthday in 2013, the museum is a place where, apart from some dolls and their houses in glass display cases, the visitor is encouraged to touch, push, twist, and shove the

exhibits, to blow bubbles and to clamber on suspended sculpture.

The museum also attempts to instill visitors with social conscience. In the *Boston Black: City Connects* exhibit, children learn about race, ethnicity, identity, and community. This learning process is furthered by another complete exhibit, the two-story Japanese silk merchant's home,

a gift from Kyoto, Boston's sister city.

The museum has a great variety of exhibits. In the New Balance Climb, children find their way through a three-story climbing puzzle made of brightly painted curved platforms. The Construction Zone is a kid-sized construction world inspired by the Big Dig (see page 39). The Art Studio is a messy, hands-on activity space, and Peep's World is a science exhibit for preschoolers.

Engaging as it is, the Children's Museum will likely represent a fair outlay of time and energy for youngsters, so it is best set aside as a separate destination, or at least one that follows lunch or a rest period – especially if kids have spent a busy morning at the Aquarium.

Institute of Contemporary Art ⑫

Address: 100 Northern Avenue, www. icaboston.org
Tel: 478-3100
Opening Hrs: Tue–Sun 10am–5pm, Thur–Fri until 9pm
Entrance Fee: charge

LEFT: at the Children's Museum.
BELOW: Children's Museum.

South Station, at Atlantic Avenue and Summer Street, is a grand 1900 structure that serves as a multimodal transportation hub and entry point for Amtrak and commuter trains from points west and south of Boston. Oddly, even in the great days of railroading, the city never had a single station to handle train traffic heading both north and south.

BELOW: the Institute of Contemporary Art.

Transportation: World Trade Center, Courthouse

Leaving the Children's Museum, turn left to cross Seaport Boulevard and reach Northern Avenue. The **Seaport District**, which begins here, is the locus for some of Boston's most ambitious 21st-century revitalization projects. Between Northern Avenue and the water is **Fan Pier**, site of a new Federal Courthouse named after the late beloved Congressman Joseph Moakley, and the site of a dramatic structure (opened in 2006) that houses the **Institute of Contemporary Art** (**ICA**). The ICA displays contemporary art in a variety of media, from visual art to music to film and performance art. Changing exhibits feature local artists, emerging artists, and selections from the permanent collections.

SOUTH BOSTON

South and east of the Seaport District is **South Boston**, a peninsular neighborhood that has long been a special province of Boston's Irish community. Of course, the Irish presence is strong throughout the Boston area, and has been ever since the great migrations of the 1840s and '50s; but here in 'Southie' the bonds of ethnicity, culture, politics,

and religion remained especially strong. One reason for its insularity was geography: South Boston was long separated from the city proper by vast gray industrial blocks, by Fort Point Channel, and by a tangle of highways and railroad tracks.

Now, the rehabilitation of the warehouse and industrial zones, coupled with the influx of young professionals drawn not only by the proximity of new businesses but by real estate prices substantially below those in Beacon Hill, Back Bay, and the South End, have begun to crack the old Irish hegemony. While no one expects the world of lattes, bistro dining, and gourmet delicatessens completely to supplant a realm of Catholic school uniforms, corner taverns, and neighbors waving at neighbors from the porches of double-decker houses, change is no doubt in the air.

South Boston's top attraction is **Fort Independence** ⑬, built in 1801 on what was then an island just offshore; since 1891 the fort has been connected to the mainland. There have been fortresses on this site since 1634, but its only military involvement was during the last days of the siege of Boston in 1776, when British

artillery unsuccessfully bombarded the Americans on Dorchester Heights.

A promenade encircles the massive stone fort, and continues around landlocked **Pleasure Bay**. Here are splendid views of the outer harbor and islands, a fishing pier, and ample grounds for picnicking. An obelisk commemorates Donald McKay, the East Boston clipper builder, whose ships once sailed past this point on their way to the ends of the earth.

Because Fort Independence isn't near any 'T' stops, and since most visitors won't be driving, it's best suited for those who enjoy a long walk – roughly 2.5 miles (4km) from the Children's Museum by way of Summer and East First streets to Day Boulevard. If harbor views are the object, less ambitious perambulators should instead consider a boat ride out to the Harbor Islands.

A young Edgar Allen Poe was stationed on Fort Independence during his brief military career; supposedly, he heard a story about a soldier who had been sealed up alive in a dungeon at the fort by his enemies. This may have been the source for Poe's tale A Cask of Amontillado.

LEFT: Louise Bourgeois's *Spider* at the Institute of Contemporary Art.

RESTAURANTS, BARS, AND CAFES

American

Meritage
Boston Harbor Hotel,
70 Rowes Wharf
Tel: 439-3995
www.meritagetherestaurant.com
D daily, B Sun $$$$ ㊺
[p272, F3]
Each New American dish is available in a small or large portion and is linked to one of six wine categories. Thus diners know that pan-seared Diver scallops are best with a full-bodied white wine, and a spicy/earthy red is best for the cocoa-rubbed roast Kobe beef flank steak. Award-winning, 15,000-bottle cellar.

International

Menton
354 Congress St
Tel: 737-0099
www.mentonboston.com
D daily $$$$ ㊻ [p268, E2]

Named for a small French village on the Italian border, Barbara Lynch's impressive French-Italian fine-dining temple is likely to deliver one of the best meals of your life. In addition to the impeccably executed cuisine, which can be enjoyed in a four or seven-course prix-fixe dinner, the service is gracious and the setting beautiful.

Italian

Sportello
348 Congress St
Tel: 737-1234
www.sportelloboston.com
L Mon–Fri, D daily $$–$$$ ㊼
[p268, E2]
This sleek re-imagining of the classic lunch counter serves Barbara Lynch's trattoria-inspired menu, including simple soups, fresh salads,

house-crafted pastas, and creamy polentas.

Japanese

Oya
9 East St
Tel: 654-9900
www.oyarestaurantboston.com
D Tue–Sat $$$ ㊽
[p272, D2]
A magnet for food gurus, Oya offers a sushi meal to remember for a lifetime, with an incredible fusion of flavors, along with superb service and Zen-like atmosphere.

Mexican

Temazcal Tequila Cantina
250 Northern Ave
Tel: 439-3502
www.temazcalcantina.com
L Mon–Sat, D daily, brunch Sun $$ ㊾ [p268, E2]
This upscale Liberty Wharf cantina offers a lively atmosphere,

menus on iPads, and 300 types of tequila. Go for the lobster guacamole, bean dip, margaritas, and view.

Seafood

James Hook & Co. Lobsters
15–17 Northern Ave
Tel: 423-5500
www.jameshooklobster.com
Mon–Thur, Sat 9am–5pm, Fri 9am–6pm, Sun 9am–2pm $
㊿ [p268, E1]
Here you can get one of the best lobster rolls in Boston, as well as clam chowder, and live lobsters.

Prices for a three-course dinner per person, with tax and tip:

$$$$ = over $75
$$$ = $50–75
$$ = $25–50
$ = under $25.

THE HARBOR ISLANDS

After years of being largely ignored, the 34 islands and peninsulas have been designated as a national park area and recreational facilities are being expanded.

The Boston Harbor Islands were added to the national park system by the federal government in 1996. Their designation as the **Boston Harbor Islands National Recreation Area** follows a nearly four-century history of use, abuse, and neglect of what is one of the most interesting, yet little-known, parts of metropolitan Boston.

Some of the islands, created by retreating glaciers 16,000 years ago, are now connected by bridges or causeways to the mainland, and three (Governors, Apple, and the aptly named Bird) have become one and are now Logan Airport. The farthest Boston Harbor Island is The Graves, a rocky outcrop with a lighthouse, 11 miles (18km) from Boston's Long Wharf.

A checkered past

The islands' first visitors, Native Americans (the Massachusett and others), came for hunting. But, as the islands' strategic importance as guardians of the harbor and the city itself was appreciated, forts were constructed on Peddocks (Fort Andrews), Lovells (Fort Standish), and Georges (Fort Warren). These remained active from King Philip's War of 1675 to the 20th century. Some of the islands served as hospitals, almshouses, quarantine facilities, prisons, and reformatory schools.

In the 18th century, the islands were popular with Bostonians, who would visit to enjoy not only the sea air but also the illicit pleasures of gambling and boxing matches. Others hosted summer homes for the wealthy, lighthouses, and makeshift encampments for fishermen, while some islands were later used for the disposal of sewage, trash, and deceased horses. And as one would expect of any decent archipelago, the islands are said to harbor

Main Attractions
GEORGES ISLAND
SPECTACLE ISLAND
PEDDOCKS ISLAND
LOVELLS ISLAND
GRAPE ISLAND
BOSTON LIGHT

Maps and Listings
MAP, PAGE 132

LEFT: an excursion to Little Brewster Island.
RIGHT: sailing into Boston Harbor.

ABOVE: island tour boat.

buried pirate treasure (Lovells Island) and ghosts (Georges Island). Although much of the Harbor Islands' future remains to be defined, a handful are the focus of visitor activity.

Georges and Spectacle islands

Georges Island ❶, the main gateway to the other Harbor Islands, is a 45-minute boat ride (7 miles/11km) from Downtown Boston. You can fish along its shores for bluefish and striped bass, and learn about the harbor's military history at Fort Warren (built in 1833), a training ground for Union soldiers and a prison for Confederate captives. Georges has a refreshment stand, picnic areas, guided tours, and magnificent views of the Boston skyline, Boston Light, and nearby Gallops and Lovells islands.

Spectacle Island ❷ is also reachable by ferry from Boston, and features a marina, a lifeguarded swimming beach (open daily late June–Labor Day), a visitor center, and 5 miles (8km) of walking trails leading up a hill 157ft (48 meters) high, which rewards hikers with panoramic views of the harbor and city.

Peddocks, Lovells, Grape, and Bumpkin islands

These islands are accessible by daily (June–Oct) ferryboat service from Georges and Spectacle islands, with a weekend service in spring and fall.

Peddocks Island ❸ lies a little more than a mile south of Georges, and consists of four drumlins connected by sand or gravel bars. Human bones 4,100 years old were discovered on it, the oldest archeological find in New England. In addition to a brackish pond, a marsh, and many walking trails, Peddocks houses the remains of Fort Andrews, built under the shadow of the Spanish American War and garrisoned during World Wars I and II.

Lovells Island ❹ was runner-up to New York as the site for the Statue of

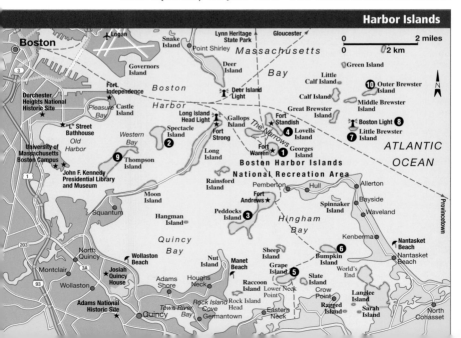

Liberty. Overnight camping (special permit required) is popular near the ruins of Fort Standish, built in 1900. In addition to dunes, woods, and picnic areas, Lovells has one of the Harbor Islands' few inviting beaches.

Grape and Bumpkin are in Hingham Bay and are protected by the long arm of Nantasket Beach and the town of Hull. **Grape Island ❺** is one of the finest camping islands in the harbor, offering a wealth of trails for inquisitive visitors who may encounter skunks, rabbits, and birds among the wild berry trees. **Bumpkin ❻** lies close to the Hull peninsula, and hosts the remains of a children's hospital and a farmhouse now overgrown with local vegetation including bayberries and wild raspberries. There is a choice of campsites among its walking trails.

Little Brewster

Little Brewster ❼ lies farther out, beyond the crook of the peninsula. It offers magnificent panoramas of the inner harbor and the open Atlantic, but its chief attraction is **Boston Light ❽** (tel: 223-8666; 3-hour group tours spring–fall depart from the Boston Harbor Islands Pavilion near Quincy Market, reservations required). Its original beacon, built in 1716, was the first in the nation, but the present building was constructed in 1782 after the British blew up the original before departing Boston in 1776. The lighthouse, a National Historic Landmark, is the oldest continually used lighthouse site in the country. Near here, during the War of 1812, the British ship *Shannon* engaged the American frigate *Chesapeake*. The British won the battle but not immortality: that went to Captain James Lawrence of the *Chesapeake* with his command: 'Don't give up the ship!'

Off the beaten path

Access to many of the other harbor islands is possible by private boat or tours arranged by organizations including the Friends of Boston Harbor (www.fbhi.org) and the New England Aquarium (see page 124). **Thompson Island ❾** is owned and managed by private, non-profit Thompson Island Outward Bound Education Center, which operates a ferry service (departing from the EDIC pier in South Boston, June–Sept Sun only) and free guided tours of the island's salt marsh.

In addition to hiking and camping, the islands are used for activities as varied as apple festivals, winter cruises, and Civil War reenactments.

For the more adventurous, islands such as **Outer Brewster Island ❿** and The Graves (north of Outer Brewster) offer excellent scuba diving; and wildlife cruises to the islands offer a chance to view sea ducks, barn owls, redwing blackbirds, double-crested cormorants, great blue herons, harbor seals, and a variety of seashore life in easily accessible tide pools. There is recreational fishing throughout the islands (equipment rentals available on Spectacle Island) for striped bass, mackerel, winter flounder, and bluefish.

TIP

Trips to the islands embark from Long Wharf, as well as from South Boston's EDIC Pier, Quincy's Fore River Shipyard, Hingham's Hingham Shipyard, and Hull's Pemberton Point. For more information on visiting the islands, log on to www.boston harborislands.org or call 223-8666.

BELOW: Fort Warren on Georges Island.

WATCHING FOR WHALES

One of the world's greatest gatherings of humpback whales takes place off the coast of Massachusetts. Today their hunters take aim with cameras rather than guns.

Colt and Cardhu, Tear and Trident, and Tornado and Regulus make a great spectacle as they lunge, breach, and flipper. You can see them by joining one of the whale-watching boats that leave Boston and Provincetown from April to October (see Boat Tours and Cruises, page 255, and see www.whalecenter.org).

Their destination is Stellwagen Bank, a shallow underwater deposit of sand and gravel, to which these humpback whales return after spending the winter in their Caribbean breeding grounds. Experts recognize the different humpbacks, which often reach lengths of 40–50ft (12–15 meters) and weights of 30 tons, by their distinctive body markings, especially those on their tail flukes.

Huge quantities of plankton and an infinite number of small sand eels are the magnets that attract the world's largest concentration of whales to Stellwagen Bank. The vast majority of the hundreds of individual whales that visit each year are humpbacks, but there are minkes, finbacks, and a few right whales.

The humpback is basically a bulk feeder which dives deep below the schools of sand eels and then lunges upward through the school with its mouth open to engulf large quantities of fish and water. These voracious eating machines are capable of capturing hundreds, if not thousands, of small fish with every lunge they make.

ABOVE: whale-watchers look on as a humpback whale 'breaches'.

BELOW: humpback whales and other wildlife can be seen on boat tours departing from Provincetown and Cape Cod.

BELOW: a whale-watching tour ticket booth.

THE HEYDAY OF YANKEE WHALING

The dramatic painting by Robert Walter Weir, Jr, on show at the Kendall Whaling Museum in Sharon, Massachusetts, is a reminder that whales as a source of income are not new to New England. Nor is their annual visit to Stellwagen Bank. In the 1770s local fishermen hunted the northern right whales that populated Stellwagen and started the decline in their numbers from 50,000 to the 400 or so that remain in the North Atlantic. (Right whales are so-called because they were the right whales to hunt: they swim slowly, enabling the hunters to keep abreast of them in rowboats. Once harpooned, right whales float on the surface rather than sink.)

Whale oil lit the lamps of the world, and New England vessels – 735 of them at their peak – prowled the globe. Then petroleum-based kerosene was discovered in Pennsylvania in 1859. Whaling began to decline, and soon the opening-up of the West offered more alluring opportunities to the adventurous than a hazardous life at sea.

ABOVE: Robert Walter Weir, Jr's dramatic painting of whale hunting, called *Taking a Whale/Shooting a Whale with a Shoulder Gun.*

ABOVE: a humpback whale, just off Cape Cod, shows off his huge mouth.
RIGHT: feeding time for a humpback whale.

CHARLESTOWN

The USS *Constitution* and the Bunker Hill Monument attract the Freedom Trail trekkers, and the Warren Tavern allows you to combine historical research with having a drink.

Charlestown, which today is a northern neighborhood of Boston, was founded in 1629, one year before Boston, when 10 men with their families and servants were sent by the Massachusetts Bay Company to occupy the company's New England holdings. One year later this scant band was joined by John Winthrop, who would become the colony's first governor, and his shipload of 800 Puritans.

Conditions were difficult, disease was rife, the water was foul, and fear of Indians was ever-present. In 1631 Winthrop and many of his followers headed south across the Charles River estuary and settled on the Shawmut peninsula, today's Boston proper. However, the doughty few who remained on the Charlestown side prospered, and by the end of the 17th century had established a democratic town meeting, founded a church and school, built a mill, and even hanged Massachusetts's first witch. The town thrived and became the fourth-busiest port in the country. However, in 1775, it was razed by the British and, consequently, none of the buildings bordering its tree-lined streets pre-dates 1800.

In more recent years, Charlestown, like many Boston neighborhoods, has lured professionals seeking homes with plenty of character, within a short distance of Downtown. In addition to this new affluent social component, Charlestown has also drawn lower-income citizens to public housing projects modeled on traditional row-house design. The ethnic and racial diversity is welcome – but some worry that Charlestown risks becoming a quarter of rich and poor, with little middle ground.

Main Attractions

CHARLESTOWN NAVY YARD
USS CONSTITUTION, 'OLD IRONSIDES'
BOSTON MARINE SOCIETY
BUNKER HILL MONUMENT
WARREN TAVERN
PHIPPS STREET BURYING GROUND

Maps and Listings

LEFT: young sailor aboard 'Old Ironsides'.
RIGHT: a bust in the window of a row house.

Charlestown Bridge

Charlestown is usually reached via the Charlestown Bridge, an extension of Washington Street in Boston's North End, although a more pleasant and exciting approach is to board the ferry at Long Wharf for a short voyage to the USS *Constitution* National Park. (Alternatively, take the Orange Line of the 'T' to the Community College stop; if you choose this option, the route described below will have to be taken more or less in reverse.) A forerunner of today's Charlestown Bridge was the very first span across the river, which opened in 1786 with mighty cannon salutes and shouts of: 'You Charlestown pigs, Put on your wigs, And come over to Boston town.'

That original Charlestown Bridge, with an enormous span of 1,053ft (321 meters) and a width of 423ft (129 meters), was considered the greatest feat of engineering yet undertaken in America. Within 15 years, a further

three privately funded bridges had firmly linked Boston to the mainland; until then, the city had been a peninsula with something of the character of a tight little island.

Immediately upstream from the bridge, the **New Charles River Dam** controls the water level in the river basin. Here there are three locks: two for recreational boats, and a third for larger commercial vessels. Beyond, on the Cambridge (north) side, is the Charlesgate Yacht Club, one of a handful of powerboat marinas on the river.

City Square ❶

The Charlestown Bridge leads directly into Charlestown's City Square. Immediately to the northwest is small, leafy **John Harvard Mall**, in the center of which stands a granite memorial to this Charlestown man who 'was sometimes minister of God's word' and who, when he died in 1638 aged 27, bequeathed

BELOW: City Square.

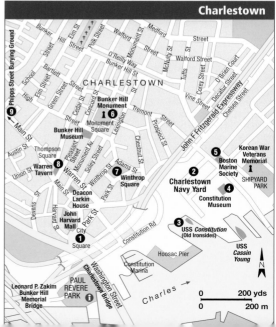

his library of 300 books and half his estate to the college that now bears his name. Harvard Mall is where the first settlers built their fort. Eight plaques embedded in the walls recount the subsequent early history of the settlement.

Immediately to the right of the mall is tiny **Harvard Square**, where No. 27, built around 1800, is one of the very few stone houses in Charlestown. It originally served as the town dispensary. Above the mall is **Harvard Street**, a dignified curving street where many notables lived in still-standing, handsome, mid-19th-century houses with mansards and bow windows. Turn left on Harvard Street and return to City Square, passing No. 16, once occupied by Edward Everett (1794–1865), Governor of Massachusetts and President of Harvard.

Charlestown Navy Yard ❷

From City Square, head northeast along Chelsea Street until you reach the decommissioned Charlestown Navy Yard, which during its heyday (1825–68 and World War II) employed thousands of men. Largely abandoned during the postwar era, it is enjoying a resurrection not only because of the famous ship it berths and other tourist attractions, but also because many buildings have been recycled into handsome apartments and high-tech laboratories.

USS Constitution ❸

Address: Charleston Navy Yard, www. history.navy.mil/ussconstitution/
Tel: 246-1812.
Opening Hrs: Apr–Oct Tue–Sun 10am–6pm, Nov–Mar Thur–Sun 10am–3.30pm
Entrance Fee: free
Transportation: North Station, Community College

The towering masts of the USS *Constitution* dominate the Charlestown Navy Yard, and are a magnet for

ABOVE: sailboats moored in front of Charlestown Bridge.

visitors. Commonly referred to as 'Old Ironsides,' the ship was built in Boston, and her copper sheathing, bolts, and fittings were made by Paul Revere. She first sailed from the harbor in 1798 in a shakedown cruise. Thirty years later, she was retired after being involved in 40 victorious engagements, including the sinking of the British warship *Guerrière* in 1812. It was during this battle that the *Constitution* earned her nickname 'Old Ironsides.' A British sailor, on seeing cannonballs apparently bouncing off her side, exclaimed 'Her sides are made of iron!' The *Constitution* had been constructed of extremely durable 'live oak,' from the Sea Islands of Georgia. The ship's imperviousness to cannon fire was also due to her ribs being placed closer together than was the usual custom, and the extra thickness of her planking.

The fact that the *Constitution* is moored in Boston and was not

ABOVE: the Constitution Museum
BELOW: the USS Constitution.

their pennies to a drive that spread throughout the land. In 1954, legislation was enacted making Boston the permanent home port of the *Constitution*, and here she proudly sits, the oldest commissioned warship in the world and liable – in theory, anyway – to be called into active service. It's unlikely, though: since 1897, she has rarely left her berth. The few trips include a 22,000-mile (35,000km) voyage in 1921 and a short overnight trip in 1997 to Marblehead. Now, each July 4, tugs pull her into the harbor for her annual celebratory 'turnaround.'

A tour of the *Constitution* is a must for anyone remotely interested in naval history, let alone rabid devotees of Patrick O'Brian's Aubrey–Maturin novels. Along with Lord Nelson's *Victory* in Portsmouth, England, 'Old Ironsides' offers one of the few opportunities in the world to walk the decks of one of the great wooden fighting ships of more than two centuries ago. Regardless of whether the fascination lies in imagining the cacophony of the great guns and the impact of enemy fire,

scrapped years ago is the result of several land battles. In 1830 she earned a reprieve from the shipbreaker's yard when the young Oliver Wendell Holmes penned a poem with the lines 'Ay! pull her tattered ensign down,/Long has it waved on high,' which pulled the nation's heartstrings.

Holmes, portrayed by an actor, can be seen in stovepipe hat wandering about the Navy Yard, often accompanied by Captain Isaac Hull, who commanded the *Constitution* in her engagement with the *Guerrière*. The actor playing Hull, by the way, will likely be a mere shadow of the original – the captain was an immensely fat man. The guides who escort visitors around the great vessel are, like her, very much on the official rolls. Each is an active-duty sailor in the US Navy.

In 1905, the venerable ship again faced destruction. This time she was to be used for target practice by the Navy. A group of concerned citizens intervened, and finally, in the 1920s, when she was in need of restoration, Boston schoolchildren contributed

or in wondering what it would be like for hundreds of sailors to share such close quarters, she is a ship to conjure with.

Constitution Museum ❹

Address: Charlestown Navy Yard, Building 22, www.ussconstitution museum.org
Tel: 426-1812
Opening Hrs: daily Apr–Oct 9am–6pm, Nov–Mar 10am–5pm
Entrance Fee: donation
Transportation: Community College

Further insight into the *Constitution* and life aboard her can be gained by visiting the **Constitution Museum**, about 600yds/meters east of the mooring. Between the two, and a couple of hundred yards to the south, the sleek, gray World War II destroyer USS *Cassin Young* DD-793 also welcomes visitors. Although she was built in California, she represents 14 sister-ships launched in the Charlestown Yard during World War II; at that time, the yard employed 50,000 workers who constructed 141 ships and serviced 5,000 others.

Boston Marine Society ❺

Address: Charlestown Navy Yard, Building 2, www.bostonmarinesociety.org
Tel: 242-0522
Opening Hrs: Mon–Fri 9am–4pm
Entrance Fee: free
Transportation: Community College

Just beyond the Constitution Museum, you can rest your feet in the wardroom of the **Boston Marine Society**. The two main purposes of this Society, formed in 1742 by Boston sea captains, were to start a collection box – it can still be seen and still functions – to provide assistance to members and their families in times of distress, and 'to make navigations more safe.' Even today, the Society appoints the Pilot Commissioners who, in turn, appoint the Boston Harbor pilots.

The Museum's two rooms are rich in paintings, models of ships (including the great clippers built across the harbor at the boatyard of Donald McKay), and nautical memorabilia.

Bunker Hill Monument ❻

Follow the Freedom Trail markers inland from the Navy Yard to

ABOVE: Navy insignia.
BELOW: park ranger and visitors at the Bunker Hill Monument.

The Battle of Bunker Hill

On the hot afternoon of June 17, 1775, the Americans inflicted more than 1,100 casualties on the approaching British regulars. The British seized the hill, but the colonists took heart from their own stubborn stand, which left 440 of them dead or wounded. Both sides lost notable officers. Major Pitcairn had led British troops at the Battle of Lexington two months earlier; American Dr Joseph Warren, a valued revolutionary activist and close friend of Paul Revere, died fighting as a private although he had just been commissioned a major-general. Several months later, Revere – once a dentist – identified his friend's remains from dental work he had done.

ABOVE: Bunker Hill Monument.

After taking Bunker and Breed's hills from American forces in the costly battle of June 17, 1775, the British fortified this commanding section of Charlestown. A strategic component of the stalemated siege of Boston for the next nine months, it was abandoned by the Redcoats as part of their evacuation of the area under threat of George Washington's guns on Dorchester Heights.

Breed's Hill where, in Monument Square, a granite obelisk soars 221ft (67 meters) high. The **Bunker Hill Monument** (daily Jul–Aug 9am–5.30pm, Sept–June 9am–4.30pm; tel: 242-5641) stands in the heart of an immaculate sward the size of three football fields, which is surrounded by iron rails and four sets of gates. This is where, on an area probably twice as large, the Battle of Bunker Hill was fought. (The designation is a misnomer; Bunker Hill itself actually lies about 300yds/meters to the north.)

The cornerstone for the Monument was laid by the Marquis de Lafayette on the 50th anniversary of the battle and the finished obelisk was dedicated in 1842 with a speech by Daniel Webster. Its construction resulted in the first commercial railroad (horse-drawn) in the nation. This was required to haul the massive granite blocks from their Quincy quarry to the Neponset River, from where they were floated on barges to Charlestown.

Alongside the Monument is a small museum with several exhibits, including an excellent diorama of the battle. A strenuous climb of 294 stone stairs leads the visitor to the top of the Monument. The views were the most breathtaking in Boston when the structure was new; today, the Downtown skyline, rather than the open sea, offers the most dramatic vista.

At the park's south end, between the obelisk and the main entrance gate, the Massachusetts Gate, stands a bronze statue of Colonel Prescott, who uttered the famous 'whites of their eyes' command.

Winthrop Square ⓻

Leave Monument Square by heading south on Winthrop Street and you immediately enter **Winthrop Square**, which, for a century, was the training field where Charlestown boys learned the art of war. From here, soldiers were sent to fight in the Revolution, the War of 1812 and the Civil War. Monuments and plaques at the north of the Square remember those who did not return. The Old Training Field School from 1827 at the south border of the square is now a handsome private residence.

Descend Winthrop Street for a couple of hundred yards and turn right onto Main Street. At Nos. 55–61 is the post-revolutionary home of Deacon Larkin, who lent Paul Revere a horse for his famous ride to Lexington. Incidentally, the horse was not returned.

Warren Tavern ⓼

Continue along Main Street to Pleasant Street. At No. 2 is the immaculately restored three-story **Warren Tavern** (see below), one of the first buildings erected (1780) after the burning of Charlestown by the British. It is also the oldest tavern in continuous use in Boston and probably the oldest extant building in Charlestown. It was named for General Joseph Warren, who died at Bunker Hill and was described by British Prime Minister Lord North as 'the greatest incendiary in North America.' The low-ceiling, beamed timbers and wall sconces evoke a colonial atmosphere.

Phipps Street Burying Ground ❾

Further along Main Street is the **Phipps Street Burying Ground**, Charlestown's first cemetery, which dates back to 1630. At least 100 graves are pre-1700 burials, and about 10 times that number date to before 1800. It provides the best historical record of pre-revolutionary Charlestown. This is because of a unique layout: families were buried in rectangular plots that were arranged to correspond to the locations of their homes. A granite obelisk commemorates preacher John Harvard, who died in 1638; it was erected by Harvard graduates in 1828 because his original gravestone had been lost. From here, it is just a couple of hundred yards to the Community College stop of the 'T.'

ABOVE: a tavern with a history.

RESTAURANTS, BARS, AND CAFES

Restaurants

American

Ironside Grill
25 Park St,
Charlestown
Tel: 242-1384
www.ironside-grill.com
L & D daily **$$–$$$** ❺❶
[p266, D2]
After a visit to the USS *Constitution*, enjoy a lunch of classic pub grub – burgers, seafood, pizzas – on the outdoor patio of this neighborhood grill.

Tavern on the Water
One 8th St,
Charlestown
Tel: 242-8040
www.tavernonthewater.com
L & D daily ❺❷ **$$–$$$**
[p266, E2]
The number-one reason to come here: the wonderful harbor and city views, sure to distract you from standard pub offerings (fried calamari, spinach and artichoke dip, fish fillets, sandwiches, salads).

French

Navy Yard Bistro and Wine Bar
Charlestown Navy Yard, cnr 1st and 6th streets, Charlestown
Tel: 242-0036
www.navyyardbistro.com
D daily **$$** ❺❸ [p266, D2]
Enjoy a cozy, neighborhood vibe, an extensive wine list, and French cuisine with an international twist. Entrées include lobster risotto, grilled hangar, and steak ginger-sake salmon.

Italian

Figs
67 Main St, Charlestown
Tel: 242-2229
www.toddenglish.com
L, D daily **$$** ❺❹ [p266, D2]
Pizza snobs flock to restaurateur Todd English's Charlestown outpost for its famous thin-crusted pizzas, with topping combos such as fig, prosciutto, and Gorgonzola cheese; handmade pastas; salads; and more elaborate dishes such as truffled wild mushroom risotto with warm duck and fig ragu.

Mediterranean

Olives
10 City Square, Charlestown
Tel: 242-1999
www.toddenglish.com
D Mon.–Sat. **$$$** ❺❺ [p266, D2]
The original establishment of celebrity chef Todd English (see also Figs, above) specializes in rustic Mediterranean bistro fare in 'casual-elegant' surroundings. Among the specialties: intricate hand-crafted dishes such as rabbit cacciatore with crispy polenta filled with farmhouse ricotta, roasted tomato, and roasted pine-nut cream.

Moroccan

Tangierino Restaurant and Lounge
83 Main St, Charlestown
Tel: 242-6009
www.tangierino.com
D daily **$$$** ❺❻ [p266, D2]
Plush red tapestries, chandeliers, and red-velvet seats set the mood in this romantic Moroccan chophouse, whose specialties include lamb with almond couscous and a honey-nutmeg reduction, tagines, and Moroccan duck confit. There's a hookah lounge downstairs.

Bars

Warren Tavern
2 Pleasant St, Charlestown
Tel: 241-8142
www.warrentavern.com
L & D daily. ❽ [p266, D2]
Paul Revere may not have slept here, but he certainly quaffed a few brews here. This has been a popular watering hole since 1780, and a popular destination for great burgers and terrific clam chowder.

Prices for a three-course dinner per person, with tax and tip.

$$$$ = over $75
$$$ = $50–75
$$ = $25–50
$ = under $25.

BACK BAY AND FENWAY

This varied area encompasses the Public Garden, grand houses, Newbury Street, Copley Plaza, the Prudential Center, the Boston Public Library, the Christian Science complex, the Museum of Fine Arts, and Fenway Park.

Main Attractions
PUBLIC GARDEN
MAKE WAY FOR DUCKLINGS STATUE
NEWBURY STREET
JOHN HANCOCK TOWER
BOSTON PUBLIC LIBRARY
CHRISTIAN SCIENCE CENTER
MUSEUM OF FINE ARTS
ISABELLA STEWART GARDNER
    MUSEUM
FENWAY PARK

Maps and Listings

Time and again, visitors from more carefully planned cities have suggested that Boston's streets were laid out by wandering colonial cows. The **Back Bay** is the Hub's answer to those wags. The neighborhood was laid out very carefully by mid-Victorian true believers in the urban grid pattern. The French formal influence – for the Back Bay was built in the era when Baron Haussmann was creating the grand boulevards of Paris – is more evident here than in any other part of Boston, and the cool logic of the layout is reflected even in the alphabetical progression of the cross streets from Arlington to Hereford.

But two things have kept the Back Bay from being severe and unimaginative. The first is the progression of architectural styles characterizing the row houses that dominate its streets – walking from the Public Garden to the Fenway is like taking a seminar in the evolution of 19th-century taste, from Italianate through Beaux Arts to Colonial Revival. The second is the progression of time: succeeding generations have made the Back Bay their own, creating sleek shopping districts along Newbury and Boylston streets and turning a once-staid quarter of

single-family homes into a chic warren of condominiums and apartments.

Taming the tide

Originally the Back Bay was exactly what its name suggests – a shallow estuary that reached well beyond Columbus Avenue. In 1814, developer Uriah Cotting built a dam across the bay from the Boston Common to Sewall's Point, near today's Kenmore Square. His plan was to harness the bay's tidal currents in order to power some 80 mills.

LEFT: view from the Tower Skywalk.
RIGHT: Back Bay brownstones.

Back Bay

200 yds
200 m

N

Charles River

Harvard Bridge

Charlesgate East

BACK BAY FENS

Charlesgate

Ipswich Street

Marlborough Street

Back Street

Fenway

Boylston Street

Hemenway Street

Burbank St

Norway Street

Haviland St

Clearway St

Edgerly Road

Massachusetts Historical Society

Massachusetts Avenue

Commonwealth

Hereford Street

Gloucester Street

Fairfield Street

Exeter Street

Dartmouth Street

Clarendon Street

Berkeley Street

Arlington Street

Commonwealth Avenue

Newbury Street

Boylston Street

Beacon Street

Marlborough Street

Back Street

Esplanade

Storrow

Storrow Drive

Church Court

Ames Mansion

Burrage Mansion

John F. Andrew House

Charles Francis Adams House

Boston Architectural Center

Hynes

Cambria St
Cecilia St
Scotia St
Back Bay Hilton Hotel

St Germain Street

Massachusetts Avenue

Berklee Performance Center

Dalton Street

St Botolph Street

Belvidere

West Newton St

Colonnade Hotel

Huntington Avenue

Columbus

Carleton St
Holyoke St
Follen St

Garrison St
W. Canton St

Clearway St

Berklee St

Horticultural Hall

Mother Church & Extension

Christian Science Center

Publishing Society Building

Administration Building

Broadcasting Center

Sheraton Boston Hotel

Hynes Convention Center

Prudential

Prudential Center

Prudential Tower

Saks Fifth Avenue

Lord & Taylor

Lenox Hotel

Former Exeter St Theater

St Botolph Club

Algonquin Club

Cushing-Endicott House

Ames-Webster Mansion

Hunnewell Mansion

First Baptist Church

Church of the Covenant

New England Life Building

Emmanuel Church

Taj Boston Hotel

Hooper Mansion

Gibson House Museum

Boston Public Library

New Old South Church

Copley Square

Trinity Church

Copley

Fairmont Copley Plaza Hotel

Westin Hotel

Copley Place

Back Bay Station

Back Bay

Stanhope

Clarendon Street

Chandler

Lawrence

Appleton

Warren

Dartmouth

Street

Stuart Street

St James

Trinity Place

John Hancock Tower

500 Boylston

Boylston

Newbury St

BACK BAY

Exeter Street

Dartmouth Street

Clarendon Street

Berkeley Street

PUBLIC GARDEN

BOSTON COMMON

Esplanade

Lagoon

Washington Monument

Make Way for Ducklings

Hampshire House (Bull & Finch)

Gibson House Museum

Beacon Street

Brimmer

Beaver Place

Byron St

River St

Charles Street

Arlington Street

Park Square

South Charles St

Boylston St

Park St

Eliot Street

Stuart Street

Piedmont Street

Fayette St

Charles St

Columbus

Arlington Street

Berkeley Street

Isabella Street

Cortes Street

Massachusetts

BAY VILLAGE

Herald St

Marginal Rd

Tremont

Shawmut Av.

Paul Pl

Dwight Street

E. Berkeley Street

Turnpike

Boston Center for the Arts (Cyclorama Building)

Plaza Castle

Charles Playhouse

Four Seasons Hotel

Park Plaza

Arlington St Church

King's Chapel Parish House

Third Harrison Gray Otis House

Soldiers and Sailors Monument

1 Make Way for Ducklings
2 Hampshire House (Bull & Finch)
3 Arlington St Church
4 Taj Boston Hotel
5 Gibson House Museum
6 Church of the Covenant
7 500 Boylston
8 New England Life Building
9 Trinity Church
10 Boston Public Library
11 Fairmont Copley Plaza Hotel
12 Copley Place
13 New Old South Church
14 Ames-Webster Mansion
15 Prudential Tower
16 Christian Science Center

Cotting died before his mill dam was finished, but in any event, there was far less tidal power than his grand scheme would have required.

With its outlet now obstructed by the dam, the estuary became stagnant, and the sewage that had until then been channeled into the bay and flushed out with the tides began to present a problem, especially when the wind shifted east. In 1849 the mayor declared the Back Bay 'offensive and injurious to the large and growing population,' and after eight years of political wrangling a plan was finally approved to fill it in.

The rush of speculation that accompanied the project was tempered with public concern. Most people accepted that the city needed more space for parks and civic institutions, and a remarkable 40 percent of the new land was reserved specifically for these purposes. Generous though it was, there were definite limits to public beneficence. With so much at stake, there was never any question about who was in control. The Back Bay would ultimately bear the stamp of society's upper crust.

By the mid-19th century, Boston's upper class was beginning to pull away from its Puritan moorings. The Brahmins' inclination for thrift was being challenged by a new spirit of self-indulgence and the rise of the *nouveaux riches*.

By 1900, construction of the Back Bay was virtually complete, and apart from a few isolated structures, it remains essentially unchanged. Today, its homes and churches comprise perhaps the finest cache of Victorian architecture in the US.

Mapping out the territory

Geographically, today's Back Bay falls into two distinct areas. North of Boylston Street, the old Back Bay proper is criss-crossed by the perfect grid ordained by its original planners. Other than Newbury and Boylston streets, this area is almost exclusively residential. The northern border is marked by the busy traffic of Storrow Drive, although footbridges provide access to the riverside green space beyond.

South of Boylston, the tidy grid gives way to the logic of public spaces.

Filling in the stagnant estuary was a major undertaking. The first trainload of gravel from West Needham was dumped into the fetid water in 1857, and for more than 30 years a new load arrived every 45 minutes, 24 hours a day. (Contrary to common belief, the fill was not taken from the top of Beacon Hill, which had been lowered more than half a century earlier.) The project created 450 acres (180 hectares) of new land.

BELOW: the Swan Boats in Public Garden.

This is where the Back Bay gets 'lumpy', each lump defined by a large, self-contained development: Copley Square, Copley Place, the Prudential Center, and the Christian Science Headquarters. Although several large apartment buildings stand here, the area is predominantly occupied by department stores, hotels, shops, restaurants, and offices.

BACK BAY

The Public Garden

One other section of the Back Bay stands alone: the **Public Garden**. Adjacent to the Common, it was designed by George Meacham and built on landfill in 1859, some 200 years after the Common was established. This lush 24-acre (10-hectare) rectangle is probably Boston's prettiest, most relaxing park, with flower beds, exotic trees, and several splendid works of sculpture, including the magnificent equestrian statue of George Washington that faces the Arlington Street gate at Commonwealth Avenue. The Garden is a perfect spot to begin a Back Bay tour.

BELOW: a toddler plays on the *Make Way for Ducklings* statue.

The Garden's central attraction is the **Lagoon ❶**, surrounded by enormous willow trees. Inspired by the opera *Lohengrin*, the swan boats that make lazy figure eights in the water have been operated by the same family, the Pagets, for three generations, and have given as many generations of young swan pilots the opportunity to develop heroic quadriceps: the boats are pedal-powered. A short suspension bridge crosses the pond at its center.

Near the corner of Charles and Beacon streets is a set of bronze statues depicting the Mallard family of *Make Way for Ducklings ❷*, Robert McCloskey's classic children's book set along the Charles River and on the Public Garden Lagoon. Small children adore clambering over the eight ducklings or riding on Mrs Mallard's back. Elsewhere in the park, statues of interest include that of Edward Everett Hale, author of *The Man Without a Country* (at the Charles Street entrance opposite the Boston Common), and Charles Sumner, who led abolitionist forces in the US Senate before the Civil War (on the Public Garden's Boylston Street perimeter).

The Public Garden is fronted by an impressive line of buildings, including the **Arlington Street Church** ❸ (351 Boylston Street) and the prestigious **Taj Boston Hotel** ❹ (15 Arlington Street). The Arlington Street Church was the first building to rise in the Back Bay, and its elaborate spire and brownstone facade are a departure from the chaste Georgian meeting houses favored by the previous generation. The Taj Boston is in the opulent landmark hotel building that was formerly the first hotel in the Ritz-Carlton chain, built in 1927.

The Grid

The Back Bay grid is immediately west of the Public Garden and connected to it by the **Commonwealth Avenue Mall**. A long but rewarding stroll through the Back Bay requires moving up and down the grid of streets. **Beacon Street** has too much auto traffic to carry off its traditional reserve, while **Marlborough Street**, in spite of a lively contingent of students, is still quiet and shady. Commonwealth Avenue is one of the most pleasant strolls in the city, and **Newbury Street** and **Boylston Street** are home to excellent stores and sidewalk cafés, though Boylston lacks the quiet ambience of the rest of the Back Bay. Start this tour on Beacon Street near the Garden and finish at the corner of Boylston Street and Massachusetts Avenue. Fortunately – as this walk will take several hours if done at the proper leisurely pace – those Newbury Street cafés will intervene at just the right time.

Gibson House Museum ❺

Address: 137 Beacon St, www.thegibsonhouse.org
Tel: 267-6338
Opening Hrs: tours Wed–Sun 1pm, 2pm, 3pm
Entrance Fee: charge
Transportation: Arlington

ABOVE: strollers in the Public Garden.

From the Public Garden, walk down Beacon Street to the 1860 **Gibson House Museum**, a brick home from the first period of Back Bay construction, complete with original Victorian furnishings, preserved intact through the tenure of the last owner, a scion of the Gibson family who died in the 1950s. The sumptuously furnished dining room is set with a Rockingham service and English Regency chairs; downstairs, the kitchen and laundry room are much as they were when to maintain even a modest row house like this one required a corps of servants. A tour of the Gibson House is highly recommended for anyone interested in social history as well as architecture and decor; it offers a rare encounter with a place frozen in time.

Commonwealth Avenue

Continuing down Beacon Street, turn left at Berkeley Street. At **Commonwealth Avenue**, the Back

The attractions of the Back Bay were not appreciated by some conservatives. Even in the 20th century, one Beacon Hill gentleman told his prospective son-in-law, who was hoping to build a house in the Back Bay, that he could not allow his daughter to live on 'made land.' He got his way: the couple elected to settle on Beacon Hill.

ABOVE: the John Hancock Tower, New England's tallest building.

'On the one hand an almost brutal, certainly primitive, boldness, arrogance, power; on the other a serene Classicism, reserved, scholarly, delicately conceived in all its parts, beautiful...'

In *My Life in Architecture* Ralph Adams Cram favorably compared the new Boston Public Library with the adjacent Trinity Church.

Bach cantatas performed during the Sunday 10am service between September and May (tel: 536-3355). Then, turn right on Newbury to find the magisterial structure which now houses **Louis Boston**. The building was completed in 1864 as the Museum of Natural History, the forerunner of Boston's Museum of Science. Its serene classical design is by William Gibbons Preston. Inside, you'll find Boston's finest men's clothing and accessories.

Continue on Newbury to reach the plain granite face of Ralph Adams Cram's **New England Life Building** ❻, built on the original site of MIT. Evoking both corporate power and a mausoleum, the insurance firm's building, begun in 1939, inspired poet David McCord to write: 'Ralph Adams Cram / One morning said damn, / And designed an Urn Burial / For a concern actuarial.' Some of the chill has disappeared as the first floor has been converted into stores on Newbury and Boylston.

Reaching Clarendon Street, look to the right for a glimpse of Richardson's Romanesque **First Baptist Church** (110 Commonwealth Avenue; www.first baptistchurchofboston.org; tel: 267-3148; call for hours; free). The tower's frieze was designed by Frédéric-Auguste Bartholdi (sculptor of the Statue of Liberty) in Paris and was carved by Italian craftsmen. The faces in it are said to be likenesses of noted Bostonians, including Longfellow, Emerson, Hawthorne, and Sumner. The trumpeting angels on the corners have earned the building the sobriquet of 'Church of the Holy Bean Blowers.'

Now turn left onto Clarendon Street and walk one block to Boylston Street to reach **500 Boylston** ❼, designed by noted American architects Philip Johnson and John Burgee in 1988. The designers apparently took an ironic approach to the problem of relating a modern skyscraper to its old neighbors. They

Bay comes gloriously into its own. A shady mall runs down the middle of this nearly 100yd/meter-wide boulevard, whose openness would have been impossible in the tight quarters of Old Boston. Although the houses tend to be uniform in proportion and ambience, the play of styles on 'Comm Ave' covers more architectural ground than elsewhere in the Back Bay and gives the street an almost whimsical quality.

The parade of spectacular buildings continues on Newbury Street, but for most visitors, Newbury's architecture is secondary to its ritzy shops, galleries, and outdoor cafés, the last of which add a Continental *élan* to the neighborhood and provide the best vantage for the chic to see and be seen.

Look to the left on Newbury, between Berkeley and Arlington streets, to see the first Gothic Revival Church in the Back Bay, **Emmanuel Church**, famed for its cycle of transformed the simple elegance of a Palladian window – a common feature in old Boston houses – into an enormous, looming, black-glass facade. The building is fronted by an equally monstrous colonnade which, again, gives it a certain ironic continuity with the classical 19th-century revival. When it first appeared, it was compared to a 1930s parlor radio.

John Hancock Tower ⑧

Between the east and west sections of Boylston Street is **Copley Square**, one of America's most celebrated public spaces. Its appeal derives not from the square itself, but from the structures that flank it on three sides.

The eastern side of the square is dominated by the bold juxtaposition of **Trinity Church** (see below) and the 1976 **John Hancock Tower**. When the plan for the Hancock Tower was unveiled, there was a fear that the giant, rhombus-shaped skyscraper designed by I.M. Pei and Henry Cobb would overpower its neighbor, Trinity Church. At 790ft (241 meters), the Hancock Tower is the tallest building in New England, but the design has an intriguing twist. Sheathed with reflective glass, it acts like an enormous mirror and, in a sense, is both conspicuous and invisible: it steals Trinity's glory but reflects it right back.

Trinity Church ⑨

Address: 206 Clarendon St, www.trinity
churchboston.org
Tel: 536-0944
Opening Hrs: Mon, Fri–Sat 9am–
5pm, Tue–Thur 9am–6pm, Sun 7am–
7pm; guided tours during these open
times, except Sun, when tours are
offered 1–5pm
Entrance Fee: charge
Transportation: Copley, Back Bay

The Hancock Tower is an eye-catcher, but Copley Square belongs to Trinity Church. With this 1877 masterwork, Henry Hobson Richardson's adaptation of the Romanesque style came into full blossom. The ingenious arrangement of large-scale masses, coupled with an artful use of polychrome masonry and ornamentation, make this one of the great ecclesiastical buildings in the US.

Visit the interior, resplendent with intricate woodwork and with

Back Bay's Social Mix

Originally, the wealthiest old families resided on Beacon Street, the less affluent old families on Marlborough, the *nouveaux riches* on Commonwealth Avenue, and the social climbers on Newbury Street. After the 1930s Great Depression, such distinctions became less clear, and many houses were subdivided into apartments or rooming houses. In the 1970s and 1980s, condominium conversions gutted the interiors even further. While few single-family homes remain, more recently, more care is being taken to preserve historic details. A new generation of wealth has also moved in – along with Beacon Hill, the Back Bay is now one of the most expensive residential neighborhoods in the city.

BELOW: architecture on Commonwealth Avenue.

stained glass and frescoes by John La Farge, William Morris, and Edward Burne-Jones; this lavishly decorated space is a dramatic Pre-Raphaelite/Arts and Crafts reversal of the old New England ecclesiastical esthetic that produced all those stark Puritan meeting houses. A bronze statue by Augustus Saint-Gaudens of the Rev. Phillips Brooks – author of the Christmas carol 'O Little Town of Bethlehem' – stands outside the north transept of the church.

Boston Public Library ⑩

Address: 700 Boylston St, www.bpl.org
Tel: 536-5400
Opening Hrs: Mon–Thur 9am–9pm, Fri–Sat 9am–5pm
Entrance Fee: free
Transportation: Copley, Back Bay

Across the Square from Trinity Church is the **Boston Public Library**, a Renaissance Revival palace designed by Charles Follen McKim, and built between 1887 and 1895. A 1972 addition by Philip Johnson, quoting the original in shape and size but devoid of its magnificent Beaux Arts detail, fronts Boylston Street.

RIGHT: Trinity Church's stained glass windows.
BELOW: the ornate interior of Trinity Church.

Explore the sumptuous interior of the old library. The **John Singer Sargent Gallery** on the third floor features a series of murals on subjects of religion that some critics rank among his most powerful work. At the head of the main staircase and in a second-floor gallery, murals by Pierre Puvis de Chavannes depict the Nine Muses; in an adjacent room is Edwin Austin Abbey's treatment of the Holy Grail legend. **Bates Hall** is a magnificent 218ft (66-meter) -long, barrel-vaulted reading room wrapped in marble, oak, and sandstone.

Fairmont Copley Plaza and Copley Place

On the south side of Copley Square stands the **Fairmont Copley Plaza Hotel ⑪**, an elegant 1912 Renaissance-style palace with a sumptuously decorated lobby, well worth a peek. Designed by Henry Hardenbergh, who is famed for both the Plaza Hotel and Dakota apartments in New York and the Willard Hotel in Washington DC, the Fairmont Copley Plaza serves as a stately and subtle foil to the show-stopper architecture of Trinity Church and the Library.

Poised at the southwest corner of Copley Square is a starkly modern and frankly commercial counter-point to all of these grand old piles. **Copley Place** ⓬ is a sprawling, 9-acre (3.6-hectare) development that combines shops, offices, hotels, and parking facilities. Inside, gleaming glass canopies and crisscrossing superstructures are visually exciting, and a stone waterfall in the central atrium adds a surprisingly restful quality. The stores – including Tiffany & Co., Burberry, Jimmy Choo, and Neiman Marcus – are clearly targeted at a high-end market. A glass-sided footbridge over Huntington Avenue connects Copley Place with the Prudential Center.

New Old South Church ⓭

The beautifully ornamented, poly-chromatic **New Old South Church** (645 Boylston Street; www.oldsouth.org; tel: 536-1970; Mon–Fri 8am–7pm, Sat 10am–4pm, Sun 8.30am–4pm; free) is an 1875 Gothic gem with a Roxbury puddingstone exterior, which sits across from the Boston Public Library. Anywhere else, it would be the center of attention, but here, its flashy neigh-bors make it something of an after-thought. The tower, dating from 1938, is not the original but retains much of its predecessor's stonework. The first tower turned out to be Boston's Leaning Tower of Pisa; when dis-mantled in 1931, it had already tilted almost 3ft (1 meter).

Back on Commonwealth Avenue, observe the site of the former **Hotel Vendôme** (No. 160). Once the most prestigious hotel in the Back Bay, the Vendôme hosted Presidents Grant, Harrison, Cleveland, and McKinley. Diagonally across from the hotel on the Commonwealth Mall is a memo-rial to firefighters who died battling a blaze at the Vendôme while it was undergoing conversion to condomin-iums in 1972.

Myriad mansions

Facing Commonwealth with an entrance on Dartmouth is the brick-and-brownstone **Ames-Webster Mansion** ⓮ (306 Dartmouth Street), designed by architects Peabody and Stearns in 1872 for the railroad tycoon and congressman Frederick L. Ames. Now converted into a hand-some office building, this palatial space features stained-glass windows by John La Farge and murals by Benjamin Constant.

Around the corner, Marlborough Street has a number of charm-ing Queen Anne houses including numbers 276, 257, and 245, all built between 1883 and 1884. Although Marlborough is generally more modest than the rest of the neigh-borhood, there are a few exceptions. The 1878 **Hunnewell Mansion** (303 Dartmouth Street) and the mansarded 1871 **Cushing-Endicott House** (165 Marlborough Street) represent two very different styles but are equally

Like the palazzi of Venice, the older houses and public buildings of the Back Bay rest upon wooden piles driven into the soft earth of the neighborhood's 'made land' to hard gravel below. Stone foundations rise from granite blocks placed atop the pilings. Some 4,500 pilings support the great mass of Trinity Church, whose tower alone weighs 8,500 tons.

BELOW: the reading room in the Boston Public Library.

grand in size and bearing. Bainbridge Bunting, in his authoritative book *Houses of Boston's Back Bay*, suggests that the latter is perhaps the most handsome house in the district.

Back on the Commonwealth Mall, note the **statue of Samuel Eliot Morison** (1887–1976), a sailor, historian, and lifelong Bostonian, who penned two Pulitzer Prize-winning biographies. The statue shows Morison dressed in foul weather gear and seated on a rock, and sits across the street from the **St Botolph Club**, of which Morison was a member.

Old mansions

Nearby are the turreted, medieval-looking **Charles Francis Adams House** (1886), at 20 Gloucester Street, and the Italian Renaissance **John F. Andrew House** (1884), at 32 Hereford Street. (Not unexpectedly, some of the grandest houses occupy the corners of blocks.)

Further toward the river are some other unusual houses. The 1882 **Ames Mansion** (No. 355) on Commonwealth Avenue and Massachusetts Avenue, now occupied

ABOVE: the Prudential Tower overlooking the Charles River.
BELOW: interior of Old South Church.

by offices, informally welcomes visitors. A few blocks away, at the corner of Massachusetts Avenue and Beacon, Graham Gund's 1980s **Church Court** development integrates the facade of a 19th-century church into a lively condominium complex. The 1899 **Burrage Mansion** (314 Commonwealth Avenue) bristles with turrets, towers, and Gothic ornamentation, suggesting a French chateau.

The modern concrete structure at the corner of Hereford Street and Newbury is the **Boston Architectural Center**. The Richard Haas *trompe-l'œil* mural on its rear wall is a cross-section of a Renaissance duomo. The two-story buildings on the rest of the block are converted stables where Back Bay families originally kept their horses and carriages. Be sure to take a look at the surrealist 'Tramount' mural near the end of the block. Beyond this, the Hynes/ICA subway station at 360 Newbury is in a dramatic modern recycled building designed by Frank Gehry (prior to his titanium period).

Prudential Tower and Prudential Center

Looking south, one sees the Back Bay's skyline dominated by the 52-story **Prudential Tower** , a monument to 1960s urban renewal and the International style. Below is the **Prudential Center**, or 'Pru,' a mixed project completed in the early 1960s.

The **Skywalk** Observatory (Mon–Sat 10am–9pm, Sun 11am–6pm; tel: 859-0648) on the 50th floor has stunning 360-degree views, and the central shopping core – with over 75 stores – was renovated in the 1990s, and the notoriously drafty mall areas enclosed. Back on Boylston and merging with the Prudential is the spacious **Hynes Convention Center**. Rounding out the Pru are apartment buildings and the Mandarin Oriental, Boston Hotel.

Christian Science complex

Adjacent to the Pru is Boston's most monumental space, the **Christian Science Center** ⑯. Designed by I.M. Pei, it was created in the early 1970s by the Christian Science Church, a worldwide movement founded by Mary Baker Eddy and headquartered in Boston since 1882. The centerpiece is a 670ft (204-meter) long reflecting pool. Its south side in summer is ablaze with flowers that border a stately row of linden trees. Dominating the other long side of the pool is a domed 1906 Renaissance-style basilica and a modern, five-story colonnaded building.

Tucked in between the two and engulfed by the basilica is the original Mother Church, built in 1893–4 as a Romanesque affair with a square bell tower and a rough granite facade. A five-story elliptical Sunday school at the southwest corner of the pool and a 28-story administrative building at the southeast complete the ensemble. The interior of the basilica – the church annex, entered through a handsome portico of 10 limestone columns – is a glorious column-free

affair that can seat 5,000 people on three levels. The impressive organ is the largest pipe organ in the Western hemisphere.

The Christian Science media organization is housed in the classically inspired **Publishing Society Building**, which contains a comfortably appointed reading room and the **Mapparium**, a remarkable walk-in stained-glass globe of the world with fascinating acoustic properties (200 Massachusetts Ave, tel: 450-7000; www.marybakereddylibrary.org; Tue–Sun 10am–4pm; charge for Mapparium, other rooms free).

Massachusetts Avenue

At the corner of Massachusetts Avenue and Huntington Avenue is **Horticultural Hall**, a handsome Baroque building dating from 1900–01 and housing the venerable Massachusetts Horticultural Society, founded in 1829.

Opposite, **Symphony Hall** ⑰ puts the finishing touches to the Back Bay. The modest 1900 McKim, Mead, and White brick Renaissance exterior isn't as impressive as the interior. A

ABOVE: Christian Science Plaza.
BELOW: inside the Christian Science Center.

Mary Baker Eddy's Empire

Mary Baker Eddy (1821–1910) opened her first church in 1894. Today Christian Science has some 2,000 churches in 80 countries and reaches millions more people through print, radio, television, and the internet. Eddy believed that numbers are not a measure of spiritual vitality and kept the Mother Church's statistics secret. That attitude remains, but it is known that this very wealthy Church is an aging organization that has failed to attract enough new members and that its media activities have sustained some heavy losses. Its newspaper, the *Christian Science Monitor,* does not have a religious bias and is highly respected. It is published daily online and weekly in print.

ABOVE: antique furniture and classical art in the Museum of Fine Arts.

moved into a grand new mansion at 1154 Boylston Street in 1899 and **Harvard Medical School** followed its lead in 1906. Today, the Fenway is home to several important museums and theaters, and a number of major hospitals and colleges, including part of the sprawling campus of Northeastern University.

The geographical focus of the area is the **Back Bay Fens** ⓲, a reedy marshland along the Muddy River (a creek, actually) and a major link in Frederick Law Olmsted's Emerald Necklace. Unfortunately, a busy road encircles the Fens and isolates it from the neighborhood. Joggers and community gardeners still make good use of the area, but it could do with more attention – not from tourists after dark, however.

Moving away from the Christian Science Church and Symphony Hall on Huntington Avenue are some of Boston's most beloved arts institutions. **The Boston University Theater** is home to the Huntington Theater Company, a professional resident company noted for its classic and contemporary drama. Nearby is **Jordan Hall** at the **New England Conservatory of Music** ⓳, internationally renowned for both its acoustics and the music performed.

Museum of Fine Arts ⓴

Address: 465 Huntington Ave, www.mfa.org
Tel: 267-9300
Opening Hrs: Sat–Tue 10am–4.45pm, Wed–Fri 10am–9.45pm
Entrance Fee: charge, free Wed 4–9.45pm
Transportation: Museum, Ruggles

Huntington Avenue opens up somewhat with the buildings of the **Northeastern University** campus, but what attracts most visitors to the Fenway are the **Museum of Fine Arts** (**MFA**) and the Isabella Stewart Gardner Museum. The former's collection, one of the world's greatest,

young professor of physics, Wallace Sabine, was hired to guarantee that the hall would be acoustically perfect, and there isn't a bad seat in the house. The Boston Symphony plays Oct–Apr, the Boston Pops May–June.

FENWAY

Beyond Massachusetts Avenue, the densely packed Back Bay yields to the **Fenway**, a loose collection of institutions and apartment buildings joined by the meandering path of the Back Bay Fens. These islands of activity form an urban archipelago that drifts out to Brookline without any real focus or organizing theme.

The Fenway first became fashionable in the early 1900s, when the Back Bay was nearing completion. The area was especially attractive to civic and to educational institutions that had outgrown downtown quarters and were looking for a place to expand. The **Massachusetts Historical Society** (founded in 1791)

Boston is named after Boston, Lincolnshire, in England, whose name is an abbreviation of St Botolph's Town.

is housed in a massive classical structure completed in 1909, and also in I.M. Pei's West Wing, built in 1981, and in a new Art of the Americas wing designed by Foster + Partners and opened in 2010. The new 53-gallery wing allows 5,000 artworks to be displayed, more than twice the number formerly exhibited at one time.

Visitors pressed for time might concentrate on the Old Kingdom Egyptian treasures; the Asiatic collection, especially the Japanese items; Impressionist paintings, especially those of Monet; the Boston school of painters (Stuart, Sargent, and Copley); and the early American silver collection. In the **Japanese Garden**, an attempt has been made to recapture the spirit of the 18th-century New England coastline (see also page 162).

Isabella Stewart Gardner Museum ㉑

Address: 280 The Fenway, www.gardnermuseum.org

Tel: 566-1401

Opening Hrs: Wed–Mon 11am–5pm, Thur until 9pm

Entrance Fee: charge, free for US military and families, and for those named 'Isabella'

Transportation: Museum, Ruggles

The **Isabella Stewart Gardner Museum** is within easy walking distance of the Museum of Fine Arts. The Venetian palace in which the museum is housed was built by Gardner for the specific purpose of displaying her art collection. A native New Yorker of clearly extravagant means, Isabella Stewart married John 'Jack' Lowell Gardner – of an equally wealthy Boston family – in 1860. Until her death in 1924, 'Mrs Jack' cultivated a reputation for unconventional behavior in the primly conventional society of Victorian Boston. Although she apparently did not keep lions in her cellar or walk them on a leash down Beacon Street (as legend has it), Mrs

Isabella Stewart Gardner engaged many performers, such as Paderewski and Nellie Melba, for private concerts, and her museum still presents more than 125 concerts a year.

BELOW: the interior courtyard at the Isabella Stewart Gardner Museum.

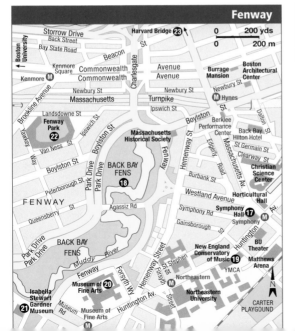

SHOPPING

The Back Bay is the city's premier shopping district. **Newbury Street** is lined with glassy boutiques, designer outposts, salons, and galleries. **Copley Place** and the **Shops at the Prudential Center** are glass-enclosed malls with high-end retailers and specialty shops. Major department stores are also present, including **Saks Fifth Avenue** (800 Boylston Street), **Neiman-Marcus** (5 Copley Place), and **Lord & Taylor** (760 Boylston Street).

Antiques

Brodney Antiques
145 Newbury St.
Tel: 536-0500
www.brodney.com
This eclectic collection includes estate jewelry, sculptures, silver, pillboxes, furniture, paintings, and bronzes.
Marcoz Antiques
177 Newbury St
Tel: 262-0780
www.marcozantiques.com

Elegantly handcrafted pieces including silver, jewelry, and 18th- to 20th-century European furnishings.

Art Galleries

Copley Society of Boston
158 Newbury St
Tel: 536-5049
www.copleysociety.org
The country's oldest non-profit art association displays the works of its more than 600 members, as well as noted artists of the 19th and 20th centuries.
International Poster Gallery
205 Newbury St
Tel: 375-0076
www.internationalposter.com
Here are more than 10,000 one-of-a-kind vintage posters from around the world, especially heavy on French inventory.

Home

Simon Pearce
103 Newbury St
Tel: 450-8388

www.simonpearce.com
Ooh and ah over fine glassware and pottery made by the artisans at Simon Pearce's flagship store, in Vermont.

Jewelry

Also look for outposts of **Cartier** (40 Newbury Street) and **Tiffany & Co.** (100 Huntington Avenue).
Dorfman Jewelers
24 Newbury St
Tel: 536-2022
www.dorfmanjewelers.com
This elegant shop displays a superb collection of first-class jewelry, watches, pearls, and diamonds.
Shreve, Crump, and Low
39 Newbury St
Tel: 267-9100
www.shrevecrumpandlow.com
In 2011, North America's oldest jewelry store (established in 1796 across from Paul Revere's silversmith shop) moved to Newbury Street.

Men's Clothing and Shoes

The Back Bay hosts high-end outposts including **Emporio Armani** (210 Newbury Street) and **Thomas Pink** (100 Huntington Avenue).
Alan Bilzerian
34 Newbury St
Tel: 536-1001
www.alanbilzerian.com
A go-to for cutting-edge European and Japanese fashions.
Riccardi
116 Newbury St
Tel: 266-3158

www.riccardiboston.com
Fashion-forward clothes, shoes, and accessories, from lines such as Chrome Hearts, Commes Des Garçons, Dior Homme, and Balmain.

Music

Newbury Comics
332 Newbury St
Tel: 236-4930
www.newburycomics.com
At this flagship store, you'll find music, DVDs, autographed CD booklets, and rock posters.

Women's Clothing

Newbury Street, Copley Place, and the Shops at Prudential Center are all packed with high-end designer stores for women's fashion.
Anthropologie
799 Boylston St
Tel: 262-0545
www.anthropologie.com
Clothing, jewelry, gifts, homeware, and furniture with a bohemian slant.
Dress
221 Newbury St
Tel: 424-7125
www.dressboston.com
Up-to-the-minute trends and hard-to-find lines, including 3.1 Phillip Lim, Giles & Brother, Issa, and Vanessa Bruno.
Poor Little Rich Girl
166 Newbury St
Tel: 425-4874
www.poorlittlerichgirl.com
With clothes and accessories from every era, this vintage shop is one of the best in town.

LEFT: a local bookstore.

Gardner had wide-ranging interests, from oriental philosophy to the Boston Red Sox.

Her will stipulated that everything be preserved exactly as she left it – and so it was until March 1990, when thieves disguised as policemen made off with 13 works of art valued at $300 million, including Vermeer's *The Concert*, three Rembrandts, five drawings by Degas, and a Manet. To date, they're still missing.

The Gardner opened a new wing in 2012. Designed by Pritzker Prize-winning architect Renzo Piano, it houses special exhibits and the new Calderwood Performance Hall.

The museum still has plenty of eclectic European and American items. Exceptional works include paintings and drawings by Titian, Rembrandt, Bellini, Matisse, Botticelli, Whistler, and Sargent. Titian's *Europa* is considered by some to be the most important work of art in Boston. In the center of the palace is a glorious courtyard with a Roman mosaic pavement, a skylight, and an abundance of lush, green landscaping and flowers.

Fenway Park ㉒

North of the Fens is an institution closer to the hearts of most Bostonians: **Fenway Park**. Built in 1912, this is the smallest and oldest stadium in the major leagues. Baseball legends like Ted Williams and Carl Yastrzemski played their entire careers at Fenway, which novelist John Updike called a 'lyrical bandbox.' Red Sox fans, heartbroken since 1918, the last year Boston won a World Series, rejoiced when the team brought home the trophy in 2004. A repeat World Series win followed soon after in 2007.

Kenmore Square is two blocks away from Fenway Park. The intersection is a major link for commuter lines and is usually choked with traffic and pedestrians.

Boston University stretches along Commonwealth Avenue at the western end of the square and also spills into Bay State Road, a quiet strip of ivy-covered townhouses. Kenmore Square's real claim to fame is the giant '**Citgo**' sign flashing from a nearby rooftop; local devotees convinced the city to give the sign protected status.

River vistas

Conclude a Back Bay tour with a reminder that it is really the waterside neighborhood that its name implies. Head back to Massachusetts Avenue and walk north to the **Harvard Bridge ㉓**, also called the Massachusetts Avenue Bridge, and also called the MIT Bridge because its northern end leads directly to that institute's campus. Here the Charles River is at its widest, and the view eastward is magnificent. The river is vibrant with sailing boats and shells, and the pathways along the **Esplanade** teem with strollers, joggers, cyclists, rollerbladers, and, in winter, cross-country skiers. This is Boston at its best.

If you can't score Red Sox tickets, get an inside look at Fenway Park on a 50-minute walking tour of the stadium, offered daily 9am–5pm on the hour, or until three hours before game time (tel: 226-6666).

BELOW: Fenway Park, one of the USA's oldest stadiums.

Restaurants, Bars, and Cafes

Restaurants

American

Abe & Louie's
793 Boylston St
Tel: 536-6300
www.abeandlouies.com
L Mon–Fri, D daily, Br Sat–Sun
$$$–$$$$ ⑤⑦ [p268, A2]
This upscale steakhouse is the place to tuck into chilled oysters, a corn-fed, Midwestern USDA prime porterhouse steak, or the two-pound lobster savannah.

Asana
Mandarin Oriental Boston, 776 Boylston St
Tel: 535 8800
www.mandarinoriental.com
B, L, & D daily **$$$** ⑤⑧ [p268, A2]
A creative menu of refined American cuisine and authentic Asian fare draws on both organic, seasonal New England ingredients and traditional flavors of the Orient. The stylish, elegant dining room features floor-to-ceiling windows affording prime views of lively Boylston Street. An exclusive private chef's table offers up to ten guests a customized culinary journey and a view of chef Rachel Klein's kitchen.

B. Good
131 Dartmouth St
Tel: 424-5252
www.bgood.com
L & D daily **$** ⑤⑨ [p268, B3]
'Fast food' with a healthy twist. Burgers (beef, veggie, or turkey) and sandwiches are a standout, served with a variety of toppings (such as the West Side, with avocado, Aacilantro, tomato, and chipotle salsa) and oven-baked french fries or sweet-potato fries. Several salads are also on the menu.

Boston Public Library
700 Boylston St
Tel: 385-5660
www.bpl.org
See Library opening hours, page 152. **$** ⑥⓪ [p268, B2]
There are two restaurants on the first floor of the BPL: the Courtyard Restaurant, adjacent to the Italianate courtyard, offers luncheon dining Mon–Fri 11.30am–2.30pm and tea service Wed–Fri 2–4pm; the more casual Map Room Café, in the original 1895 map room, serves breakfast, lunch, and snacks Mon–Sat 9am–5pm.

Citizen Public House & Oyster Bar
1310 Boylston St
Tel: 450-9000
www.citizenpub.com
L Sun, D daily **$$** ⑥① [p270, D3]
This American gastropub near Fenway Park puts a modern spin on traditional tavern cuisine (think steak tartare sliders, English pea soup with truffle croutons and candied bacon, and a pan-seared organic half chicken with herb spaetzle). You can also book a 10-person pig roast in advance. The bar, meanwhile, has microbrews, specialty cocktails, and 100 types of whiskey.

Top of the Hub
Prudential Center,
800 Boylston St
Tel: 536-1775
www.topofthehub.net
L & D daily, Br Sun **$$$** ⑥② [p268, A2]
One of the most romantic spots in Boston is high atop the Pru on the 52nd floor. The ambience is classic, with candlelight and linen; the food, New American, features dishes such as spicy lobster soup, macadamia nut-crusted tuna, and braised lamb shank. For the undecided, five- and seven-course tasting menus (at $75 and $95 per person) are offered. There's a lively bar, live jazz, and dancing. Sunday brunch (fixed price $39) is a treat.

French

Bistro du Midi
The Heritage on the Green, 272 Boylston St
Tel: 426-7878
www.bistrodumidi.com
D daily, Br Sat–Sun **$$$** ⑥③ [p268, C2]
Located across from the Public Garden, this welcoming upscale bistro delivers modern Provence-inspired cuisine, from slow-cooked crispy pork belly with ratatouille to shellfish bouillabaisse, roasted chicken, and a Grand Marnier soufflé.

Clio
370 Commonwealth Ave
Tel: 536-7200
www.cliorestaurant.com
B daily, D Tue–Sun **$$$$** ⑥④ [p270, E2]
At one of Boston's most sophisticated restaurants, award-winning chef/owner Ken Oringer prepares New French-New American dishes such as toasted bread soup with Reblochon cheese and black truffle; glazed Kobe beef short ribs; and caramelized croissant bread pudding. The Uni Sashimi Bar is also a foodie destination.

Eastern Standard
528 Commonwealth Ave
Tel: 532-9100
www.easternstandardboston.com
B, L, D daily **$$** ⑥⑤ [p270, D2]
Just blocks from Fenway, Eastern Standard has something for everyone – from foodies craving seasonal fare and craft cocktails to Red Sox fans looking for a post-game beer.

L'Espalier
774 Boylston St
Tel: 262-3023
www.lespalier.com
D Mon–Sat. **$$$$** ⑥⑥ [p268, A2]
The menu of sophisticated, modern New England-French cuisine emphasizes artisanal and New England ingredients, with entrées such as Painted Hills Farm beef tenderloin with grilled radicchio, confit potatoes, and red pepper and walnut pesto, or Indian-spiced marlin with cucumber yogurt, tamarind-glazed carrots, and mango. A three-course prix-fixe menu and a seven-course degustation menu are available.

Italian

Crazy Dough's
1124 Boylston St
Tel: 266-5656
www.crazydoughs.com

L & D daily **$** **47** [p270, E3]
When you're in the mood for a slice of pizza topped with roasted portobellos and goat's cheese or simply pepperoni, this is the place. Add a salad, maybe a second slice topped with pastrami and sauerkraut, or eggplant and roasted red peppers, a glass of wine, and you've got a unique Boston treat.

Coppa
253 Shawmut Ave
Tel: 391-0902
www.coppaboston.com
Daily L & D **$$$** **68** [p268, C3]
An enoteca by Ken Oringer and Jamie Bissonnette, Coppa supplies delectable Italian bar snacks (meatballs, fried risotto balls with fontina, crostini with whipped ricotta), house-cured salumi, wood-fired thin-crust pizzas, roasted steaks and fish, and house-made pastas. Dishes are served as small plates.

Sorellina
1 Huntington Ave
Tel: 412-4600
www.sorellinaboston.com
D daily **$$$–$$$$** **69** [p268, B2]
Sorellina pairs a lively, sophisticated environment with high-concept Italian-Mediterranean fare, such as Columbia River wild king salmon, Berkshire double rib roast with mascarpone polenta, Kobe beef meatballs, and a warm chocolate *budino* or lemon custard for dessert.

Japanese
Douzo
131 Dartmouth St
Tel: 859-8885

www.douzosushi.com
L & D daily **$$$** **70** [p268, B3]
Meaning 'Please come in,' Douzo is a modern, innovative Japanese restaurant and lounge specializing in fresh fish and ingredients, artistic presentation, and a chic ambience and decor.

Middle Eastern
Café Jaffa
48 Gloucester St
Tel: 536-0230
www.cafejaffa.net
L & D daily **$** **71** [p268, A2]
Expect very little ambience but huge servings of authentic Middle Eastern dishes such as lamb shawarma, tabouleh, dolmas (stuffed grape leaves), and falafel.

Seafood
Legal Sea Foods
Copley Place, 100 Huntington Ave
Tel: 266-7775
www.legalseafoods.com
L & D daily **$$–$$$** **72** [p268, B3]
A once-small Cambridge fish store has grown into a small industry, having earned a reputation as the best place around for fresh seafood. No reservations; waits can be long. (Also at 26 Park Square, tel: 426-4444; 5 Cambridge Center, Kendall Square, Cambridge, tel: 864-3400; 20 University Rd, Charles Square, Cambridge, tel: 491-9400; 255 State St, tel: 742-5300; Prudential Center, tel: 266-6800.)

Thai
Bangkok City
167 Massachusetts Ave

Tel: 266-8884
www.bkkcityboston.com
L Mon–Sat, D daily **$$** **73** [p268, A3]
Classic Thai fare in an intimate, candlelit setting with both Western and traditional (low-tabled) seating. Among the favorites are pad Thai and crispy duck.

Bars and Cafés

Bukowski Tavern
50 Dalton St
Tel: 437-9999
Tel: 497-7077.
10 [p268 A3]
Locals and tourists enjoy beers, burgers, and loud conversation at the gritty Bukowski Tavern. Also at 1281 Cambridge St, Cambridge.

Tealuxe
108 Newbury St
Tel: 927-0400
www.tealuxe.com
11 [p268 B2]
If you're after non-alcoholic refreshment, Tealuxe offers more than 100 loose teas from

around the world, along with a creative selection of sandwiches and sweets. The outdoor patio is perfect for people-watching on Newbury Street while sipping a nice iced tea or boba, known here as 'bubble tea.' Also 0 Brattle St, Harvard Sq, Cambridge; tel: 441-0077.

Top of the Hub Restaurant & Skywalk
Prudential Center,
800 Boylston St
Tel: 536-1775
12 [p268 A2]
The view from the 52nd-floor bar at the Top of the Hub Restaurant & Skywalk will even make teetotalers giddy. There's live entertainment Tue–Sat.

RIGHT: spectacular views from the Top of the Hub.

THE MUSEUM OF FINE ARTS

Few museums in the world rival this one for its decorative and fine art collections, as well as its acclaimed 'super shows.'

One of America's first museums, the Museum of Fine Arts was founded in 1870, opened its doors in 1876, and in 1909 moved into the present location. Today its 450,000-object collection represents all periods and cultures.

The outstanding Asiatic collection – featuring everything from woodblock prints and paintings by Japanese ukiyo-e masters to Chinese Buddhist stone sculptures – includes treasures of 19th-century Boston's highly cultured citizens, many of whom were keen collectors and passionate about all things Asian.

Other early Bostonians traveled to Europe, and the museum acquired one of the foremost holdings outside Paris of Impressionist painting, in particular works by Monet, Pissarro, Sisley, Renoir, and Manet. The MFA also has the world's most extensive collection of paintings and pastels by Jean-François Millet.

The American art collection, including John Singer Sargent murals and John Singleton Copley paintings, is one of the world's best. In 2010, a new Art of the Americas wing opened to showcase 5,000 artworks from North, Central, and South America. The recent expansion also included the new Linde Family Wing for Contemporary Art.

Above: Edward Hopper's watercolor *Lighthouse and Buildings, Portland Head, Cape Elizabeth* (1927). The varied New England landscape is also captured in the museum's collection by other well-known American artists such as Winslow Homer.

Left: one of the many highlights of the excellent Asiatic collection is this little 12th-century AD (Jin Dynasty) Chinese Buddha, made of lacquered wood with painting and gilding.

The Essentials

Address: 465 Huntington Avenue, www.mfa.org
Tel: 267-9300
Opening Hrs: Sat–Tue 10am–4.45pm, Wed–Fri 10am–9.45pm
Entrance Fee: charge, free Wed 4–9.45pm, donation suggested.
Transportation: Museum, Ruggles

ABOVE: admiring the rich display of artworks at the MFA.

BELOW: the Impressionists: Renoir's *Dance at Bougival* (1883) shares wall space with equally important works by such European painters as Van Gogh, Degas, and Gauguin.

TREASURES OF THE ANCIENT WORLD

For 40 years from 1905, Harvard University and the Museum of Fine Arts collaborated on an archeological excavation in Egypt, based at the Great Pyramids at Giza. From this, the museum acquired a world-famous collection of Egyptian treasures. Among many Old Kingdom sculptures is a beautiful statue of King Mycerinus, who built the Third Pyramid at Giza, and his queen, dated to around 2548–2530 BC. Other treasures include gilded and painted mummy masks, and some remarkably well-preserved hieroglyphic inscriptions.

The Giza expedition's director, Dr George A. Reisner, also worked in the Sudan and brought home a dazzling collection of Nubian artifacts, the best in the world outside Khartoum. Particularly awe-inspiring is the exquisite gold jewelry, inlaid with enamel and precious stones, and the sculptures, varying in size from huge statues of Nubian kings to tiny *shawabtis* (funerary figurines).

ABOVE: restoration work underway at the MFA.

ABOVE: Cyrus Edwin Dallin's bronze equestrian statue *Appeal to the Great Spirit* was placed in the forecourt in 1913.

ABOVE: the MTA's rotunda was decorated by John Singer Sargent.

THE SOUTH END

This area, an ethnic cocktail of more than 40 nationalities, includes the massive Cathedral of the Holy Cross, distinguished residential areas, and buzzed-about restaurants.

‘Thunderation, there is a man in shirt sleeves on those steps.’

That was the reaction of the title character's Brahmin father in John P. Marquand's famous satire on upper-class Boston, *The Late George Apley*. Apley Senior, observing the construction of stately row houses in the recently developed district in the 1870s, concluded that here was another Back Bay, and promptly bought in. When he saw the South End taking a middle-class turn away from frock-coat propriety, he just as promptly left.

If Marquand's character could see everything that has transpired in the South End since that famous decampment, he might wish he had made a long-term investment in the place – even if shirtsleeves, in the 21st century, would be the least of his sartorial worries. Perhaps no Boston neighborhood has gone on such a roller-coaster ride of respectability and real estate values, or boasted such a diversity of residents, as the South End.

The South End – not to be confused with South Boston – is that area adjacent to, and south of, the Back Bay. It is delineated by the Southwest Corridor, Berkeley Street, and Harrison and Massachusetts avenues. This area, where landfill and building began in the 1830s, was originally called Shawmut Neck. By the middle of the 19th century its layout was very similar to that seen today, and by the 1870s the area was fully developed into a grid pattern with blocks of homogeneous red-brick three- and four-story stooped row houses. These houses lined short, often discontinuous, streets running perpendicular to the main thoroughfares. It has often been said that if

LEFT: South End brownstones.
RIGHT: the South End in winter.

During the early part of the 20th century, many of the African-American owners of South End homes were porters working on the railroads' Pullman sleeping cars. Pullman porters were relatively well paid by the standards of the black working class of that era, and ownership of a South End row house was a clear mark of upward mobility.

BELOW: the Boston Center for the Arts.

the Back Bay is French-inspired, the South End is English, with more park-centered squares and a rather more florid style of architecture.

Some of the new houses had mansard roofs. Indeed, the first such roof – now so much part of the Boston architectural scene – appeared in the South End in the freestanding Deacon House, which was acclaimed as 'one of the wonders of the mid-century.'

The South End enjoyed a fleeting decade of prosperity. But when its wealthier residents abandoned it for the new and fashionable Back Bay, it became home to the *nouveaux riches* (in shirtsleeves, no less), and then the working class and the latest immigrants. True, some Yankee stalwarts, such as Walbridge A. Field, who had been Chief Justice of Massachusetts, remained loyal and still resided in the South End at the turn of the 20th century. But by this time, many private homes had

been turned into rooming houses, and only seven of the 53 houses in elegant Union Park (see page 169) remained private. Desuetude engulfed the district.

A phoenix and a polyglot

As recently as the 1950s, when the Massachusetts Turnpike cut a swath along the edge of the South End, the run-down rooming houses in its path were scarcely lamented; their owners were compensated as little as $5,000 for each building when they were taken by eminent domain and demolished. But in the late 1960s and early '70s, the old brick row structures began to appeal to 'urban pioneers' who saw their intrinsic value and were willing to restore them – even at the end of the 1970s, it was still possible to buy an old rooming house for just $40,000.

New buyers with a taste for city life but without the means for Back Bay or Beacon Hill began the task

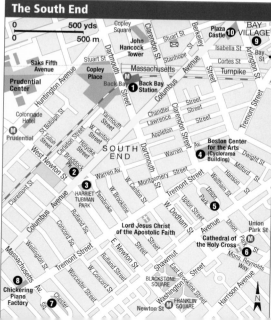

The South End

of turning one South End block after another back into single-family homes. Often, these gentrified sections rubbed shoulders with quarters that were still inhabited by poor black and Hispanic families; the trend toward gentrification produced some friction as values climbed and rental units became more scarce.

In the late 1980s the South End entered yet another phase of its evolution. As property values skyrocketed and the original pioneers of restoration saw their children grow up and move out, many of the row houses were again partitioned – this time, into attractive condominiums rather than seedy rooms for rent. It's possible, in this compact quarter, to encounter every type of Boston housing, and every type of Bostonian. An impressive racial and ethnic diversity still characterizes much of the district, with substantial African American, Hispanic, Asian, and gay communities.

Leafy little squares

From Copley Square, stroll south on Dartmouth Street for about 300yds/ meters to **Back Bay Station** ❶. Facing the Station is the Southwest Corridor, a landscaped 50yd/meter wide park under which the railroad tracks run. This park, built in the 1980s, links the Back Bay and the South End: Formerly, the railroad track was a barrier that separated the two.

Enter the Southwest Corridor, immediately turn left onto Yarmouth Street and appreciate the attempts that have been made to retain the integrity of the South End. The right side of the street is lined with 19th-century red-brick row houses; the left side consists of modern, low-rent, red-brick apartments. The rounded bows, so characteristic of the older South End houses, are echoed in the new apartments by much more linear bays.

Return to the Southwest Corridor and turn left into **Braddock Park**

ABOVE: statue in Harriet Tubman Park honoring the woman behind the 'underground railway' which led thousands of slaves to freedom.

ABOVE: varied cuisine abounds in the South End.

While a doctoral student at Boston University's School of Divinity, the Rev. Martin Luther King, Jr, lived on the South End's St Botolph Street.

Baptist congregations moved to the South End, but most of its members now live in other parts of metropolitan Boston.

Tiny **Harriet Tubman Park** ❸, which stands in the lee of the church, remembers the 'Moses of the South.' Tubman was a runaway slave who organized the 'underground railway,' a network of abolitionists who helped thousands of slaves escape to freedom. They built secret passageways in their homes and held huge parties to cover the flight of their transient guests who were en route to freedom in Canada, although many escaped slaves remained in Boston.

Continue on Warren Avenue for about 500yds/meters and turn left onto Clarendon Street to enter an enclave known as Clarendon Park. Its streets carry the names – Appleton, Warren, Chandler, Lawrence – of prominent Beacon Hill residents. These streets are lined by attractive small versions of Beacon Hill houses, which were built, it has been suggested, to accommodate the servants of those whose names they bear.

❷. This park is typical – but the least known – of half a dozen leafy residential squares that pepper the South End, all of which feature a long, narrow garden, enclosed by wrought-iron railings. Each red-brick, three- or four-story row house that lines the square is entered by a steep stoop which often rises a full story to the second floor. All have a regular cornice line; some are topped by a mansard roof. Adding attraction is wrought-iron ornamentation in the form of balustrades and railings around small gardens and sometimes over windows and balconies.

Leave Braddock Park and turn right on Columbus Avenue, immediately reaching the sharp-angled intersection of Columbus and Warren avenues. Here stands the red-brick Concord Baptist Church (190 Warren Avenue), readily recognizable by its large octagonal clerestory. It was built in the 1870s, when many

The Place to Be

The diverse South End has emerged as a hip, eclectic enclave. Home to residential Victorian brick row houses and green parks, artists and art galleries, and chic boutiques selling clothes, gifts, and stylish home furnishings, the neighborhood has retained its historic appeal while growing into a vibrant, decidedly modern and diverse district. The South End's thriving restaurant scene in particular deserves notice for its impressive variety, reflecting the diversity of the neighborhood's residents: French, Italian, Greek, Korean, Thai, Japanese, Brazilian, Indian, Ethiopian, Spanish, and Southwest cuisine are all found here. Variety is matched by quality: many South End eateries have become premier destinations for Boston foodies.

Cyclorama to arts center

A right turn from Warren onto Clarendon takes the visitor to the unusual **Cyclorama Building ❹**, recognizable by the kiosk, a salvaged lantern, which stands outside it. The Cyclorama was built in 1884 to house a gigantic circular painting – 276ft (84 meters) long and 22ft (7 meters) high – of the Battle of Gettysburg by Paul Philippoteaux. Subsequently, it was used for varied purposes, from hosting sporting events to being the home of the Boston Flower Exchange. In 1907, when it was used as a garage, Alfred Champion pioneered the spark plug here. Since 1970, the building has been part of the Boston Center for the Arts. The lively complex encompasses artists' studios, galleries, and small experimental theaters, and has attracted some excellent restaurants to the neighborhood. You can take a detour from here to see Bay Village (see page 171).

Proceed southwest on Tremont Street for a couple of hundred yards and turn left into **Union Park ❺**, since 1859 one of the South End's most distinguished residential areas. Facing one another and separated by a garden with two fountains are rows of red-brick houses with swells, oriel windows, and steep stoops.

A great cathedral

Exit from Union Park, cross Shawmut Avenue and continue to Washington Street. Here is the imposing, towering facade of the **Cathedral of the Holy Cross ❻**. This, one of the

The Lebanese poet, essayist, novelist, and artist Khalil Gibran (1883–1931) came to Boston in 1885 with his parents and grew up in the South End.

SHOPPING

The South End's Tremont Street and Union Park shops are filled with home decor, clothing, gifts, and art.

Food

Olives & Grace
669 Tremont St, enter at Pembroke St
Tel: 236-4536
olivesandgrace.com
Opened in 2012, this small boutique focuses on products from skilled craftsmen – small-batch food makers, emerging artists, and gift producers.

Home Decor

Hudson
12 Union Park St
Tel: 292-0900
www.hudsonboston.com
Comfortable elegance – a mix of classic New England and casual Californian – is the key in Hudson's excellent selection of lighting, furniture, textiles, and gifts.

Michelle Willey and Vessels Gallery
8 Union Park St
Tel: 424-670
michellewilley.com and vesselsgallery.com
The high-quality home accessories in this boutique are both elegant and functional: modern monogrammed Auberge towels by Matouk, stylish and practical French porcelain by Pillivuyt, linen aprons, and jute bags for grocery shopping.

J.E.M.
470 Shawmut Ave
Tel: 391-0490
jemhome.com
Against bright blue walls, art, jewelry and lighting from independent designers mix with salvaged relics (like vintage document chests or Italian commercial baking trays).

Jewelry

M. Flynn
40 Waltham St
Tel: 292-0079
www.mflynnjewelry.com
Tucked in an artist studio building, M. Flynn's retail showroom features pieces from the sister-team of Megan and Moria, as well as accessories from the likes of Alexis Bittar and Lauren Merkin.

Market

SoWa Open Market
460 Harrison Ave
Tel: 800-403-8305
sowaopenmarket.com
May through October, visit this one-stop indie artisan fair for clothing, jewelry, and gifts.

Men's Clothing

Uniform
511 Tremont St
Tel: 247-2360
www.uniformboston.com
Interesting and current men's casualwear, shoes, and accessories from the likes of Cheap Monday, RVCA, Original Penguin, Ben Sherman, Scotch & Soda, Freitag, and Loomstate.

Women's Clothing

Flock
274 Shawmut Ave
Tel: 391-0222
flockboston.com
In a South End boutique with a fresh, down-to-earth vibe (think plants, bird cages, and antique furniture), a mom-daughter team mixes hard-to-find California brands and up-and-coming designers.

The St James, on Franklin Square, had a short life as a hotel. It opened in 1868 with more than 400 rooms but was taken over in 1882 by the New England Conservatory of Music.

RIGHT AND BELOW: the Cathedral of the Holy Cross in 1920 and as it looks today.

world's largest Gothic cathedrals, can seat 3,500 and accommodate double that number. The puddingstone exterior with granite-and-sandstone trim has an asymmetrical facade.

The exterior belies a truly Gothic interior, which has a vast clear space interrupted only by two rows of columns extending along the nave and supporting the central roof. Light enters through innumerable stained-glass windows. The largest of these

line the transept and tell the story of the exaltation of the cross by the Emperor Heraclitus and the miracle by which the cross was verified.

Until the 1980s the Washington Street 'El', the elevated train line built in the early 20th century, passed close to the Cathedral's entrance. The noise was deafening, and it is claimed that the Yankees routed the line this way in order to disturb the Irish congregants.

Elegant squares

Proceed southwest on Washington Street for three blocks. There, side by side, are Blackstone and Franklin squares, two geometrical, flat, grassy areas, and each with a splashing fountain as a centerpiece. Although not built until the 1860s, the squares had already been planned by Bulfinch at the start of that century. Blackstone is a welcoming place to relax, watch neighborhood dogs frolic; Franklin attracts seedy elements.

Each square is backed on its south side by a stately building. The elaborate French Second Empire edifice that graces Franklin Square

ABOVE: leafy streets.

was formerly one of the city's most elegant hotels, the St James, where General Grant once lodged when he was president. The building became familiar to many through the television series *St Elsewhere*. The Blackstone building, less flamboyant and more severe, consists of brownstone row houses with handsome pedimented formal windows and doors enclosed by pilasters.

Continue on Washington Street for half a dozen blocks. Turn right onto Massachusetts Avenue and enter **Chester Square ⓻**, which, until 40 years ago, was the most expansive – though faded – residential square in all Boston, and indeed could begin to be compared to the great London squares. Then Mass Ave was realigned, and rerouted through the heart of the oval park that separates the two crescents of 70 opulent row houses.

Chester Square debouches into Tremont Street. A left turn immediately leads to the **Chickering Piano Factory ⓼**, which, when opened in 1850, was the largest building in the nation, other than the Capitol. It stopped producing pianos in 1929, and was saved from extinction by being converted into artists' studios and apartments. The dominating feature of this handsome six-story building is an octagonal tower.

A right, rather than a left, turn onto Tremont leads first to **Concord Square** and then to **Rutland Square**, two more handsome residential squares.

Village in a city

If, at the Cyclorama, instead of continuing your explorations of the South End you had turned left onto Berkeley Street, proceeded for 400yds/meters and then turned right onto Columbus Avenue and proceeded a further 200yds/meters, you would have arrived at **Bay Village ⓽**, a tiny, delightful oasis that makes the South Slope of Beacon Hill look like a bustling metropolis.

The name Bay Village is a relatively modern one, conjured up by real estate developers. Many of the painters, housewrights, and cabinetmakers who created the grand homes on Beacon Hill built and lived in these much more modest homes, and a number of these houses have been sensitively renovated by people who can't quite afford a Beacon Hill property.

RIGHT: Columbus Avenue.
BELOW: the Plaza Castle now houses a restaurant, instead of an armory.

An alternative way to enter this haven is from the intersection of Columbus, Arlington, and Stuart streets, which is dominated by a massive rusticated granite Italian Renaissance fortress whose hexagonal tower is a landmark. This building, now the **Plaza Castle** , was once an armory; today, it's an annex of the nearby Park Plaza Hotel and home to the Smith & Wollensky restaurant (see page 173).

Bay Village, where Edgar Allan Poe once lived, has been described as Beacon Hill on mudflats. It was developed in the 1820s when the Back Bay was still a tidal basin, and a quarter of a century would elapse before the first buildings appeared in the South End. Today, the neighborhood, consisting of half a dozen short, gas-lit streets lined by uniform, almost toy-like red-brick row houses, still has a 19th-century ambience.

Enter the Village by **Piedmont Street**, which faces the Plaza Castle's Arlington Street facade. There's nothing special here, but at No. 52 stood the 'Napoleon Club,' one of America's first gay bars. It owed its location to the fact that Bay Village is near the city's Theater District, which was filled with speakeasies during Prohibition.

A half-block down Piedmont is a plaque in the sidewalk commemorating one of Boston's – and America's – worst disasters. Here stood the Coconut Grove nightclub where on the evening of November 28, 1942, 492 people died when a fire spread throughout the building.

Turn right onto Church Street and, proceeding along it, wander into Winchester and Melrose streets before arriving at lovely **Fayette Street**, the oldest street in the district, with immaculate window boxes filled with colorful blooms.

These streets and homes you admire were originally 12–18ft (3.7–5.5 meters) lower. When the Back Bay was filled in, Bay Village (then called the Church Street District) flooded and, in a mammoth undertaking, about 500 buildings were raised. From Fayette Street, turn onto Arlington Street and resume the hurly-burly of life in Boston.

RESTAURANTS, BARS, AND CAFES

Restaurants

American

Charlie's Sandwich Shoppe
429 Columbus Ave
Tel: 536-7669
B & L Mon–Sat **$** 74 [p268, B3]
The landmark diner (since 1927) serves breakfast all day, terrific pancakes, and signature turkey hash. Cash only.

Grill 23 & Bar
161 Berkeley St
Tel: 542-2255
www.grill23.com
D daily **$$$** 75 [p268, B2]
Since 1983, Grill 23 & Bar has been a destination for prime, dry-aged beef, fresh seafood, and fabulous desserts. Housed in the former Salada Tea building, this sets the standard for steakhouse dining.

Smith & Wollensky
Park Plaza Castle, 101 Columbus Ave
Tel: 423-1112
www.smithandwollensky.com
D daily **$$$$** 76 [p268, C2]
The renowned steak chain has a branch in the renovated armory built in 1891 to headquarter the First Corps of Cadets. The specialties include dry-aged steaks and enormous lobsters.

Tremont 647
647 Tremont St
Tel: 266-4600
www.tremont647.com
D daily, brunch Sat–Sun **$$** 77 [p268, B4]
The atmosphere here is offbeat – on Sundays there's a Pajama brunch – while specialties feature big flavors, such as Too Stinky Cheeses.

Don't miss Taco Tuesdays – a half dozen or more types of tacos to choose from, and all for just $2.

Ethiopian

Addis Red Sea
544 Tremont St
Tel: 426-8727
www.addisredsea.com
L Sat–Sun, D daily **$–$$** 78 [p268, C3]
Dishes include tantalizing vegetarian options, many eaten in the traditional method – scooped up with spongy *ingera* bread by hand. For a true sampling, choose one of the combination platters.

French

Hamersley's Bistro
553 Tremont St
Tel: 423-2700
www.hamersleysbistro.com
D daily **$$$** 79 [p268, B3]
Upscale hearty fare in an elegant, banquette-lined room. The house special is roast chicken with garlic, lemon, and parsley.

Italian

Giacomo's
431 Columbus Ave
Tel: 536-5723
D daily **$$** 80 [p268, B3]
Small and busy, Giacomo's offers terrific seafood and classic Italian dishes, including fine homemade pastas at a great price. Cash only.

Stella
1525 Washington St
Tel: 247-7747
www.bostonstella.com
D daily, Br Sun **$$** 81 [p268, B4]
A pretty and energetic Italian restaurant, with a large outdoor patio, Stella offers pastas, roasts, and

braises representing nearly all of Italy's regions.

Latin American

Orinoco
477 Shawmut Ave
Tel: 369-7075
www.orinocokitchen.com
L & D Tue–Sat, Br Sun **$$–$$$** 82 [p268, B4]
Inspired by the *taguaritas* (family-run Venezuelan roadside eateries), casual and lively Orinoco serves up a mix of bold flavors from Andean and Caribbean countries.

Polish

Café Polonia
611 Dorchester Ave
Tel: 269-0110
www.cafepolonia.com
B, L, & D daily **$$** 83 [p268, D4]
Polka music and bread served with lard set the mood at this small, informal eatery where specialties include stuffed cabbage and *pierogis*.

Southwestern

Masa
439 Tremont St
Tel: 338-8884
www.masarestaurant.com
D daily, Br Sat–Sun **$$** 84 [p268, C3]
A stellar concoction of Southwestern flavors, with sophisticated flair, such as cornmeal-crusted fried skate with spicy mango slaw, or blackened rare ahi tuna.

Spanish

Toro
1704 Washington St
Tel: 536-4300
www.toro-restaurant.com
L Mon–Fri, D daily, Br Sun **$$** 85 [p268, B4]

Prices for a three-course dinner per person, with tax and tip:

$ = under $25
$$ = $25–50
$$$ = $50–75
$$$$ = over $75

Small, loud, and lively, Ken Oringer's authentic and innovative Spanish-style tapas restaurant draws a trendy crowd.

Bars and Cafés

The Bee Hive
541 Tremont St
Tel: 423-0069
13 [p268, C4]
Underground and upscale, this bohemian bar and eatery serves up live jazz and New American fare.

JJ Foley's
117 E. Berkeley St
Tel: 728-9101
14 [p268, C3]
A great old-school tavern.

L Street Tavern
58 E. 8th St
Tel: 268-4335
15 [p268, D4]
Fans of the 1997 movie *Good Will Hunting* will want to make a pilgrimage here, the Southie bar featured in the film.

Sister Sorel
645 Tremont St
Tel: 266-4600
16 [p268, B4]
Sister Sorel shares the Tremont 647 kitchen, but also offers snacks and a more lounge-like setting.

Wally's Café
427 Massachusetts Ave
Tel: 424-1408
17 [p268, A4]
Wally's Café is a great South End spot for live music, particularly jazz.

The Streetcar Suburbs

Many of Boston's outlying neighborhoods are accessible on the 'T' and worth a visit for their parks, green areas, and sights of interest.

Urban historian Sam Bass Warner, Jr, coined the term 'streetcar suburbs' for neighborhoods outside of Boston's core made easily accessible by late 19th-century advances in transportation. Some lie within the city limits; Brookline and Watertown are separate municipalities. Many of these areas were beautified as part of the landscape architect Frederick Law Olmsted's 'Emerald Necklace,' a 5-mile (8km) skein of green spaces that covers over 1,000 acres (400 hectares) of parkland, and that gave a growing city much-needed breathing room.

The Emerald Necklace begins at the Public Garden, extends along Commonwealth Avenue and continues through the Back Bay Fens (see page 156), ending at Franklin Park in Roxbury. From the Back Bay, it's fairly easy to walk as far as the Fens; to head farther, use MBTA (see page 238) buses.

The marshy Fens begin at the intersection of Boylston Street and the Fenway, just west of Massachusetts Avenue. Beyond, the Fenway loops into the Riverway, which soon becomes the Jamaicaway, passing Olmsted Park on the right. Just ahead lies Jamaica Pond, a small jewel ringed by tree-lined paths. Sailboats and rowboats can be rented at Jamaica Pond's boathouse.

Follow the Jamaicaway to the Arborway and the entrance to Harvard University's 265-acre (107-hectare) **Arnold Arboretum** ('T' Orange Line Forest Hills stop), designed by Olmsted and Charles Sprague Sargent. Open during daylight hours throughout the year (tel: 524-1718), the Arboretum is home to more than 15,000 plants, including rare trees and shrubs, 300-year-old bonsai trees and one of North America's oldest and largest collection of lilacs, in glorious bloom during each May and June.

Franklin Park, a couple of miles farther along the Arborway (the Forest Hills terminus of the 'T' Orange Line is within a mile of the park's entrance), was intended to be the crown jewel of the Emerald Necklace. Years of neglect left the park a hostile wilderness, but recent efforts have returned it to something of its intended beauty.

The **Franklin Park Zoo** (1 Franklin Park Rd; www.zoonengland.org; tel: 541-5466; Apr–Sept Mon–Fri 10am–5pm, Sat–Sun 10am–6pm, Oct–Mar daily 10am–4pm; charge) has been revived, and a handsome addition is a tropical rainforest exhibit, home to free-flying birds, gorillas, a pygmy hippopotamus, and thousands of plants. Other attractions include an aviary, a butterfly exhibit, and a children's petting zoo. In 2012, the zoo welcomed three colobus monkeys, which are native to equatorial Africa.

Memories of the New Frontier

Accessible via the Red Line (JFK/UMass stop and shuttle bus) is the striking **John F. Kennedy Presidential Library and Museum** (www.jfklibrary.org; tel: 514-1600; daily 9am–5pm; charge), designed by I.M. Pei and occupying a stunning location on Columbia Point. The Library contains the president's papers; public exhibits cover

LEFT: gorilla in Franklin Park Zoo.

his life and the history of the US during his era. Personal items on display include JFK's desk and the coconut shell on which he carved a cry for help after his PT boat was sunk during World War II. An introductory film narrated by John F. Kennedy is part of the tour. The *Ventura*, the president's sailboat, sits behind the library.

Two miles (3km) north of Columbia Point, in South Boston's Thomas Park ('T' Red Line, Broadway stop) is **Dorchester Heights National Historic Site**, where Washington's army placed cannon to force the British from Boston in 1776. A 115ft (35-meter) white marble monument commemorates the victory and offers splendid views.

Brookline

Nestled between Boston's outlying neighborhoods to the north and south, **Brookline** by the 19th century was Boston's wealthiest suburban enclave. The heart of Brookline is Coolidge Corner, a stop on the 'T' Green Line (be sure to board the correct train, as the line splits into several routes past Copley).

A 10-minute walk northwest on Harvard Street leads to Beals Street; turn right to reach No. 83, the **John F. Kennedy National Historic Site** (www.nps.gov/jofi; tel: 566-7937; May–Sept Wed–Sun 10am–4.30pm, tours until 3pm; charge), the 1917 birthplace of the president. His parents lived in this modest, two-story house from 1914 to 1921. Under the supervision of the late Rose Kennedy, the president's mother, the house was restored to its 1917 appearance.

A bit over a mile (1.6km) south of Cleveland Circle, the Green Line terminus, is the **Olmsted National Historic Site** (43 Warren Street; www.nps.gov/frla; tel: 566-1689; tours Wed–Sun, see website for times), where Frederick Law Olmsted had his office during and after the construction of the Emerald Necklace.

Another 1.5 miles (2.4km) beyond is the **Larz Anderson Auto Museum** (15 Newton Street; www.larzanderson.org; tel: 522-6547; Tue–Sun 10am–4pm; charge). The Museum houses a superb collection of early automobiles and related exhibits in the

carriage house of diplomat Larz Anderson's former estate. Across the road is The Country Club, founded in 1881 and the forerunner of hundreds of such establishments throughout the nation.

Watertown

North of Brookline and the Boston neighborhood of Brighton, the suburb of **Watertown** lies on the other side of the Charles River. Just west of Watertown Square (bus from Harvard Square) is the **Armenian Library and Museum of America** (65 Main Street; tel: 926-2562; Thur–Fri noon–8pm, Sat–Sun noon–6pm; charge for museum), containing a diverse collection of Armenian textiles, ceramics, coins, and religious art.

If you're driving, continue on Route 20 for 2 miles (3km), then turn left on Gore Street to reach **Gore Place** (52 Gore Street, Waltham; www.goreplace.org; tel: 781-894-2798; tours Mon–Fri 1pm, Sat noon–3pm), a treasure trove of early 19th-century European and American decorative arts. This brick mansion was designed by Rebecca Payne Gore – one of the first women to design a great home – and built in 1805 by her husband, Christopher Gore. The home has some of America's first flush toilets and showers. A later innovation is the flying staircase that spirals three flights upward.

RIGHT: memorabilia at the JFK Presidential Library.

CAMBRIDGE

Academia is the vital heartbeat of this city, home to Harvard and MIT universities, but the former New Towne also has its share of history, cemeteries, and architectural gems.

ambridge, separated from Boston by the Charles River and linked to it by half a dozen bridges, was founded in the same year as Boston. Originally called New Towne, it was the Bay Colony's first capital. It is still a city in its own right: its population of 106,000 makes it one of the largest in Massachusetts. Each fall this number is swollen by about 25 percent by students attending Harvard University or Massachusetts Institute of Technology (MIT), both of which also attract many tourists to the city.

HARVARD

Harvard Square ❶, the focal point of Cambridge for the visitor, can be reached readily from Boston on the Red line of the 'T'. The square and its immediate surroundings crowd with restaurants, cafés, and stores, including a notable concentration of bookshops. Newspapers from around the world are available at the large Out of Town News kiosk in the middle of the square.

A tall, abstract, granite sculpture entitled *Omphalos* stands next to the kiosk. If the sculpture had been commissioned by Harvard rather than by the Massachusetts Bay Transportation Authority, one would have cried hubris, knowing that it was the intent of the sculptor's patron to indicate that Cambridge and not Delphi was the navel of the world. In the square pierced and tattooed skateboarders mingle with undergraduates and tourists, and music fills the air as street musicians play at every corner. (There are more than four corners because the square is amorphous.)

LEFT: students outside the Comparative Zoology building, Harvard. **RIGHT:** shops in quaint Harvard Square.

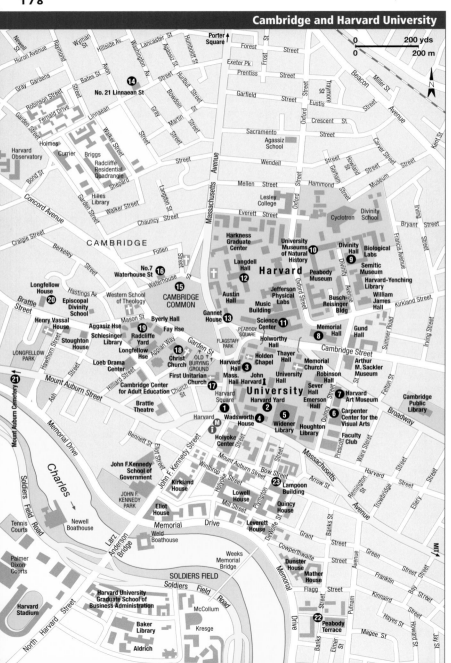

Harvard Yard ❷

Begin an exploration of the heart of Harvard by walking through the gate on Massachusetts Avenue north of Harvard Square, to enter **Harvard Yard**. Harvard Yard is a delightful shady oasis rather than the 'unkempt sheep-commons' that John Kirkland saw when he became president of the college in 1810. Then it was cluttered with a brewery and sundry privies. Kirkland is responsible for the trees, the footpaths, and the tradition of care that still prevails.

Straight ahead is **University Hall**, an 1816 granite building designed by Charles Bulfinch. It now houses university offices but originally had dining rooms, classrooms, a chapel and the president's office. Fortunately, the architect anticipated the future, and designed the rear of this building to be almost as handsome as the front. And it is this rear that is now the western side of the New Yard or Tercentenary Quadrangle.

The larger-than-life-sized bronze statue of John Harvard that sits below the American flag in front of University Hall is often referred to as 'the Statue of Three Lies.' The statue is not of John Harvard but an idealized representation, modeled by an undergraduate in 1884, the year that the figure was sculpted by Daniel Chester French. The inscription on the base refers to John Harvard as the founder of Harvard College. He was not: he was the first major benefactor. The inscription also says that the College was founded in 1638, the year of the John Harvard bequest. It was not: the correct date of its founding is 1636.

The two halls you passed between to enter the yard are Massachusetts and Harvard halls. Massachusetts Hall, erected in 1720, is the oldest Harvard building still standing, and the College Clock, part of the original structure on the western gable, has been painted to resemble its 18th-century appearance. During the Revolutionary War, Continental Army soldiers were billeted here.

Harvard Hall ❸

Harvard Hall (1766) is the third college building to stand on this site. Its predecessor was razed by a 1764 fire

Law School students, when in Harvard Square, will gleefully point out to you the joke window above the Curious George bookstore advertising the law firm of Dewey, Cheetam, and Howe (try saying it out loud).

BELOW: statue of John Harvard.

John Harvard

John Harvard, a butcher's son, was born in London in 1607. Shortly after he was married in 1637, he sold the Queen's Head inn in Southwark bequeathed to him by his mother and set sail for the New World. Although he was never formally ordained as a minister, he served for a time as assistant pastor in the First Church of Charlestown. But, within a year of his arriving in New England, he died of tuberculosis. In his will he left half of his £1,600 of inherited wealth, together with his library of classical and theological literature, to a school in New Towne, soon to be renamed Cambridge. The future of the school was assured, and in 1639 it was named Harvard College.

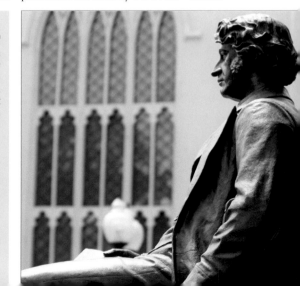

Continental Army troops occupied Harvard Hall in 1775–6, removing 1,000lbs (450kg) of lead from the roof to make bullets. The hall's fine Georgian architecture was compromised in 1842 and 1872 by new extensions.

which was called 'the greatest disaster in the history of the College', destroying as it did the largest library in the colonies, including John Harvard's books. One of the latter was saved because, on the night of the fire, an undergraduate had removed it from the library. Next day, realizing the treasure he possessed, he took the book to President Holyoke who thanked him graciously, accepted the volume and expelled the student for removing it without permission.

North of Harvard Hall is **Holden Chapel** (1742), Harvard's third-oldest building. The chapel, in glorious High Georgian style, with its pediments decorated with the elaborate crest of the Holdens, was called 'a solitary English daisy in a field of Yankee dandelions.' Even though Harvard was originally a ministerial school, Holden was its first chapel – built more than a century after the college was founded. Later, it was the home of the Medical School; it now houses offices of choral groups.

The north side of the Old Yard is occupied by four freshmen dormitories, including the twin dormitories

BELOW: Harvard buildings.

of Hollis and Stoughton. The former, Harvard's fourth-oldest building (1763), was home, at different times, to President John Quincy Adams, Ralph Waldo Emerson, Henry Thoreau, and Charles Bulfinch. During the war 600 Colonial troops were quartered here.

Wadsworth House ❹

To the south is **Wadsworth House**, a yellow clapboard building near another gate from Massachusetts Avenue. Built in 1727, Wadsworth House was the home of Harvard presidents until 1849. It was George Washington's headquarters for a few nights when he arrived in Cambridge. Today it houses the Alumni Office and other university offices.

Grander by far than the Old Yard is the Tercentenary Quadrangle or **New Yard**, dominated on the south by the Widener Library's massive Corinthian colonnade standing atop a monumental flight of stairs and on the north by the soaring, delicate, white spire of Memorial Church, which honors the Harvard dead in both world wars. H.H. Richardson's

Sever Hall, its entrance flanked by turreted towers and the entire building rich in decorative brickwork, was built in 1880; it has been called 'a turning point in the course of American architecture.'

Widener Library ❺

Widener Library is the third-largest library in the US and the world's largest university library (see panel). Three interesting Cambridge dioramas (1677, 1755, and 1936) can be seen in the building, whose Widener Memorial Room, a glorious affair of wood paneling and stained-glass windows, contains Harry Widener's original private library, which includes a copy of the Gutenberg Bible and a First Folio of Shakespeare. Some claim that John Singer Sargent's murals in the anteroom to the Memorial Room 'are the worst works of public art ever done by a major American painter.' The adjacent **Houghton Library** has a brilliant collection of incunabula and the libraries of, among others, Cotton Mather and John Masefield. The John Harvard collection has the one book

that survived the 1764 fire and 'sisters' of many other works destroyed.

An artistic hodgepodge

Exit onto Quincy Street from Sever Quadrangle. To the right is the striking **Carpenter Center for the Visual Arts** ❻ (24 Quincy St; tel: 495-3251; Mon–Sat 10am–11pm, Sun 1–11pm), the only Le Corbusier building in North America, and just one of a variety of modern buildings on the Harvard campus. When James Stirling, the English architect and designer of the Sackler Museum, was severely criticized for his design, he was reported to have exclaimed: 'Doesn't fit in! I've simply created another animal for the Harvard architectural zoo!' And, indeed, the Carpenter is incongruous among the conventional buildings to its north and south and facing it from across the road.

The most striking features of the Carpenter Center, which proper Bostonians have compared to two

ABOVE: the Widener Library.
BELOW: a futuristic dormitory building on the MIT campus.

The Widener Library

The library contains more than 3 million volumes stacked on over 50 miles (80km) of shelves. It is the administrative center of the university network of nearly 100 libraries which house 15.6 million books and is the largest university library system in the world. The Widener Library holds one of the few remaining perfect copies of the Gutenberg Bible and a First Folio of Shakespeare. The library is a memorial to Harry Elkins Widener, a young bibliophile who drowned in the sinking of the *Titanic*. As he had already indicated that he would donate his library to Harvard, his mother gave the university his books and the money to build space for millions more.

ABOVE: the steps of the Widener Library.
RIGHT: Fogg Art Museum.

rhinos wrestling, are the sweeping ramp that leads from the street to the heart of the building on the upper level; the Le Corbusier trademarks of tall pillars, upon which the building appears to float; and concrete sun breakers that admit natural light while blocking out the sun's direct rays. Ascend the ramp and look down into the studios where artists are at work, or visit one of the many temporary exhibitions the Carpenter hosts. In the basement of the building is the **Harvard Film Archive** (tel: 495-4700), dedicated to screenings of both new and classic films.

Next to the Carpenter Center, a new **Harvard Art Museum** designed by architect Renzo Piano is being built at 32 Quincy Street, expected to open in 2014. It will house the collections of three Harvard museums: the Fogg Art Museum, the Busch-Reisinger Museum, and the Arthur M. Sackler Museum. During renovation, the Arthur M. Sackler Museum (485 Broadway; www.harvardartmuseums. org; tel: 495-9400; Tue–Sat 10am–5pm; charge) is housing all three collections.

The **Sackler** collection is devoted to works of ancient, oriental, and Islamic art, including Japanese prints and woodblocks, Persian miniatures, Greek and Roman statues and vases, and what many agree is the most magnificent collection of Chinese jades in the world.

Outstanding in the **Fogg** are the Ingres canvases, the best collection outside France; a splendid assembly of pre-Raphaelite works and French Impressionists; 27 Rodins; a Fra Angelico crucifixion; 54 Blake watercolors; and a print room with 300 Dürers and 200 Rembrandts. The Fogg also has an excellent collection of Western sculpture, featuring Romanesque works from the late 11th and 12th centuries and a dazzling display of silver.

The **Busch-Reisinger** collection is devoted to the art of Germany, with some works from other North European countries. Outstanding is the 20th-century Expressionism, with canvases by Klee and Kandinsky and Max Beckman's *Self-Portrait in Tuxedo*. Here, too, are a wonderful *Pear Tree* by Gustav Klimt and the largest collection outside Germany of Bauhaus material, including the archives of Gropius and Feininger. Among older paintings, the collection is especially strong in 15th- and 16th-century items from the German, Dutch, and Flemish schools. Romanesque and Gothic ecclesiastical sculpture, 18th-century Rococo porcelain, jewelry, textiles, furniture, and metalcraft are also in the collection.

Farther north, across Cambridge Street, is the slender-pillared **Gund Hall**, home of the Graduate School of Design. The vast studio area, which is four levels high and devoid of interior walls, is a stunning highlight of this 1972 design by John Andrews. Gund is home to the Frances Loeb Library, specializing in books about architecture and urban design.

Memorial Hall and Divinity Avenue

Across from Gund is **Memorial Hall** ❽, a huge Ruskinian Gothic pile which, like nearly all great Harvard buildings, has its admirers and detractors. Among the latter is G.E. Kidder Smith, the architectural historian: 'Though not lovely [it] is loved, a mammoth ugly duckling, an almost fantastic statement of the taste of its time.' Memorial Hall was built in the last quarter of the 19th century to honor Harvard men who fell in the Civil War. Its steep polychromatic roofs were at one time topped by a soaring clock tower whose bells called and dismissed classes. The tower was destroyed in 1956 in a spectacular conflagration.

Although from the outside Memorial Hall looks like a cathedral and although its interior is tripartite, one has only to enter to realize that this is a secular building. The vast, oblong nave was used for commencement exercises and as an undergraduate dining hall. The transept, in ecclesiastical terms, is the memorial part of the hall, and its 17 stained-glass windows are a veritable museum of American stained glass: note especially the 'Battle Window' by John la Farge. The apse, again in ecclesiastical terms, is Sanders Theater, which, with seating for 1,200, is still the largest auditorium in the university. It has superb acoustics and sightlines.

Continue northward, crossing Kirkland Street, and enter Divinity Avenue. At the corner stands a building that might look more at home in Bavaria than New England: the **Busch-Reisinger** building, which formerly housed the university's collection of German art. On the other side of Divinity Avenue stands the 15-story **William James Hall**, which houses the university's

BELOW: the Gothic Memorial Hall.

ABOVE: Botanical Museum.

behavioral sciences department. It was designed by Minoru Yamasaki, whose work included the twin towers of New York's former World Trade Center.

Homogeneity is the keynote to the other buildings on 300yd/meter-long Divinity Avenue, even though they were built over a span of 150 years and serve a wide variety of purposes. To the right are the Harvard-Yenching Library and the Semitic Museum. The **Semitic Museum** lacks the mass appeal of its neighbors; its main attraction is a collection, changed from time to time, of old photographs of the Middle East.

Divinity Hall ❾ is the last building on the east of Divinity Avenue, and is the oldest Harvard building (1816) devoted to its original purpose: a dormitory for divinity students. It was built because President Kirkland believed that divinity students should be isolated from the rest of the university in case they adopted 'more of the spirit of the University than of their profession.'

Closing the avenue at its northern end is the **Farlow Herbarium**, which has the world's largest orchid collection.

Museums of Natural History ❿

With their primary entrance on Oxford Street, the **University Museums of Natural History** (tel: 495-3045; daily 9am–5pm) are comprised of the Peabody Museum of Archeology and Ethnology, the Museum of Comparative Zoology, the Geological and Mineralogical Museum, and the Botanical Museum.

Giant totem poles, Navaho blankets, Hopi ceramics, and African masks are among the items on display at the **Peabody Museum of Archeology and Ethnology**, the oldest such museum in the Americas and the most important of the four museums. Outstanding is the Hall of the North American Indian, which focuses on the interaction between Native Americans and newcomers. The Tozzer Library is said to contain America's best anthropological collection.

The Natural History Museums' top attraction is the Ware Collection of Glass Flowers in the **Botanical Museum**. These 847 remarkably accurate models are a unique collection made near Dresden, Germany, by the Blaschkas, father and son, between 1871 and 1936.

The **Museum of Comparative Zoology** contains such treasures as Kronosaurus, a fossil sea-serpent from Australia, 42ft (13 meters) long; the 25,000-year-old Harvard mastodon; a 65-million-year-old dinosaur egg; extinct birds such as the great auk and the passenger pigeon; and hundreds of stuffed birds and animals.

Rounding off this quartet of museums is the **Geological and Mineralogical Museum**, which

exhibits a large collection of gems, minerals, and ores, and over 500 meteorites.

The Science Center ⓫

Farther down Oxford Street, toward Memorial Hall, is the airy glass and concrete **Science Center**, the largest of all Harvard buildings and winner of an American Institute of Architecture award for its architect, Josef Louis Sert, once dean of the university's Graduate School of Design. A mini-museum in the Science Center houses a permanent exhibition of fascinating early scientific instruments dating back to c.1550. The collection illustrates the history of instrumentation in a broad range of subjects, from astronomy to navigation, and includes telescopes and early computing devices.

Walk down Oxford Street on the eastern flank of the Science Center and turn left to see three entirely disparate buildings. To the west is the discreet, almost genteel, Music Building. Inscribed above its entrance are the words: 'To Charm, To Strengthen and To Teach, These are the Three Great Chords of Might'. To the east is the all-glass Gordon McKay Building of Engineering and Applied Physics and the Jefferson Physical Laboratory, a large red-brick Victorian monster. Here, in the 1920s, a laboratory was made available to Edwin Land, a bright young undergraduate who subsequently made his fortune by inventing the Polaroid camera.

The Law School

Walk westward and immediately enter an irregular yard, part of which is a parking lot. It is flanked by a variety of buildings. Prominent is the white limestone **Langdell Hall ⓬**, which is the heart of the Law School and delineates the west side of Law School Yard. Because of the great length of Langdell and the lack of depth of the yard, it is impossible to appreciate fully the glory of the grand ivy-covered portico of this building with its Ionic columns and pilasters. It houses part of the

Harvard has two celebrated student publications. The Harvard Crimson is the undergraduate newspaper, located at 14 Plympton Street, and the Harvard Lampoon is a humor magazine, housed in castle-like offices on Mount Auburn Street built on land donated by William Randolph Hearst, once its business manager.

LEFT: the entrance to the Peabody Museum. **BELOW:** displays at the Peabody Museum of Archeology and Ethnology.

TIP

The Porter Square
subway station is only a
few blocks north of
Linnaean, and the 'T'
will make the return trip
to Harvard Square in
five minutes. Free
campus tours leave
from the Harvard
Information Center in
Holyoke Center, 1350
Massachusetts Avenue.
For schedules, call 617-
495-1573.
Reservations are
needed for groups of
more than 20.

largest law library of any university
in the world (1.4 million volumes).
The Law School, established in 1817
with six students, is America's oldest
law school.

The back of Langdell Hall, almost
as handsome as the front, forms the
east side of a small, leafy quadrangle, around and spreading out from
which are the 17 other buildings that
constitute the Law School. Much
appreciated in winter are the tunnels that connect some of these to
Langdell Hall.

The Law School's polychromatic
Austin Hall is somewhat evocative
of Sever Hall and bears the characteristic Richardson imprint. The
portico of this Romanesque building, completed in 1881, has three
glorious round arches supported by
groups of intricate colonettes and a
conical-capped asymmetrical turret.

To the west, and unsuccessfully
attempting to close this pseudo-
yard from Massachusetts Avenue,
is the somewhat incongruous
Gannet House ⑬, a small white
Greek-Revival building from 1838,
home of the renowned *Harvard*

Law Review. The north side of the
Law School Yard is enclosed by the
modern buildings of the **Harkness
Graduate Center**, opened in
1949 and designed by Architects
Collaborative under the leadership
of Walter Gropius (see panel).

Old Radcliffe Residential Quadrangle

To visit the old Radcliffe Residential
Quadrangle, turn right on
Massachusetts Avenue, which in
recent years has seen an increase of
exotic restaurants and boutiques,
many of which recall the atmosphere
of Harvard Square in the 1960s and
1970s. Walk north on Massachusetts
Avenue and turn left on Shepard
Street to reach the quadrangle, a
pleasant affair of neo-Georgian
buildings. The handsome, modern
Hilles Library, in the southwest corner of the quadrangle, is much more
than a library: It includes a movie
theater and art gallery and is the site
of the quadrennial Music-Listening
Orgy, during which hundreds of classical CDs are played from beginning
to end without interruption.

BELOW: an aerial shot of
Harvard Campus.

On Linnaean Street, about 600yds/meters off the northeast corner of the quadrangle, is **No. 21** , a simple white two-story structure that dates back to the second half of the 17th century; it is the oldest entire dwelling place in Cambridge.

CAMBRIDGE COMMON TO MOUNT AUBURN STREET

Colonial memories

Reach the Cambridge Common from the old Radcliffe Quadrangle by turning left onto Garden Street, and walking four blocks. Alternatively, those that skip the Radcliffe Quadrangle can simply exit the Harvard Campus onto Massachusetts Avenue and cross the street.

The **Cambridge Common** ⓯ is a reminder that Cambridge has a long and proud colonial history, quite apart from its university associations. It hosts a treasure trove of markers, memorials, and monuments and a place inexorably associated with George Washington. It was here on July 4, 1775, that he took command of the Continental Army. Make

ABOVE: summer loving on Cambridge Common.

for the flagpole and the cluster of three cannons, abandoned when the British left Boston on March 17, 1776, and placed about cobblestones on the west side of the Common.

On the north side of the Cambridge Common is the two-story gray clapboard house at **No. 7 Waterhouse Street** ⓰. It was here that Dr Benjamin Waterhouse lived and 'cut the claws and wings of smallpox' by introducing into the US, in 1800, a vaccination with 'vaccine threads' that he had received from Dr Edward Jenner.

Walk to the Common's southern border of Garden Street, noting the traffic island with a granite lectern topped by a bronze plaque honoring William Dawes, sent at the same time as Paul Revere to warn outlying villagers of the coming of the British. Footprints of his galloping horse are simulated in brass on the pavement.

Adjacent to the **First Unitarian Church** ⓱ is the Old Burying

Harkness Graduate Center

All the buildings in the center are dormitories except the Harkness Commons; it contains dining areas, public rooms and some unusual works of art. The Commons faces a sunken quadrangle, frozen in winter for ice-skating. The central work of art and the focal point of the complex is the 27ft (8.2-meter) high stainless steel *World Tree* by the sculptor Richard Lippold. Nicknamed 'Jungle Gym,' 'Clothes Rack,' and 'Plumbing,' it represents a primitive religious symbol common among such people as the Australian Aborigines, who believe that their sacred *World Tree* is the hub of the universe. To welcome the spring, law students have been known to indulge in strange fertility rites around this tree.

Harvard's Farlow Herbarium, founded by William G. Farlow, who held the first chair of cryptogamic botany in the US in 1879, contains more than 1.3 million specimens of lichens, fungi, algae and bryophytes. It also has a large library of associated books and manuscripts.

Ground, known as 'God's Acre,' in which Harvard's first eight presidents are interred. Several veterans of the Revolution, including two black soldiers, also lie here. Next to the cemetery on Garden Street is **Christ Church** ⑱ (see panel).

Education for women

Continue on Garden Street and enter the old **Radcliffe Yard** ⑲, where the renowned women's college began life in 1879. To the right and left are Byerly Hall and Fay House. The latter, a Federal-style building from 1806, is the oldest structure in the Yard and once housed the entire college apart from student rooms.

Across the Yard is striking **Aggasiz House**, with its Ionic portico. Named after Radcliffe founder Elizabeth Cary Agassiz, it contains a 350-seat theater where Eugene O'Neill's first play opened and failed and where Jack Lemmon got his start. On either side are the Radcliffe Gymnasium and

the Schlesinger Library. The Murray Research Center, which studies the impact of social changes on lives, especially those of women, now occupies

Christ Church

Christ Church is Cambridge's oldest house of worship, built in 1761 by Peter Harrison, who also designed Boston's King's Chapel. Its simple design fulfilled the congregants' request for 'no steeple, only a tower with a belfry.' When most of the Tory congregation fled in 1774, the church was used as a barracks and the organ pipes were melted down for bullets. A bullet hole in the vestibule is said to be from the rifle of a Redcoat as he marched toward Lexington in the early hours of April 18, 1775. The church was reopened on New Year's Eve, 1775, when George and Martha Washington attended worship. A century later, Teddy Roosevelt taught Sunday School here while studying at Harvard.

the first floor of the gymnasium. Upstairs is the Radcliffe Dance Center.

The **Schlesinger Library** has an outstanding collection of literature on the history of women in America and is the country's top research center devoted to women's studies. The library, open to the public, includes a culinary collection with more than 2,300 cookbooks. On the other side of the Yard is **Longfellow House**, a long red-brick neo-Georgian affair with paired entrances framed by pilasters. It houses the Graduate School of Education.

Tory Row

Exit from Radcliffe Yard onto Brattle Street, once known as Tory Row because in the 18th century most of its houses were owned by loyalists. It was also called Church Row, because its residents both built and worshipped at Christ Church. This is the most prestigious street in Cambridge, famous for both history and architecture. A walk of just under a mile (1.2km) fully justifies these claims. Here, all the hubbub is gone and the leafy, tranquil street is lined by splendid large clapboard houses fronted by elegant porticoes, most from the 19th century but some dating to the 18th, each standing in its own spacious grounds. Many bear blue plaques commemorating the greats who have lived in them.

Across Brattle Street is the modern **Loeb Drama Center** (64 Brattle Street). Down Brattle Street to the left, an outdoor café fronts No. 56, a simple two-story, hip-roofed, Federal-style building, home to Longfellow's 'village blacksmith.' But don't search for the chestnut tree under which Longfellow met Dexter Pratt: It suffered the fate of Washington's elm and was chopped down in 1870 when Brattle Street was widened.

Farther along, at No. 42, stands the first of the famous mansions that line the length of the street. Aside from the projecting entrance, this three-story gambrel-roofed clapboard house is true to its 1727 origins. It was built by the future Major-General William Brattle, doctor, lawyer, and minister, commander of all the militia of the province and one of the wealthiest men in Cambridge.

For many years, women who attended Harvard were required to apply to Radcliffe, but in 1999 Radcliffe College as such was fully integrated with Harvard, with the Radcliffe name retained by an Institute of Advanced Study within the university.

LEFT: City Hall, Cambridge.
BELOW: graduation day, Harvard.

He fled to England in 1774. The mansion is now the **Cambridge Center for Adult Education**.

Next door is the **Brattle Theatre**. Paul Robeson and T.S. Eliot trod the theater's boards, as did Jessica Tandy and Hume Cronyn, Hermione Gingold and Zero Mostel. Since 1953 it has been a movie revival house.

Retrace your steps along Brattle to the Radcliffe Yard and continue. **Stoughton House**, the dark building on the left at No. 90, was designed by H.H. Richardson of Boston's Trinity Church fame, and is renowned as one of the first and best examples of domestic American shingle style. Next door at No. 94 stands the **Henry Vassal House**, originally built in the 17th century; its eponymous owner gambled away his fortune. It was the medical headquarters for the first American Army during the Revolution.

Across the road is the red puddingstone Episcopal Divinity School, whose faculty house (No. 101), with its curved central bay, has the grace of an English Regency villa. Continue to the **Longfellow House** ⑳ at No.

RIGHT: the leafy streets of Harvard.
BELOW: Longfellow House.

105 (www.nps.gov/long; tel: 876 4491; guided tours Jun–Oct Wed–Sun), a yellow clapboard building that is the most historic house on Tory Row. The Georgian mansion, started in 1759, originally stood amid 116 acres (47 hectares); it was one of seven Tory estates occupying the area between Brattle Square and Elmwood Avenue, whose lands stretched down to the river. The house was abandoned by its owner, John Vassal, Jr, in 1774, when patriots made life difficult for loyalists in Cambridge, and it was George Washington's headquarters for nine months during the siege of Boston.

Longfellow first arrived here as a lodger in 1837. After receiving the house as a wedding gift from his father-in-law, he remained until 1882. Tragically, his young wife Fanny was fatally burned here in 1861. The gardens, old carriage house and the house are kept virtually as they were in Longfellow's time, with myriad memorabilia including a chair made

from the 'spreading chestnut tree.' Across the street is Longfellow Park, through which the poet would walk on his way to bathe in the river.

Brattle Street tour extension

Those who thoroughly enjoy seeing famous homes can continue on Brattle Street, passing many distinguished residences. These include the houses that Longfellow built for his two daughters (Nos. 113, 115), and the Hooper-Lee-Nichols House (No. 159), built in the 1680s and now owned by the Cambridge Historical Society (open to the public on occasion). Farther on, across Kennedy Road (named after a Cambridge cookie manufacturer and not the President), is No. 163, former home of Edwin Land, inventor of the Polaroid camera, and No. 165, built in 1870 by John Bartlett, the Cambridge bookseller responsible for *Bartlett's Familiar Quotations*. Turn left onto short Elmwood Avenue to see No. 33, a splendid three-story Georgian affair from 1767. It was used as a hospital for Americans during the Revolutionary War and has since been occupied by an illustrious line of owners. Today, it is owned by Harvard and occupied by its president.

Mount Auburn Cemetery ㉑

Those who take the Brattle Street tour extension can, from Elmwood, head west along Mount Auburn Street for about 600yds/meters to the main entrance of **Mount Auburn Cemetery**. Otherwise, reach the cemetery by foot or bus from Harvard Square.

Consecrated in 1831, this is America's oldest and most beautiful garden cemetery, its grounds planted with a glorious collection of trees and shrubs. Among more than 70,000 people interred here are Charles Bulfinch, Oliver Wendell Holmes, Henry W. Longfellow and Mary Baker Eddy (whose tomb is rumored to contain a telephone with an unlisted number). In recent years novelist Bernard Malamud, inventor Edwin Land, and engineer R. Buckminster Fuller have all been laid to rest here. Fuller's grave displays an image of his geodesic dome and the cryptic epitaph, 'Call me trimtab', and lies near his relative, American 19th-century transcendentalist Margaret Fuller.

Although most tombs in this non-sectarian cemetery are modest, others are grand, and the cemetery has been a showpiece of American funerary art for the past 150 years. A climb to the top of the George Washington Tower located at the cemetery's center affords wonderful views of the landscape.

Return to Harvard Square either by walking or taking a bus along Mount Auburn Street.

Along the Charles River

Harvard's domain also extends south of the Square. Back at Harvard Square, walk south on John F.

ABOVE: Mount Auburn Cemetery.
BELOW: wall painting on Massachusetts Avenue.

ABOVE: Henry Moore's *Three-Piece Reclining Figure, Draped,* MIT.
RIGHT: Lampoon HQ.

A stele on the corner of Otis and Second streets in East Cambridge marks where 800 British Redcoats landed on April 19, 1775, to begin their march on Lexington and Concord.

Kennedy Street for 600yds/meters to the river. The first half of this street is occupied by stores and restaurants, while the right side of the lower half is occupied by the **John F. Kennedy School of Government**, which, like most of Harvard, just grows and grows. A small, attractive public park lies between this school and the river.

On the left side of John F. Kennedy Street are **Kirkland** and then **Eliot**, two of Harvard's seven original neo-Georgian residential houses, distinguished by their graceful cupolas, enclosed courtyards, and mellow red-brick walls. The houses, together with newer, more modern fellows, stretch to the left along the river, ending in the contemporary **Peabody Terrace** ㉒ a 21-floor, three-towered complex for married students; the building came from the drawing board of Josef Luis Sert.

Across the Larz Anderson Bridge sprawls, on the left, the **Business School** campus and, on the right,

Harvard's vast playing fields, which are both in Brighton, a suburb of Boston.

At the rear of a wide triangular area on Mount Auburn Street, the whimsical building (44 Bow Street) with a gaudy door and topped by an ibis is the headquarters of the *Lampoon* ㉓, Harvard's famous humor magazine. Also on Mount Auburn Street, note a red-brick building with a six-pillared entry. This is the Fly Club, one of eight once-snooty Harvard 'final clubs', which have shed much of their exclusivity in recent years. Theodore and Franklin Roosevelt were both members here, presumably because even they couldn't pass muster at the lordliest Harvard club of all, the Porcellian.

MASSACHUSETTS INSTITUTE OF TECHNOLOGY

Half a mile beyond Central Square, you reach the first MIT buildings. On the left is the **MIT Museum** Ⓐ (265 Massachusetts Avenue; http://

web.mit.edu/museum; tel: 253-5927; daily 10am–5pm; charge), which was founded in 1971 and contains treasures that have made MIT a leader in computer, electronic, and nuclear technologies.

Another MIT museum open to the public is the **Hart Nautical Museum** (55 Massachusetts Avenue, Building 5; http://web.mit.edu; tel: 253-5942; daily 10am–5pm; free), which features model craft ranging from Donald McKay's great Yankee clipper *Flying Cloud* to modern guided missile warships by way of America's Cup defenders.

Continue from the MIT Museum along Massachusetts Avenue and cross the railroad to reach the main campus. The west campus, on the right, is devoted to the students' social life; the larger east campus, to the left, is the workplace of MIT.

Kresge Auditorium and the Chapel are two outstanding buildings designed by a Finnish architect, Eero Saarinen. The former, completed in 1953, is an enormous tent-like structure rising out of a circular brick terrace; its roof appears to be supported at only three points by delicate metal rods, and it is enclosed by thin-mullioned curtains of glass. It is very much an outward-looking building.

The much smaller non-denominational chapel, a windowless, brick cylinder set in a moat and adorned with a sculptural bell tower, is inward-looking. Light reflected from the moat illuminates the interior, where a delicate bronze-toned screen hangs behind the white marble altar block. Slightly farther west is **Baker House** ⓑ, an undulating dormitory designed by the Finnish architect Alvar Aalto so that all its rooms have a view of the river.

Back on Massachusetts Avenue is the imposing domed neoclassical facade of the **Rogers Building** ⓒ, completed in 1937 and named after William Barton Rogers, who

TIP

The Friends of the Mount Auburn Cemetery offer special walks and talks – tel: 547-7105. A map of notable graves and memorials is available at the front gate of the cemetery, which is also one of New England's favorite spots for bird-watching, especially during the spring migration.

BELOW: Ray and Maria Stata Center for Computer, Information, and Intelligence Sciences.

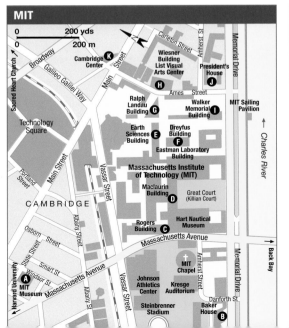

The Education Industry

Boston has been firmly linked to learning ever since William Blackstone, the first white settler, lugged 200 books to his cabin.

There are over 50 colleges and universities in and around Boston, adding several hundred thousand students to the region's population.

Harvard University is the oldest and richest university in the US. It has over 40 Nobel laureates among its current and former faculty and over 25,000 students.

Massachusetts Institute of Technology has around 10,000 students, more than half of whom are enrolled in graduate programs.

Boston University has more than 31,000 full and part-time students, and more international students than any other US university. Alexander Graham Bell taught here while he was developing the telephone. BU has 19 schools and colleges, including communications, medicine, law, theology, and dentistry.

Boston College, one of 28 Jesuit colleges in the US, is the nation's largest Catholic university, with an enrollment of nearly 15,000. A university in all but name, it has nine schools and colleges.

Northeastern University, with more than 20,000 students, has six undergraduate and eight graduate schools. The best-known are in law and criminal justice.

Emerson College is the only private four-year college in the US devoted exclusively to the study of communication and the performing arts at the undergraduate and graduate level. Famous alumni include Jay Leno, Henry Winkler, Spalding Gray, and Dennis Leary.

Suffolk University, situated Downtown, was founded to serve students otherwise denied access to college because of income, religion, or class; its fees are about half those of competing schools.

Tufts University, 5 miles (8km) north of Boston in Medford, has about 5,000 undergraduate students. P.T. Barnum of Barnum & Bailey's Circus was one of its founders.

Wellesley College, about 13 miles (21km) west of Boston, has remained women-only, with 2,400 students. Its pastoral 500-acre (200-hectare) campus is one of the finest in America, with its own lake, a nine-hole golf course and 24 tennis courts.

Babson College, also in Wellesley, has one of the top MBA programs in North America and Europe; 2,000 of its students are in the graduate school, and most of the 1,500 undergraduates plan careers in business.

Brandeis University, in the western suburb of Waltham, is known for its Gordon Public Policy Center, and its Judaic Studies program is the largest outside Israel.

Simmons College, in Fenway, has five graduate schools, including the world's first graduate business school for women.

New England Conservatory, with around 800 graduate and undergraduate students, stages free concerts.

Berklee College of Music has become the world's largest independent music college, and has 4,000 students from 80 countries.

University of Massachusetts Boston, across town on Dorchester Bay, has about 16,000 students, all commuters and many working full-time to subsidize their educations.

LEFT: graduation day at Harvard.

founded MIT in 1861. Its steep stairway and four pairs of Ionic columns provide the main entrance to the teaching buildings of the School of Architecture and Planning and lead to an extensive system of tunnels linking many of the east campus buildings.

Rather than entering here, continue on Massachusetts Avenue for a further couple of hundred yards to the Charles River. Turn left onto Memorial Drive and immediately on the left is the aptly named Great Court (also called Killian Court) in front of the monumental **Maclaurin Building**  with its Pantheon-like dome and broad Ionic portico. (Richard C. Maclaurin, a Scot, was the president of MIT who moved the institute from Boston to Cambridge.)

Farther eastward is McDermott Court, dominated by the **Earth Sciences Building** , the tallest structure on campus and readily recognized by the large white sphere on its roof. In front of it stands Alexander Calder's *Big Sail*, a giant free-form metal sculpture. The Earth Sciences Building is just one of four on campus designed by I.M. Pei, a Harvard graduate who also studied at MIT. The others are the **Dreyfus Building**  and the **Ralph Landau Building** , which flank Earth Sciences, and, somewhat farther east, the **Wiesner Building** , home to the **List Visual Arts Center** (20 Ames Street, Building E15; http://listart.mit.edu; tel: 253-4680; Tue–Wed noon–6pm, Thur noon–8pm, Fri–Sun noon–6pm, closed holidays; free).

Established in 1985, this is MIT's contemporary art gallery, which presents up to eight outstanding exhibitions each year. The List Visual Arts Center also oversees MIT's permanent collection, which includes more than 1,500 paintings, sculptures, photographs, and other artworks. The sculpture collection includes works by artists such as Alexander Calder, Pablo Picasso, Henry Moore, and Jorge Pardo.

Farther along Memorial Drive it is back to neoclassicism with the **Walker Memorial Building** . Facing this is the MIT Sailing Pavilion. And then, still on Memorial Drive, is the austere, limestone, ivy-covered **President's House** .

Main Street and Kendall Square, to the east of Wiesner, are tree-bordered areas lined by handsome, soaring buildings, most of which are of red brick. A few years ago they were a desolation. Visit the landscaped garden atop the parking lot in the heart of the **Cambridge Center** , a modern hotel, laboratory, and office complex. Farther west, across the rail tracks, is more of the same in **Technology Square**, an urban redevelopment project in which MIT joined with the city to clear away old factories and tenements.

The name Polaroid on some of these buildings reflects the birth of the instant camera in Cambridge. Polaroid's rival, Eastman Kodak, is well represented on the MIT campus with the Eastman Laboratory

ABOVE: Tony Smith's *For Marjorie* sculpture, MIT. **BELOW:** the Maclaurin Building.

SHOPPING

Independent shops line Massachusetts Avenue and the squares; but the Harvard Square area is the city's main shopping district. The Cambridge-Side Galleria (100 Cambridgeside Place) is an upscale shopping mall.

Antiques

Cambridge Antiques Market
201 Monsignor O'Brien Hwy
Tel: 868-9655
More than 150 dealers on five floors sell reasonably priced furniture, lighting, glass, books, and vintage clothing.

City Lights
2226 Massachusetts Ave
Tel: 547-1490
For 1860–1950 working antique wall sconces and chandeliers.

Bookstores

Grolier Poetry Book Shop
6 Plympton St
Tel: 547-4648
www.grolierpoetrybookshop.org
Poetry specialists since 1927, with more than 15,000 titles.

Schoenhof's Foreign Books
76A Mt Auburn St
Tel: 547-8855
www.schoenhofs.com
Founded in 1856, Schoenhof's boasts one of North America's largest selections of foreign titles, and is especially strong in French, Spanish, German, and Italian titles.

Food

Cardullo's Gourmet Shop
6 Brattle St
Tel: 491-8888
www.cardullos.com
A long-established purveyor of regional and global treats: olive oil, marzipan, maple syrup, tea, honey, caviar, and chocolate, to name a few.

Formaggio Kitchen
244 Huron Ave
Tel: 354-4750
www.formaggiokitchen.com
An impressively vast assortment of 3,000 cheeses, artisanal oils, charcuterie, handmade sweets, hard-to-find spices, and delicacies from around the world. The cheeses are aged in a special 'cave.' Smaller location at 268 Shawmut Ave, tel: 350-6996.

Gifts

Joie de Vivre
1792 Massachusetts Ave
Tel: 864-8188
www.joiedevivre.net
Cute, quirky gifts and games for children and adults, from wind-up toys and singing goats to music boxes and expensive kaleidoscopes.

Home

Abodeon
1731 Massachusetts Ave
Tel: 497-0137
www.abodeon.com
Home goods inspired by the mid-20th century and curated vintage finds, including furniture, lighting, tableware and gifts.

Music

Cheapo Records
645 Massachusetts Ave
Tel: 354-4455
www.cheaporecords.com
Savvy staff, CDs, cassettes, vinyl, and DVDs, with music ranging from soul and jazz to hip hop, rock, and disco.

Toys

Henry's Bear Park
361 Huron Ave
Tel: 547-8424
www.henrybear.com
Toys, games, and items for infants and pre-teens.

Stella Bella Toys
1360 Cambridge St
Tel: 491-6290
www.stellabellatoys.com
Traditional and educational toys, and special activities such as a Saturday Sing-Along at 11am. Also at 1967 Massachusetts Ave, tel: 864-6290.

Women's Clothing

Forty Winks
56 John F. Kennedy St
Tel: 492-9100
Shopfortywinks.com
An inviting lingerie store with friendly staff, Forty Winks stocks brands like Nu-Bra, Cosabella, and Eberjay.

LEFT: in Harvard Square.

Building and Eastman Court. George Eastman left much of his not inconsiderable estate to MIT.

MUSEUM OF SCIENCE

Perched on the Charles River Dam (Monsignor O'Brien Highway, just across the Lechmere Canal from the Galleria Mall) is the **Museum of Science**  (www.mos.org; tel: 723-2500; Sat–Thur 9am–5pm, Fri 9am–9pm, July 5–Labor Day Sat–Thur 9am–7pm, Fri 9am–9pm; charge). The museum began life in 1830 as the Boston Society of Natural History, and moved here in 1951.

The giant museum is very much a hands-on affair, and contains hundreds of exhibits in major fields such as astronomy, computing, energy, anthropology, industry, and nature. Visitors can determine their weight on the moon, listen to a transparent talking woman, see bolts of lightning created indoors, and watch chickens hatching. They can also learn how wind turbines work, or how light and color behave. The model of a Tyrannosaurus Rex, 20ft (6 meters) high, is a big draw. In addition to permanent exhibits, temporary exhibits constantly circle through, making every visit unique.

The rock garden features samples from throughout the world, including Egyptian granite, limestone from the Rock of Gibraltar, and Roxbury puddingstone.

The adjacent **Hayden Planetarium** has a projector and multi-image system offering excellent programs on astronomy, plus laser light shows.

Those prone to motion sickness should skip the museum's **Mugar Omni Theater**, where wraparound state-of-the-art movies are projected onto a domed IMAX screen 76ft (23 meters) high, with sound blasting from 84 speakers; but for the strong of stomach it's well worth a visit. There are late shows at weekends.

BELOW: exhibit at the Museum of Science.

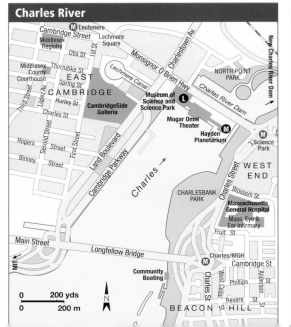

RESTAURANTS, BARS, AND CAFES

Restaurants

American

Harvest
44 Brattle St
Tel: 868-2255
www.harvestcambridge.com
L & D daily, Br Sun $$$–$$$$
86 [p272, B2]
A Harvard Square institution, specializing in contemporary New England cuisine, with a good assortment of grilled fish and meats, an open kitchen, and a sleek bar. The three-course Sunday brunch includes treats such as crab cake, eggs Benedict, and house-made challah bread French toast; and the delightful shaded garden terrace stays open well into the fall (there are outdoor heaters).

UpStairs on the Square
91 Winthrop St
Tel: 864-1933
www.upstairsonthesquare.com
Monday Club Bar: B, L, & D, Br Sun, Soirée Dining Room: D only Tue–Sat. $$$ 87 [p272, B2]
Raspberry, pink, and purple decor sets a celebratory mood at this colorful Harvard Square fine-dining destination. The Soirée Dining Room is lit by working fireplaces and features a menu of New American and Italian cuisine; the first-floor Monday Club Bar serves a cheaper 'casual haute cuisine' menu.

Chinese

Mary Chung
464 Massachusetts Ave
Tel: 864-1991
www.marychung.com
L & D Wed–Mon $ 88 [p272, C3]
Those who like their Chinese food hot are happy to cool their heels waiting for a table at this extremely plain and very popular Central Square eatery. There's a dim sum weekend brunch.

Desserts

Finale
30 Dunster St
Tel: 441-9797
www.finaledesserts.com
L & D daily $ 89 [p272, B2]
This sweet-tooth magnet serves specialty desserts and dessert wines. Desserts include a signature molten chocolate cake ($11), a strawberry tart, tiramisu, crème brûlée, and Boston cream pie.

French

Craigie on Main
853 Main St
Tel: 457-5511
www.craigieonmain.com
D Tue–Sun, brunch Sun $$$–$$$$ 90 [p266, A4]
Chef-owner Tony Maws delivers modern French bistro fare with a heavy emphasis on seasonal, organic, local ingredients. Menus change daily, the award-winning wine list consists exclusively of lesser-known, estate-bottled wines, and the cocktail list is very creative.

Salts
798 Main St
Tel: 876-8444
www.saltsrestaurant.com
D Tue–Sat $$$ 91 [p266, A4]
This cozy, elegant spot features a menu of fancy French fare inspired by American contemporary cuisine, with entrées such as lavender honey-glazed roast duck or slow-roasted halibut with heirloom potato gnocchi and black truffles.

Italian

Dante
Royal Sonesta Hotel, 40 Edwin H. Land Blvd
Tel: 497-4200
www.restaurantdante.com

D daily $$$ **92** [p266, B3]
A sophisticated space with views of the Boston skyline, serving up modern Italian cuisine with entrées such as pork shoulder Milanese, pancetta-wrapped trout, and linguini with crab and sea urchin.

Pinocchio's
74 Winthrop St
Tel: 876-4897
www.pinocchiospizza.net
L & D daily $ **93** [p272, B2]
The most popular spot in town for a slice or a whole pizza, although folks also queue up for the cheeseburger subs. Seating is limited.

Korean

Koreana
154 Prospect St
Tel: 576-8661
www.koreanaboston.com
L & D daily $–$$ **94** [p272, C2]
Grills are built right into the tables at this Korean-style barbecue. Customers can cook up dishes like Galbi (prime beef ribs with traditional sauces) or leave the cooking in the capable hands of the chefs. There's an excellent sushi bar.

Middle Eastern

Algiers Coffee House
40 Brattle St
Tel: 492-1557
B, L, & D daily $ **95** [p272, B2]
The unique north African atmosphere and a cozy upstairs draw locals to this small, eclectic coffee house, which serves coffee and teas, sandwiches, soups, hummus plates, and feta and spinach turnovers.

Moody's Falafel Palace
25 Central Square
Tel: 864-0827

L & D daily $ **96** [p272, C3]
Small and cheap, this spot draws late-night crowds, as it is open until 3am Thur–Sat, and midnight Mon–Wed, a rarity in the area.

Oleana
134 Hampshire St
Tel: 661-0505
www.oleanarestaurant.com
D daily $$$ **97** [p272, C1]
Foodies are in a frenzy over chef-owner Ana Sortun's flavorful menu, featuring entrées such as lamb with Turkish spices and fava bean moussaka, and Moroccan fish stew. The dining room is warm and inviting, and a lovely patio is open May–Oct.

Portuguese

Atasca
50 Hampshire St
Tel: 621-6991
www.atasca.com
L & D daily $$ **98** [p266, A3]
This old-world restaurant features authentic Portuguese cuisine designed to satisfy new-world tastes. Many of the dishes are available in either small or large plates, and include treats such as sautéed squid with garlic, spicy poached mussels, and baked dry salt cod with caramelized onions, roast peppers, and home fries.

Seafood

East Coast Grill & Raw Bar
1271 Cambridge St
Tel: 491-6568
www.eastcoastgrill.net
D daily, Br Sun $–$$ **99** [p266, A2]
Here's an ideal find – a restaurant whose menu includes both a raw bar

platter and oak-smoked pit BBQ. To pile on the perfection, Sunday brunch includes a 'Make Your Own Bloody Mary Bar.' This seafood restaurant, which still honors its BBQ roots, excels at both.

Southern

Hungry Mother
233 Cardinal Medeiros Ave
Tel: 499-0090
www.hungrymothercambridge.com
D Tue–Sun $$$ **100** [p266, A3]
Southern cuisine inspires much of the creative menu (cornmeal catfish, baked grits, Southern-style cornbread), but dishes like gnocchi and grilled local bluefish also make an appearance.

Tupelo
1193 Cambridge St
Tel: 868-0004
www.tupelo02139.com
D Tue–Sun $$ **101** [p266, A2]
From fried oysters with spicy remoulade to Jambalayas, New Orleans gumbo, hominy mashed potatoes, and sweet mixed berry pies, the 'comfort food with a Southern drawl' at this down-to-earth Inman Square spot is a hit.

Bars

Charlie's
10 Eliot St
Tel: 492-9646
18 [p272, B2]
If you fancy spending a relaxing summer afternoon in an outdoor beer garden, Charlie's is an excellent choice.

Enormous Room
567 Massachusetts Ave
Tel: 491-5550
19 [p272, C3]
Moroccan snacks, great drinks, and cozy divans make the Enormous

Prices for a three-course dinner per person, with tax and tip:

$ = under $25
$$ = $25–50
$$$ = $50–75
$$$$ = over $75

Room a good place to lounge in Central Square.

Green Street
280 Green St
Tel: 876-1655
20 [p272, C3]
Off Central Square, Green Street offers an upscale atmosphere and an excellent specialty cocktails menu.

Johnny D's
17 Holland Street
Tel: 776-2004
21 [p272, B1]
For a bit of off-the-beaten-path nightlife, head over to Davis Square in nearby Somerville, home to Tufts University. Johnny D's is a great venue for live music, playing everything from rock, pop and blues to folk and zydeco, and attracting a funky, cool crowd.

TOAD
1912 Massachusetts Ave
Tel: 497-4950
22 [p272, B1]
Live music seven days a week (with no cover charge) attracts locals to this small and casual Porter Square bar. In addition to a dozen beers on tap, the TOAD bar serves Angus beef burgers and veggie burgers nightly.

West Side Lounge
1680 Massachusetts Ave
Tel: 441-5566
23 [p272, B1]
Cambridge's beautiful people enjoy the ambience of the swanky West Side Lounge.

LEFT: fine New England dining at Harvest.

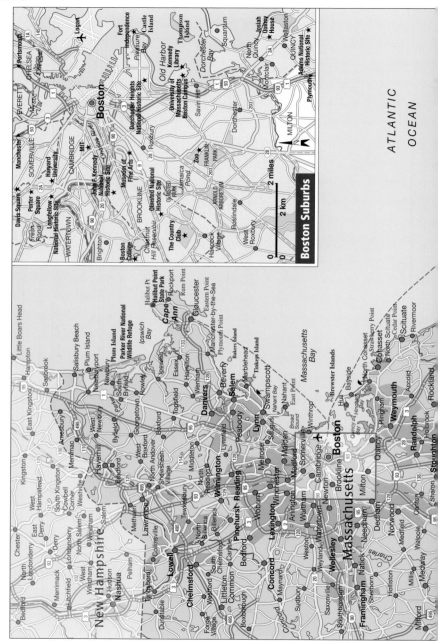

Boston Suburbs

ATLANTIC OCEAN

Massachusetts Bay

New Hampshire

Massachusetts

ATLANTIC OCEAN

0 2 km
0 2 miles

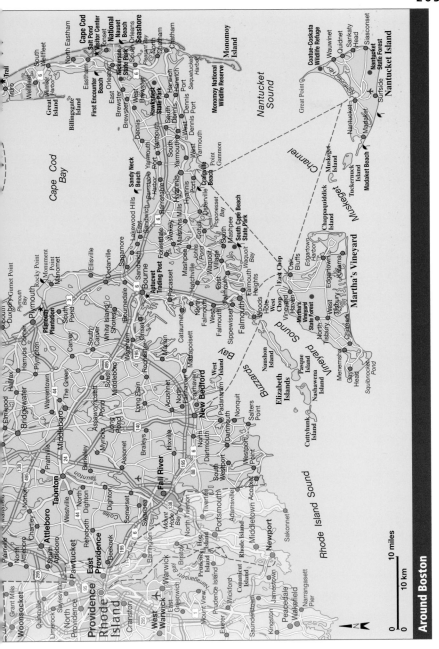

Around Boston

0   10 miles

0   10 km

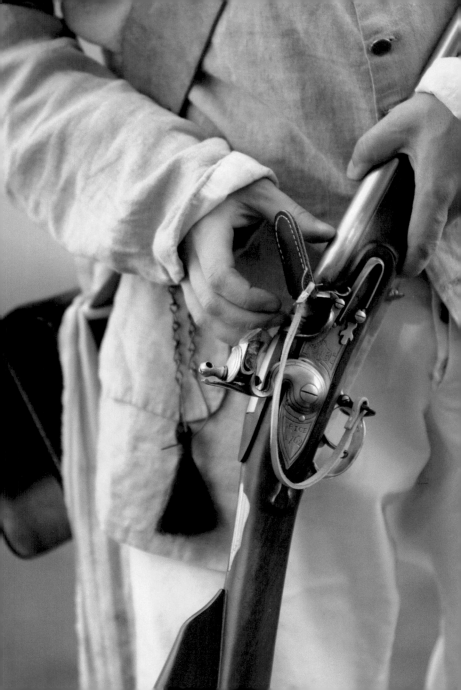

EXCURSIONS WEST

Within easy reach of Boston are the revolutionary sites of Lexington and Concord, the literary shrine of Walden Pond, and the historical reconstruction of Old Sturbridge Village.

For most visitors, an excursion into Boston's western outskirts invariably means a pilgrimage along the famed 'Battle Road' followed by combatants on those fateful days of April, 1775, when simmering American resentments flared into all-out war with Britain. But there's more out this way, including mementoes of Concord's literary immortals, the real 'Wayside Inn' of Longfellow's tales, and one of America's finest living history museums, Old Sturbridge Village.

LEXINGTON ❶

To reach **Lexington**, site of the first battle of the Revolution, leave Boston on Route 2 (Boston University Bridge to Cambridge's Memorial Drive, then west) and, after 10 miles (16km), turn right onto Route 4–225. On the left as you enter Lexington is a contemporary building which houses the **National Heritage Museum** (33 Marrett Road; www.monh.org; tel: 781-861-6559; Tue–Sat 10am–4.30pm, Sun noon–4.30pm; free), featuring changing exhibits of Americana. Soon after, still on the left, is the russet-colored 1635 **Munroe Tavern** (1332 Massachusetts Avenue; www.

lexingtonhistory.org; tel: 781-862-5598; Apr–Oct daily noon–4pm, tours every hour; charge), which served as headquarters for the Redcoats and as a hospital on their retreat from Concord. A mile farther on is the **Battle Green ❷**, properly known as Lexington Common, a triangular park in the heart of Lexington. Here, early on the morning of April 19, 1775, the colonials' Captain Parker told his men: 'Stand your ground; don't fire unless fired upon, but if

PRECEDING PAGES: Thoreau's Walden Pond. **LEFT:** a revolutionary-era musket being used at a reenactment. **RIGHT:** at the National Heritage Museum.

they mean to have a war, let it begin here!'

Atop a heap of boulders, taken from a wall behind which the Americans shot at the British, is the **Minuteman Statue** (the 'minutemen' were so called because they were members of a militia supposed to be ready at a minute's notice). To the right (east) is the 1690 **Buckman Tavern** (1 Bedford Street; lhsoc.weebly.com/; tel: 781-862-5598; Apr–Thanksgiving weekend daily 10am–4pm, tours every half-hour; charge), where several dozen minutemen gathered to await the British. Following the battle, wounded minutemen were carried here for medical attention. It has been restored to its original appearance. Guided tours highlight a bullet hole in the door, muskets, cooking equipment, and furniture.

A quarter-mile north of the Green is the mocha-colored **Hancock-Clarke House** (35 Hancock Street; lhsoc.weebly.com; tel: 781-862-5598; Apr–Oct daily 10am–4pm, tours every hour; charge) where, on April 18, 1775, wanted men John Hancock and Samuel Adams were roused from their sleep by Paul Revere and warned of the coming of the British.

Minute Man National Historical Park ❸

Leave Lexington on Route 2A – the Battle Road – from the northwest corner of Battle Green to reach Minute Man National Historical Park (daily sunrise to sunset). Stop at the **Minute Man Visitor Center** (250 North Great Road; www.nps.gov/mima; tel: 978-369-6993; daily late Mar–Oct 9am–5pm, Nov 9am–4pm; free). This is a good place to begin a Lexington–Concord exploration; a multimedia film program provides an introduction to the historic events.

Visit also the former site of the **Ebenezer Fiske Farmhouse**, whose foundation line is marked by stones.

BELOW: Obelisk honoring American war casualties, National Historical Park.

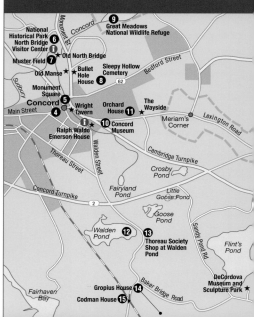

Here, after refreshing himself with a drink from a well, a minuteman found himself facing a Redcoat. 'You are a dead man,' announced the minuteman. 'And so are you,' was the reply. Both leveled their muskets, both fired, and both were killed.

CONCORD ④

Concord is 8 miles (13km) away, after several further informative stops along the Battle Road. This handsome small town, now an upscale suburb, is doubly important. Here the second engagement of the Revolution took place, and here, during the first half of the 19th century, lived a handful of renowned literati (see page 54).

Monument Square ⑤, at the center of town, is where, on April 19, 1775, a British sergeant burning a cache of captured supplies inadvertently set fire to a building. The Americans massing on the opposite side of the river saw the smoke and, assuming that the British were burning the town, decided to march to its defense 'or die in the attempt.' Their advance was blocked by a British detachment guarding the bridge. Several roads radiate from Monument Square: all should be explored.

Begin by driving north on Monument Street for a little over a mile and then turning left to reach immediately the **National Historical Park North Bridge Visitor Center** ⑥ (174 Liberty Street, Concord; www.nps.gov/mima; tel: 978-369-6993; Apr–Oct daily 9am–5pm, Nov daily 9am–4pm, reduced winter hours; free). Here, an audiovisual presentation explains the confluence of events that led to the battle. Gardens overlook the Concord River with a view of **Old North Bridge**.

Stroll the half-mile downhill past the **Muster Field ⑦** (to the right) until you reach sculptor Daniel Chester French's heroic statue of the

TIP

Concord can quickly be 'done' in a couple of hours, but to explore any house usually requires joining a guided tour, which often requires a short wait. Most tours take about 40 minutes.

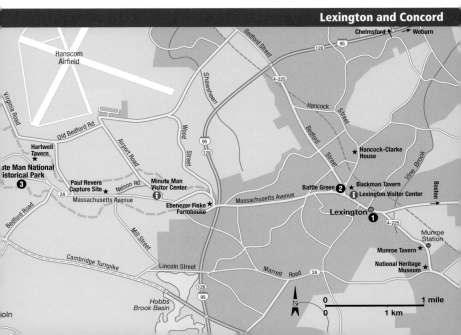

Lexington and Concord

minuteman, rifle in one hand and the other clutching a plowshare. On the plinth are Ralph Waldo Emerson's immortal words chronicling 'the shot heard round the world.' And so to 'the rude bridge that spanned the flood.' Today's bridge was built in 1956. The bloody skirmish seems distant indeed from today's idyllic surroundings.

The simple, clapboard **Old Manse** (269 Monument Street; www.the trustees.org; tel: 978-369-3909; grounds daily sunrise–sunset, house Jun–Oct Mon–Sat noon–4pm, Nov–Dec and mid-Feb–May Sat–Sun noon–4pm; grounds free, house charge), 200yds/meters south of North Bridge, was built in 1770 and was first occupied by the Rev. William Emerson, who watched the battle for the bridge from here. His grandson, Ralph Waldo Emerson, lived here for two short periods.

In 1842, newlyweds Nathaniel Hawthorne and Sophia Peabody moved in and remained for three years. During this period Nathaniel wrote *Mosses from an Old Manse*, a collection of stories that secured a literary place for both house and writer. Meanwhile, Sophia was painting and scratching the study and dining room windows with her wedding ring. The longest and most charming of her inscriptions states: 'Una Hawthorne stood on this windowsill January 22, 1845, while the trees were all glass chandeliers – a goodly show which she liked much though only 10 months old.'

Literary giants

Back in Monument Square, drive northeast on Bedford Street (Route 62) for 200yds/meters to **Sleepy Hollow Cemetery ❽**. Author's Ridge, in the northeast corner, is the final resting place of Nathaniel Hawthorne, Louisa May Alcott and her father Bronson Alcott, Ralph Waldo Emerson, and Henry Thoreau.

To escape all the history and just commune with nature, continue on Bedford Street for another mile and watch for a small sign noting the entrance to the **Great Meadows National Wildlife Refuge ❾**. Here serious birdwatchers mix with those only out for a bucolic stroll.

ABOVE: the Minuteman Statue on Battle Green, Lexington.
BELOW: bronze statue of Henry David Thoreau at Walden Pond.

A Different Drummer

Thoreau wrote seven drafts of *Walden; or, Life in the Woods* before publishing in 1854. Not all of his contemporaries agreed with the messages they saw in this mix of autobiography and social commentary. Poet John Greenleaf Whittier called it 'capital reading, but very wicked and heathenish,' and Robert Louis Stevenson thought the lifestyle described in the book was 'unmanly.' Yet *Walden* has proved powerful and timeless, and the book has never been out of print. Its popularity persists, in part due to the oft-quoted passage: 'If a man does not keep pace with his companions, perhaps it is because he hears a different drummer. Let him step to the music which he hears, however measured or far away.'

Backtrack from the Monument Square for less than a mile on the Lexington Road to the junction with the Cambridge Turnpike. Here stands the **home of Ralph Waldo Emerson** (28 Cambridge Turnpike; tel: 978-369-2236; mid-Apr–Oct Thur–Sat 10am–4.30pm, Sun 1–4.30pm), where Emerson wrote many of his celebrated essays and poems. Here also is the excellent **Concord Museum** ❿ (200 Lexington Road; www.concordmuseum.org; tel: 978-369-9763; Jan–Mar Mon–Sat 11am–4pm; Apr–Dec Mon–Sat 9am–5pm, Sun noon–5pm; open Sun 9am–5pm July–Aug; charge), which features beautifully reconstructed rooms from the 18th and 19th centuries, and Emerson's study. Its Thoreau Gallery has the largest collection of artifacts associated with the author, including furnishings from his Walden Pond abode.

One mile farther along, at 399 Lexington Road, stands the shaded brown clapboard **Orchard House** ⓫ (www.louisamayalcott.org; tel: 978-369-4118; guided tours Apr–Oct Mon–Sat 10am–4.30pm, Sun 1–4.30pm; Nov–Mar Mon–Fri 11am–3pm, Sat 10am–4.30pm, Sun 1.30–4.30pm; charge), where the Alcott family lived from 1858 to 1877. Here Louisa May Alcott wrote *Little Women*. Just beyond, at No. 455, is **The Wayside** (www.nps.gov/mima; tel: 978-318-7863; tours late May–Oct Wed–Sun 10am–5.30pm, last tour at 4.30; charge). The Wayside (not to be confused with Longfellow's Wayside Inn; see page 211) was the home of revolutionary Samuel Whitney, the muster master of the Concord minutemen.

The house is also famous for its literary inhabitants. The Alcotts resided here before moving to Orchard House. Nathaniel Hawthorne lived here after buying the house in 1852. It was later occupied by Harriet Lothrop, who authored the *Five Little*

ABOVE: Walden Pond, the inspiration for one of the greatest pieces of American literature.

Pepper books under the pen name Margaret Sidney.

AROUND CONCORD

Walden Pond ⓬

Continue to **Walden Pond** (www.mass.gov/dcr/parks/walden/; tel: 978-369-3254), reached by returning toward Concord and then traveling south on Walden Street, which crosses Route 2, for 1.5 miles (2.5km). Henry David Thoreau lived here from 1845–7, and his experiences provided the material for his famous book *Walden; or, Life in the Woods*. The pond is relatively small and can be circled on foot in about an hour. The best time to visit is in the fall, when summer crowds have thinned. A cairn of stones stands alongside the site where Thoreau lived.

Thoreau enthusiasts will also wish to visit the memorabilia-filled **Thoreau Society Shop at Walden Pond** ⓭ (915 Walden Street; tel: 978-287-5477; www.thoreausociety.

ABOVE: a group of young people learn about plants in the decorative garden at Old Sturbridge Village.

org/_shop.htm; call for hours;), which is a part of the park's visitor center. Nearby is a replica of his Walden Pond cabin.

Gropius House

Continue south from Walden Pond and, after a half-mile, turn left. Immediately to the right is the **Gropius House** ⓮ (68 Baker Bridge Road, Lincoln; www.historicnewengland.org; tel: 781-259-8098; 11am–5pm Jun–Oct 15 Wed–Sun, Oct 16–May Sat–Sun; charge). This house expresses the Bauhaus principles of function and simplicity, and was the first building that the great German architect designed when he arrived in the US in 1937.

Lincoln

Another mile leads to the attractive **DeCordova Museum and Sculpture Park** (51 Sandy Pond Road, Lincoln; www.decordova.org; tel: 781-259-8355; Tue–Sun 10am–5pm; charge),

showcasing temporary exhibitions of modern art. The 35 acres (14 hectares) of grounds, high above **Sandy Point Pond**, are a splendid setting for the Sculpture Park. In summer, outdoor concerts are held in the amphitheater.

Also in Lincoln is a gem of a three-story blue clapboard house with an Ionic portico. The **Codman House** ⓯ (34 Codman Road; www.historicnewengland.org; tel: 617-994-6690; tours June–Oct 15 2nd and 4th Saturday of month 11am–5pm; charge), its grounds landscaped like an English country estate, is a treasure trove of 18th- and 19th-century furniture and decorative arts.

Fruitlands Museum

To reach **Harvard Village** and the **Fruitlands Museum**, return to Concord and drive west on Route 2. After 13 miles (21km), turn south on Route 110 and immediately right onto Old Shirley Road. This crosses Depot Road to become Prospect Hill, where the entrance to Fruitlands is located 2 miles (3km) after leaving Route 2. **Fruitlands** (102 Prospect Hill Road, Harvard; www.fruitlands.org; tel: 978-456-3924; mid-Apr–Oct Mon, Wed–Fri 10am–4pm, Sat–Sun 10am–5pm; charge) is a handsomely landscaped property with magnificent views across the Nashua River Valley.

Fruitlands also offers excellent attractions. The first is an 18th-century farmhouse where, for some months, Bronson Alcott and his family, an English friend, Charles Lane, and others attempted an experiment in communal living. The Shaker Museum displays handicrafts and exhibits, offering insights into Shaker life, which involved celibacy, communal ownership of property, and worship joyfully expressed in dance. A third museum houses a selection of Native American (not New England) relics, arts and dioramas.

And a fine art gallery features over 100 Hudson River school landscape paintings, along with 'primitive' portraits by early 19th-century itinerant artists.

Longfellow's Wayside Inn

Head south for 6 miles (10km) past Walden Pond on Route 126, then turn right onto Route 20 and continue for 5 miles (8km) to Sudbury and **Longfellow's Wayside Inn** (72 Wayside Inn Road, Sudbury; www.wayside.org; tel: 978-443-1776), which claims to be the country's oldest operating inn. The tavern became inexorably linked with Henry Wadsworth Longfellow when *Tales of a Wayside Inn* appeared in 1863.

The inn still offers 'Food, Drink and Lodging for Man, Woman and Beast,' and can be explored by those not staying for a meal or a night. It was restored by Henry Ford in the 1920s. In its grounds stand the Red Schoolhouse supposedly attended by Mary and her little lamb of nursery rhyme fame, and a working reproduction of an 18th-century gristmill.

OLD STURBRIDGE VILLAGE

Although well beyond Boston's western suburbs, **Old Sturbridge Village** (1 Old Sturbridge Village Road; www.osv.org; tel: 800-733-1830; call or check website for daily hours; charge) shouldn't be missed by anyone with an interest in history and an extra day to spend in Massachusetts. From Boston, the best approach is via the Massachusetts Turnpike; get off at Exit 9 for Sturbridge.

More than 40 original buildings, dating from 1730 to 1840, have been collected from throughout New England and placed here to create a *c.*1830 village and a 70-acre (28-hectare) farm. A blacksmith, potter, cobbler, and other tradespeople work in period attire; there's a working general store, a restaurant, a central green, and a lake spanned by a covered bridge. A pair of oxen harnessed to a plow are used to turn the sod, and the crops grown were common to the region in the early 19th century. Houses are authentically furnished, and a variety of religious and civic events punctuate the daily and seasonal rhythm of village life and farm work.

BELOW: the Hartwell Tavern, in the Minute Man National Historical Park.

RESTAURANTS, BARS, AND CAFES

Concord

Colonial Inn
48 Monument Square. Tel: 978-369-2373. www.concordscolonialinn.com
Open: B, L, & D daily. **$$–$$$**
Classic fare at this 1716 inn includes chicken potpie, baked stuffed lobster, fresh grilled fish, and Yankee pot roast. High tea is served Sat–Sun.

Publick House
On the Common, 277 Main Street-Route 131. Tel: 508-347-3313. www.publickhouse.com Open: B, L, & D daily. **$$**
This 1771 inn's timeless menu includes prime rib with Yorkshire pudding, lobster pie, and full turkey dinner. A tavern serves a lighter menu.

Lexington

Mario's Italian Restaurant
1733 Massachusetts Ave. Tel: 781-861-1182. www.marioslexington.com
Open: L & D daily. **$**
Here simple Italian basics – pizzas, pastas, and salads – are served in a family-friendly atmosphere.

Prices for a three-course dinner per person, with tax and tip

$$$$ = over $75
$$$ = $50–75
$$ = $25–50
$ = under $25.

THE NORTH SHORE

The wild and rugged coast of Cape Ann, the characterful seaports of Marblehead and Gloucester, and the witch-filled history of Salem all cast a potent spell.

The North Shore, far more rocky and rugged than the South Shore and Cape Cod, is famed for its natural scenery and the splendid architecture and quaint streets of 18th- and 19th-century seaports such as Salem, Marblehead, Gloucester, and Newburyport. Leave Boston via the Callahan or Ted Williams tunnel (Route 1A-N), or by heading over the Bunker Hill and Tobin bridges (Route 1). The former route, which hugs the shoreline more closely, will take you through the old shoe-manufacturing city of Lynn and then into the handsome suburban precincts of Swampscott. When Routes 1A-N and 129 diverge at Eastern Avenue in Lynn, turn right to follow 129, passing grand turn-of-the-20th-century homes heading into the colonial port of Marblehead.

Marblehead

At Marblehead, turn right onto Ocean Avenue and drive across the causeway at the base of Marblehead Harbor to arrive at exclusive **Marblehead Neck ❶**. Ocean and Harbor avenues together make a 3-mile (5km) loop around the Neck, passing splendid homes and, on the harbor side, the prestigious Eastern Yacht Club. At the tip of the Neck, Chandler Hovey Park is a glorious windswept point from which to watch white sails scudding in and out of the deep, protected harbor.

Return across the Ocean Avenue causeway, then turn right onto Atlantic Avenue to arrive in **Marblehead ❷** proper, a twisting labyrinth of busy, narrow one-way streets lined with old clapboard houses.

The **Jeremiah Lee Mansion** (161 Washington Street; www.marbleheadmuseum.org; tel: 781-631-1768;

LEFT: Rockport Harbor at dusk.

June–Oct Tue–Sat 10am–4pm; charge), built in 1768, is an excellent example of Georgian architecture. Its interior features a grand entrance hall, elegant furnishings, rare hand-painted wallpaper, and original paneling. Also worth a visit is the **King Hooper Mansion** (8 Hooper Street; www.marbleheadarts.org; tel: 781-631-2608; Tue–Sat noon–4pm, Sun 1–5pm; free), an early 18th-century building with a ballroom, wine cellar, and garden. The Mansion is now home to the Marblehead Arts Association.

Washington Square, a high point in the heart of the town, provides pleasant views. The square is surrounded by private mansions once owned by sea captains and merchants, and fronted by **Abbot Hall** (188 Washington Street; www.marblehead.org; tel: 781-631-0000; call for hours), the town hall, which is home to Archibald Willard's renowned painting *The Spirit of '76*.

Bewitched Salem

Leave Marblehead by Lafayette Street (Route 114), which soon joins Route 1A and, after 3 miles (5km), enters **Salem ③**. Salem is also accessible via the MBTA Newburyport/Rockport commuter rail line from Boston. Some 200 years ago, Salem – the word is derived from the Hebrew *shalom* ('peace') – was so great a seaport that some foreigners believed New York was a town in a land called Salem. Today, Salem is a shadow, albeit a delightful one, of its former self, rich in museums and historic sites.

It is best to start your visit to the town at the **National Park Regional Visitor Center ⓐ** (2 New Liberty Street; www.nps.gov/sama; tel: 978-740-1650; daily 9am–5pm; free), just off The Mall (Essex Street), which screens a prize-winning film about Essex County, and has an excellent shop.

From New Liberty Street, turn right on Essex Street to reach the world-class **Peabody Essex**

ABOVE: Marblehead Lighthouse.

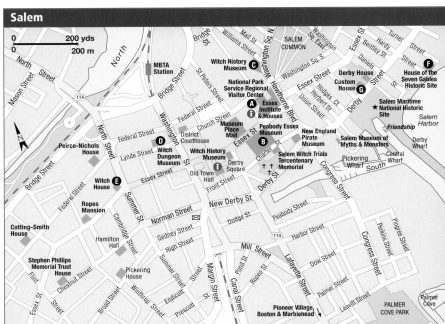

Salem

Salem's Witches

In the mid-1600s, the colonies of Rhode Island, Connecticut, and Massachusetts were caught up in a witch-killing fervor.

On a bright June day in 1648 Bostonians hanged Margaret Jones of Charlestown, and for an encore on Boston Common they hanged the beautiful and cultured Anne Hibbins, widow of the colony's former representative to England.

Against that lunatic history, the fanatical Rev. Cotton Mather sensed a great opportunity for self-promotion and professional success. He was already the colony's most highly acclaimed clergyman. He was learned, brilliant, ambitious, but he yearned for more. He longed to succeed his father, the Rev. Increase Mather, as the president of Harvard. He decided it would boost his reputation and enhance his career if he could identify assorted witches and promote their executions. So he went to work and soon focused on a witch-suspect named Goodwife Glover, the mother of a North End laundress. With Mather's help, poor Mrs Glover quickly wound up in the noose of a Boston Common gallows rope.

The Salem trials

In that same year, the fever struck Salem. The initial case involved a hot-tempered, trouble-making minister named Samuel Parris. He upset the serenity of his neighbors by arriving in town with two black slaves from the West Indies, a man named John and his wife, Tituba. Within two years, Tituba was teaching voodoo to a pair of young girls, Ann Putnam and Mercy Lewis. When they had learned all they needed to know from Tituba, they turned against the black woman with hysterical charges of witchcraft. And Tituba wound up in jail.

At this point, Salem's witchcraft surge really took off. Tituba pointed the witch-finger against two other Salem women, Sarah Osburn and Sarah Good. They in turn dragged in Rebecca Nurse and Martha Corey. And the madness kept spreading like infection, with every suspect accusing somebody else, until scores of victims awaited death. Between June and September in 1692, the Salemites executed 14 women as witches and six men as warlocks. And, to leave nothing to chance, they also convicted and hanged two dogs.

Throughout the year, Cotton Mather was a frequent visitor to the town. He never missed an execution. He was a roaring orator at all hangings and would rant and rave, and preach and pray from the gallows platform, berating and denouncing the victim who was waiting to die, and thereafter adding a modest personal statement calculated to move his steps toward the presidency of Harvard.

Such was the situation in 1693 when William Phips, who had been busy fighting the Indians and the French in the northern woods, returned to his duties as the colony's governor. Phips took one disgusted look at the witchery set-up and issued a proclamation freeing all suspects still incarcerated. Mercifully, the madness braked to an abrupt halt.

LEFT: the Salem Witch Museum.

Museum **B** (East India Square, 161 Essex Street, Salem; www.pem.org; tel: 978-745-9500; Tue–Sun 10am–5pm, closed Thanksgiving, Christmas, New Year's Day; charge). Ship models, marine paintings, nautical instruments, figureheads, charts, and maps abound in the Maritime Art and History collection, while the Asian Export collection glitters with exquisitely crafted porcelain, gold, silver, furniture, and textiles created by Chinese, Japanese, and Indian artisans. The museum's Japanese holdings in the late Edo and Meiji periods are among the world's finest. (See panel, page 217.) West of the PEM, elegant homes line Chestnut, Essex, and Federal streets; Chestnut Street is a National Historic Landmark and has been called one of the most beautiful streets in America.

North, next to Salem Common, is the **Witch History Museum** **C** (197–201 Essex Street; www.witch-historymuseum.com; tel: 978-741-7770; Apr–Nov daily 10am–5pm; charge). It and the **Witch Dungeon Museum** **D** (16 Lynde Street, Salem; www.witchdungeon.com; tel: 978-741-3570; Apr–Nov daily 10am–5pm; charge) present their versions of the witch trials that made Salem notorious in 1692–3. Learn more about this mass delusion in the **Witch House** **E** (310 Essex Street; tel: 978-744-8815; May–early Nov daily 10am–5pm, extended hours in Oct; charge), also known as the Jonathon Corwin House, where Judge Corwin questioned suspected witches.

At the other end of town, the **Salem Maritime National Historic Site**, under the auspices of the National Park Service (193 Derby Street; www.nps.gov/sama; tel: 978-740-1660; Jul–Oct daily 9am–5pm, Nov–Jun Mon–Fri 1–5pm, Sat–Sun 9am–5pm, closed Jan 1, Thanksgiving, Dec 25; free), preserves and interprets the maritime history of New England. The nearby **House of the Seven Gables Historic Site** **F** (54 Turner Street; www.7gables.org; tel: 978-744-0991; daily Jul–Oct 10am–7pm, Nov–Jun 10am–5pm, closed Thanksgiving, Dec 25, Jan 1; limited hours Dec 24 and 31; charge) was the setting for

ABOVE: the Witch House.
BELOW: Salem Maritime National Historic Site

Arthur Miller based his 1953 play The Crucible on the Salem Witch Trials, though its real target was the recent witch hunts then being carried out by Congress against supposed Communists.

TIP

Visit Salem sites by
following the red line on
the sidewalk, or board a
trackless trolley for a
one-hour narrated tour,
alighting at will and
rejoining a later car
(www.salemtrolley.com;
tel: 978-744-5469;
Apr–Oct daily
10am–5pm, call for off-
season hours).

Hawthorne's novel of that name.
There are several other houses at the
site, including his birthplace.

Across the street are the 1761
Derby House (Derby, a ship owner,
was probably the nation's first mil-
lionaire) and the 1819 **Custom
House** , with an office once used
by Nathaniel Hawthorne. To the
southeast is the desolate 2,000ft
(600-meter) long Derby Wharf, one
of 40 wharves once crowded with
merchantmen. Adjacent **Pickering
Wharf**, with its many restaurants and
stores, will delight those who enjoy
Boston's Quincy Market.

Seafront mansions

From Salem, travel north on Route 1A
to Beverly; then turn east on Route
127 to drive through Beverly Farms,
Prides Crossing, and Manchester-by-
the-Sea, all Brahmin summer retreats.
Singing Beach ❹ in Manchester
is especially attractive. It derives its
name from the crackling sound made
when walking on the sands.

Six miles (10km) past Manchester,
turn right off 127 onto Raymond
Street (which becomes Norman
Avenue and then Hesperus Avenue)
to reach the **Hammond Castle
Museum** ❺ (80 Hesperus Avenue;

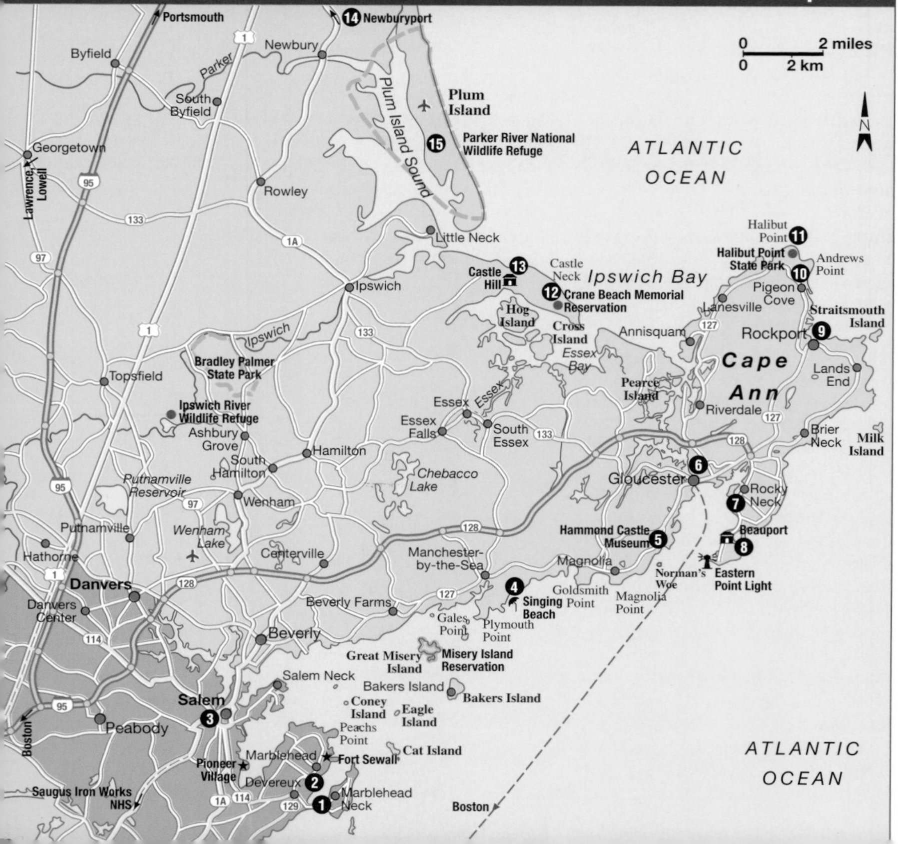

www.hammondcastle.org; tel: 978-283-2080; summer Tue–Sun 10am–4pm, winter book group tours two weeks in advance; charge). The eponymous owner of the massive mid-1920s building was an inventor; the castle was his home, his laboratory, and a gallery for his art collection. The castle has secret passageways and a long hall for a 8,200-pipe organ, and stands on a bluff overlooking the sea and Norman's Woe, a surf-pounded rock where Longfellow set his poem *The Wreck of the Hesperus*.

Gloucester ❻

Hesperus Avenue now rejoins Route 127 and enters **Gloucester**, the nation's oldest seaport, founded in 1623 by a group of Englishmen who had come 'to praise God and to catch fish.' How well they succeeded can be observed in the harbor, where local and foreign boats still unload their catch.

After crossing the bridge in Gloucester, which spans the Annisquam Canal, look for the famed **Gloucester Fisherman Statue**, depicting a helmsman firmly gripping a wheel as he scans the horizon. The statue honors those who have perished at sea. Those familiar with the book and film *The Perfect Storm*, about an ill-fated Gloucester crew, know that the poignancy of this memorial is not merely a matter of ancient history.

In town, visit the **Sargent House Museum**, the handsome Georgian home of Judith Sargent and John Murray (49 Middle Street; www.sargenthouse.org; tel: 978-281-2432; Memorial Day–Labor Day Fri–Sun noon–4pm; charge); its rooms are arranged as they might have looked in 1790. Nearby, at 10 Church Street, is the country's first Universalist church, a movement that Murray founded. A large Federal-style house at 27 Pleasant Street is home to the **Cape Ann Museum** (tel: 978-283-0455; Tue–Sat 10am–5pm, Sun 1–4pm; charge), operated by the Cape Ann Historical Association. The museum has fine seascapes by the renowned American marine painter Fitz Hugh Lane, an interesting collection of furniture, silver, and porcelain, and a maritime room.

BELOW: at the Peabody Essex Museum.

Peabody Essex Museum

The museum's collections date from 1799, when 22 Salem men who had each sailed beyond either Cape Horn or the Cape of Good Hope founded the East India Marine Society, whose mission included forming a 'cabinet of natural and artificial curiosities,' to be collected by members on their voyages. A vast 1.8 million works of art and culture comprise the collection, including African, American, Chinese, Indian, Japanese, Korean, maritime, Native American, and Oceanic art. The PEM also preserves 22 historic structures, including the Yin Yu Tang house, an 18th-century Chinese merchant's house that offers a rare perspective on Chinese art and culture. It is the only complete Qing-dynasty house outside of China.

WHERE

A more recent literary landmark in Gloucester is the Crow's Nest, the bar featured in Sebastian Junger's 1997 bestseller *The Perfect Storm*, later made into a movie starring George Clooney.

Farther inland, at 142 Prospect Street, is the Portuguese church of **Our Lady of Good Voyage**, recognizable by its two blue cupolas.

From the church, drive around the harbor to East Main Street, which leads to **Rocky Neck** ❼, an artists' colony containing lively restaurants. Rudyard Kipling worked on *Captains Courageous*, about Gloucester fishermen, while staying here.

On leaving Rocky Neck, turn right onto Eastern Point Road. After about 3 miles (5km), take the right fork to enter the exclusive Eastern Point enclave, with its score of magnificent homes. Notable is **Beauport** ❽ (75 Eastern Point Boulevard; www.historicnewengland.org; tel: 978-283-0800; June–Oct 15 Tue–Sat 10am–last tour at 4pm; charge), built and furnished between 1907 and 1934 by Henry Davis Sleeper, a prominent interior designer and collector of American art and antiquities.

RIGHT: colorful buoys at Rockport.
BELOW: the distinctive clapboard buildings of Rockport.

Farther along Cape Ann

Return to the entrance to Eastern Point, turn right onto Farrington Avenue and then left onto Atlantic Road. You are now on a counterclockwise loop of Cape Ann, following by land, if not by sea, the exploration made in 1604 by Champlain, the French explorer, and then in 1614 by John Smith, who mapped the area and named it in honor of his queen. Cape Ann combines outstanding scenery along its sometimes rocky, sometimes sandy shores, with a splendid selection of boutiques, galleries, and restaurants.

The route passes **Good Harbor, Long,** and **Pebble beaches** before reaching, after about 7 miles (11km), **Rockport** ❾. A tranquil fishing village prior to the 1920s, Rockport was discovered by artists and subsequently became a day-tripper's paradise. A main attraction is **Bearskin Neck**, a narrow peninsula densely packed with tiny dwellings and old fishing sheds, now converted into galleries, antique stores, and restaurants. A particular favorite is a red lobster shack called **Motif No.1**,

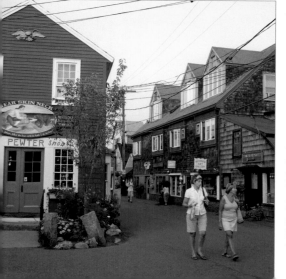

so named because of its popularity among photographers and painters. Beyond, enjoy magnificent views of the Atlantic from the breakwater at the end of the Neck.

Leave Rockport along Route 127 toward **Pigeon Cove** ⑩ , to reach **Halibut Point State Park** ⑪ . A half-mile walk from the parking lot through blueberry bushes leads to the outermost tip of Cape Ann, where huge tilted sheets of granite and fascinating tidal ponds have their devotees. A former quarry near the parking lot is a reminder that Rockport and its surroundings provided the granite for many buildings in Boston and beyond.

Continue on the loop through **Annisquam**, an exclusive summer community. Rather than returning directly to Gloucester, turn west onto Route 128 and take Exit 14 to reach Route 133 and head north.

The appearance of Woodman's, a rustic restaurant in **Essex** (see page 221), belies its contribution to mankind. This is where, on a hot July day in 1916, Lawrence Woodman tossed some cornmeal-coated clams into a pan of boiling oil and created the heavenly dish of fried clams. Essex's other main draws are its many antiques shops and the **Essex Shipbuilding Museum**, at 66 Main Street (www. essexshipbuildingmuseum.org; tel: 978-768-7541; 10am–5pm mid-May–Oct Wed–Sun, Nov–mid-May Sat–Sun; charge), displaying drawings, tools, photographs, and rigged ship models in an 1835 schoolhouse.

Turn right onto Spring Street to **Cogswell's Grant** (60 Spring Street; www.historicnewengland.org; tel: 978-768-3632; June–Oct 15 Wed–Sun 11am–last tour at 4pm; charge), the *c.*1730 summer home of Bertram K. and Nina Little, pre-eminent mid-20th-century collectors of American decorative arts. Their

riverfront farmhouse is crammed with their eclectic collection.

Just before reaching Ipswich, turn right onto Argilla Road, bordered by country estates. After about 3 miles (5km), it leads to the **Crane Beach** ⑫, with over 1,200 acres (486 hectares) of magnificent white sands, dunes, and maritime forest. (Note: Ward off pesky greenhead flies in summer and lime-disease carrying ticks with long trousers and repellent.)

Overlooking the beach is **Castle Hill** ⑬ (www.thetrustees.org; tel: 978-356-4351; grounds year-round daily 8am–sunset; tours of the house mid-May–late Oct Wed–Thur 10am–last tour at 3pm, Fri–Sat 10am–last tour at 1pm; charge). This grand 59-room Stuart-style mansion – full of Italian marble and ornate woodcarvings – was once part of plumbing-fixture magnate Richard Crane's estate. Glorious outdoor concerts are held here in summer.

Newburyport ⑭

Continue north from Ipswich on Route 1A. After 12 miles (20km), 1A

ABOVE: Rockport harbor at sunset.
BELOW: lobster pots on the dockside at Gloucester.

becomes the elegant High Street of **Newburyport**, lined by magnificent clapboard Federal-period houses. At No. 98, the **Cushing House** (www.newburyhist.com; tel: 978-462-2681; June–Oct Wed–Fri 10am–last tour at 4pm, Sat–Sun noon–last tour at 4pm), headquarters of the Historical Society of Old Newbury, has splendidly furnished rooms, a 19th-century garden, and varied artifacts ranging from paintings, maps, and photographs to clocks, silver, and antique fans.

Turn right off High Street to reach the Merrimack River and waterfront. The story of the town's 18th- and 19th-century glory days of seaborne commerce is recounted in the **Custom House Maritime Museum** (25 Water Street; www.customhouse-maritimemuseum.org; tel: 978-462-8681; May 15–late Dec Tue–Sat 10am–4pm, Sun noon–4pm; charge).

Between the waterfront and High Street is the reconstructed **Market Square** and **Inn Street Mall**, a pleasing ensemble of early 19th-century three-story brick and granite buildings that owe their architectural cohesiveness to the all-at-once rebuilding of Downtown after a disastrous 1811 fire. Both areas, along with busy State Street, are filled with shops, galleries, restaurants, and taverns. The **Old South Church** at 29 Federal Street has a whispering gallery and a bell cast by Paul Revere.

From Newburyport, a 3-mile (5km) drive across a causeway leads to Plum Island, a 4,700-acre (1,900-hectare) reservation, **Parker River National Wildlife Refuge** ⑮, with a 6-mile (10km) stretch of superb sands that is nirvana for both bird-watchers and beach bums. Turtles and toads, raccoons and rabbits, pheasant and deer thrive here.

For a quick return to Boston, take either Route 1 or – faster yet – Interstate 95 south, switching to Route 1 at Peabody. Industrial history enthusiasts can detour to the restored **Saugus Iron Works National Historic Site**, the country's first ironworks (1646), just east of Route 1 about 10 miles (16km) north of Boston (244 Central Street, Saugus; www.nps.gov/sair; tel: 781-233-0050; Apr–Oct daily 9am–5pm; free).

ABOVE: a perch at Parker River National Wildlife Reserve.
BELOW: Plum Island.

RESTAURANTS, BARS, AND CAFES

Essex

Woodman's of Essex
Route 133, 121 Main St
Tel: 978-768-6057
www.woodmans.com
L & D daily **$**
The first clam was fried here more than 95 years ago, and today the expanded seafood shack serves up lobster in the rough, steamers, fresh fish, and tasty fried clams.

Gloucester

Dog Bar Restaurant and Pub
65 Main St
Tel: 978-281-0017
www.dogbarcapeann.com
D Tue–Sun **$$**
Housed in an 1830s Federal-style brick building, Dog Bar has an intimate, inviting ambience with brick walls and a wood-burning fireplace. After dining on tasty burgers, sandwiches, or seafood, move to the tavern for more house specialty Martinis and live music.

Gloucester House Restaurant
63 Rogers St
Tel: 978-283-1812
www.thegloucesterhouse.com
L & D daily **$$–$$$**
Since 1958 the Linguata family has been serving seafood on premises overlooking a historic working wharf. Enjoy entrées such as lobster ravioli, seafood Newberg, and roasted salmon with a honey and toasted almond crust.

Marblehead

The Landing
81 Front St
Tel: 781-639-1266
www.thelandingrestaurant.com
L & D daily, Br Sun **$$**
Fresh seafood, prime beef, and poultry specialties share the menu at this pleasant spot overlooking the harbor. Dockside lunch and dinner service is available throughout boating season.

Newburyport

The Grog
13 Middle St
Tel: 978-465-8008
www.thegrog.com
L & D daily **$**
The city's premier rendezvous for burgers, seafood, chowder, and beer in a laid-back atmosphere.

Szechuan Taste Sushi Yen and Thai Café
19 Pleasant St
Tel: 978-463-0686
www.szechuantaste.com
L & D daily **$$**
A superb selection of Chinese, Japanese, and Thai delicacies, along with a sushi bar, in a handsomely decorated spot just off State Street.

Rockport

Note that Rockport is a 'dry' town, but you can bring your own wine to most restaurants.

Brackett's Oceanview Restaurant
25 Main St
Tel: 978-546-2797
www.bracketts.com
L & D daily; closed Nov–mid-Apr **$$**
Seafood, burgers, and homemade desserts in a pleasant spot overlooking the harbor.

Roy Moore Lobster Co.
39 Bearskin Neck
Tel: 978-546-6696
L & D daily **$**
This authentic shack for diehard lobster lovers is a local standby. Seating is limited, and the unpretentious setting is closer to a market than a restaurant, but the lobster, crab cakes, stuffed clams, shrimp, and clam chowder are fresh and delicious.

Salem

Finz Seafood Grill
Pickering Wharf, 76 Wharf St
Tel: 978-744-8485
www.hipfinz.com
L & D daily **$$**
With huge windows overlooking the Salem harbor, this airy, open, and upscale spot draws a loyal, local crowd who favor the great fresh oysters, innovative seafood and grill fare, lively bar, and outdoor patio.

Grape Vine
26 Congress St
Tel: 978-745-9335
www.grapevinesalem.com
D daily **$$**
Seasonal New American fare is the specialty at this bistro. Tasty items include homemade chowder, seared duck breast, mushroom spring rolls, and ravioli and risotto of the day. Dine alfresco in the garden from late May to early Sept.

Red's Sandwich Shop
15 Central St
Tel: 978-745-3527
www.redssandwichshop.com
B & L daily **$**
A terrific spot for hearty breakfasts and lunches.

Prices for a three-course dinner per person, with tax and tip:

$ = under $25
$$ = $25–50
$$$ = $50–75
$$$$ = over $75

RIGHT: Woodmans Fried Clams

The Industrial Heritage

With a manufacturing history dating back to the 17th century, Boston has played a key role in the industrialization of America.

New England's first fortunes were made on the seas, but by the early 19th century Boston money was financing America's first great wave of industrial expansion. Manufacturing was not entirely new to the region: America's first ironworks had been established in Saugus in the 1600s, and shipbuilding had long been vital to the coastal economy. But the Industrial Revolution in New England truly dates to Samuel Slater's establishment of America's first mechanized textile mill in Pawtucket, Rhode Island, in 1793.

Two decades later, Boston's Francis Cabot Lowell returned from England having memorized the details of the power loom – a device so jealously guarded by the British that the export of its plans was forbidden by law. Lowell set up his first looms at a small plant in Waltham, near Boston, and with partner Nathan Appleton soon plotted a much larger operation at a site on the Merrimack River that would bear his name.

Lowell

The mills of **Lowell** began operating in the 1820s and grew to become part of a chain of leviathan textile enterprises, all powered by the waters of the Merrimack, in New Hampshire and Massachusetts. Having reached their peak of production in the late 1800s – and having long been eclipsed by mills in the southern US and abroad – Lowell's hulking brick canalside factories have been painstakingly preserved as **Lowell National Historical Park** (Visitor Center, 246 Market Street, Lowell, www.nps.gov/lowe; tel: 978-970-5000; open daily, hours vary with season).

Begin a tour of the park at the visitor center, which offers detailed exhibits and a slide show explaining the context of the Lowell mills in the story of American industrialization. A separate exhibit, 'Mill Girls and Immigrants,' tells how the spinning machines of 'Spindle City' were first attended by girls from nearby farms who, thanks to the owners' paternalism, boarded in model dormitories and attended the city's handsome St Anne's Church each Sunday. Soon, though, the mills' capacity expanded beyond the ability of the 'mill girls' to fill labor requirements, and the operators began to recruit successive waves of immigrants, beginning with the Irish, and then the French Canadians, whose descendants still form a substantial part of Lowell's population.

National park rangers give a variety of tours through the mill buildings and along Lowell's streets and canals. The best tour involves genuine trolley rides, traveling on a barge through canals and locks and some walking. At the park's Boott Cotton Mill, vintage power looms still operate. For further understanding of the Lowell story, the national park experience can be augmented with a visit to the **American Textile History Museum** (491 Dutton Street; www.athm.org; tel: 978-441-0400; Wed–Sun 10am–5pm, closed holidays; charge), where exhibits explain the history of textile manufacturing in America, displaying textiles, machines, tools, photographs, and other artifacts. Workshops teach spinning, weaving, and quilting.

Non-mill-related Lowell sites close to the National Park Visitor Center include the **Whistler House Museum of Art** (243 Worthen Street, Lowell; www.whistlerhouse.

ABOVE: Boott Cotton Mill spools.

org; tel: 978-452-7641; Wed–Sat 11am–4pm; charge), located in the birthplace of painter James Abbott McNeill Whistler and exhibiting late 19th- and early 20th-century work by Whistler and his contemporaries. Lowell native Jack Kerouac, the central figure of the 'Beat Generation' of American authors, is commemorated in Eastern Park Plaza with a series of quotes from his work emblazoned on large steel plaques. The **New England Quilt Museum** (18 Shattuck Street, Lowell; www.nequiltmuseum.org; tel: 978-452-4207; May–Oct Tue–Sat 10am–4pm, Sun noon–4pm, Nov–Apr Tue–Sat 10am–4pm; charge) showcases antique and contemporary quilts.

From Boston, reach Lowell by taking I-93 north to I-495 south. Or, take an MBTA commuter train from North Station.

Lawrence

Downstream from Lowell along the Merrimack River is another one-time textile capital, **Lawrence** (from Boston, I-93 north to I-495 north). Lawrence, whose principal output was woolen cloth, was known as 'Queen of the Mill Towns,' and much of its old riverside factory infrastructure remains, capped by an immense clock tower that once ruled the lives of thousands. The Lawrence mills have not been as well preserved as those upriver at Lowell; the old brick buildings present a melancholy aspect, especially when seen from the Merrimack at sunset.

It was in Lawrence that 23,000 mill workers went on strike for two months in 1912. The shutdown was called the 'Bread and Roses' strike, after a line in a poem by James Oppenheim describing women workers' aspirations – 'We want bread, and roses too' – and, in fact, the strike was largely orchestrated by women. Begun in response to mill owners cutting pay after a new state law shortened the working week, the action was successful in attaining wage increases, although the owners soon increased production and, during a recession a few years later, again slashed pay. Nevertheless, the strike helped galvanize the American labor movement. The story is recounted at **Lawrence Heritage State Park** (1 Jackson Street, Lawrence; www.mass.gov/dcr/parks/northeast/lwhp.htm; tel: 978-794-1655; daily 9am–4pm; free), in a restored 1840s mill boarding house.

Watches on the Charles

Closer to Boston, in the small city of **Waltham** (MBTA buses from Boston), the **Charles River Museum of Industry** (154 Moody Street, Waltham; www.crmi.org; tel: 781-893-5410; Thur–Sun 10am–5pm; charge) occupies part of the historic Boston Manufacturing Company textile mill, predecessor of the Lowell mills and New England's first integrated textile factory – raw material went in one end and finished products came out the other. But Waltham eventually became far more famous as the 'Watch City,' with the Waltham Watch Company turning out 40 million timepieces over 100 years, in an astonishing array ranging from dollar watches to elaborate models fit for the vest pockets of tycoons. The museum exhibits Waltham watches, and also precision metalworking instruments, bicycles, and automobiles – aficionados will love the Stanley Steamer – manufactured locally.

RIGHT: Lowell was founded as a planned manufacturing center for textiles along the Merrimack River.

SOUTH SHORE AND CAPE COD

There's yet more history to be found at Quincy and Plymouth. Beyond lie the long sandy beaches and well-preserved communities of Cape Cod.

Cape Cod's glorious beaches are the prime destination for most visitors traveling south from Boston. But rather than making a beeline for the Cape via busy, bland Route 3, try clinging more closely to the shoreline, and take in a wealth of history and scenic splendor that begins just beyond the metropolis.

Leave Boston via Route 3 (the Southeast Expressway). Take Exit 12 and join Quincy Shore Drive, which crosses the Neponset River by a drawbridge, and, 9 miles (14km) after leaving Boston, arrive at **Quincy ①**, 'city of presidents.' Former US presidents John Adams and John Quincy Adams were born here. (Quincy can also be reached on the Red line of the 'T.')

Quincy's heritage

The city boasts half a dozen buildings associated with the names Quincy and Adams. The 1770 Georgian **Josiah Quincy House** (20 Muirhead Street; tel: 617-994-5930; www.historicnewengland.org; Jun–mid-Oct first Sat of month 1–5pm; charge) features an unusual monitor roof, the oldest known example surviving from the colonies. A half-mile farther south is the **Quincy Homestead** (34 Butler Road; tel: 617-742-3190; call for tour dates), a handsome country mansion dating to the 17th century. But it is the Adams legacy that shines brightest.

In Downtown Quincy, at 1250 Hancock Street, is the Visitor Center for the **Adams National Historic Site** (www.nps.gov/adam; tel: 617-770-1175; mid-Apr–mid-Nov Visitor Center and house tours daily 9am–5pm, last tour 3.15pm; charge). Come here for a thorough orientation of the remarkable story of the Adams family, which produced both

LEFT: *Mayflower II* in Plymouth Harbor.

the second (John Adams) and sixth (John Quincy Adams) presidents of the United States, as well as an illustrious line of descendants including historian Henry Adams. Shuttle tours leave the center for several Adams sites. These include the modest houses in which the presidents were born, the **Old House** that served as the Adams family residence for four generations (see panel), and the adjacent baronial **Stone Library** containing John Quincy Adams's Library of 14,000 books.

The **United Parish First Church**, 1306 Hancock Street, is known as the Church of the Presidents and contains the remains of John Adams, John Quincy Adams, and their wives Abigail Adams and Louisa Catherine Adams.

Continue south on Route 3A to the **Hingham Rotary**. Exit on Summer Street, then turn left at Martin's Lane for a 1-mile drive to **World's End**, an idyllic 251-acre (102-hectare) oasis designed by Frederick Law Olmsted. Stroll on paths lined with oak, hickory, and cedar trees and through rolling

ABOVE: the home of President John Quincy Adams in Quincy.

fields that are home to pheasant, quail, foxes, and rabbits. Herons and egrets populate the rugged shoreline, and all the while the impressive Boston skyline can be seen in the distance.

Return to Summer Street, turn left and follow Rockland Road to Washington Boulevard. This leads to **Nantasket Beach**, the best beach close to Boston (16 miles/24km). The **antique Paragon carousel**, operating in summer, is the only reminder of the Paragon Park amusement park that closed in 1985. Farther out on the peninsula, enjoy views of the Atlantic and the harbor islands. **Boston Light**, about 1.5 miles (2.4km) offshore on **Little Brewster Island**, is the successor to the nation's first lighthouse (see page 133).

Hingham

Backtrack from Hull via Washington Boulevard and Summer Street to the

The Old House

The Old House, Quincy, was built in 1731 and served as the residence of the Adams family for four generations, from 1788 to 1927. In addition to Presidents John Adams and John Quincy Adams and their wives Abigail Adams (one of the most well-read women in 18th-century America) and Louisa Catherine Adams (the only foreign-born first lady), the house was also home to Charles Francis Adams (the Civil War Minister to Great Britain) and literary historians Henry and Brooks Adams. Simple though this dwelling may be, Abigail, wife of John, wrote that she preferred the charms of 'my little cottage' to the grandeur of the London court.

The Hull Lifesaving Museum at 1117 Nantasket Avenue, Quincy (tel: 781-925-5433; call for hours) gives a good idea of the heroic measures needed when warnings from the Boston Light could not avert disaster.

ABOVE: Plymouth Rock.

polished town of **Hingham**, where the numbers on the handsome, usually white, clapboard houses on **Main Street** are not to assist mail deliveries but to announce with pride when the houses were built – more often than not, in the 19th century and, occasionally, in the 18th. The town has several inspiring churches, including the 1681 **Old Ship Church** at 107 Main Street, the oldest wooden building in the nation in continuous ecclesiastical service. The interior of its roof echoes an inverted ship's hull.

Continue south on Route 3A through **Cohasset**, where Jerusalem Road winds past mansions old and new overlooking a rocky coast. Fourteen miles (23km) farther south is **Marshfield**, where the **Daniel Webster Law Office** is located in the grounds of the 18th-century Winslow House on Careswell Street; the great orator is buried in the town's **Winslow Cemetery**, on Winslow Cemetery Road.

Immediately to the south is **Duxbury**, with its gracious colonial homes and a 9-mile (14km) long barrier beach offering superb bird-watching. The energetic might wish

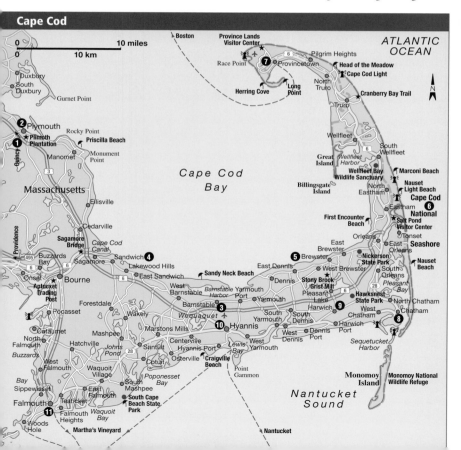

to ascend the 125 steps of the 116ft (35-meter) high Myles Standish Monument for vistas reaching from Boston to Cape Cod. Standish and other Pilgrims lie in the **Myles Standish Burial Grounds** (at Chestnut and Pilgrim by Way streets).

Plymouth

Continue on Route 3A to **Plymouth ②**, 40 miles (64km) south of Boston. This is the celebrated 1620 landing site of the Pilgrims – as the story has it, on **Plymouth Rock** – and the first permanent American settlement north of Virginia.

Plymouth is rich in Pilgrim connections; a trolley runs between the different sites. A stone's throw from the grandiose neoclassical monument over the Rock is the *Mayflower II* **Ⓐ** (www.plimoth.org; tel. 508-746-1622; late Mar–late Nov daily 9am–5pm; charge). This full-scale replica of a 17th-century vessel was built in England and sailed to Plymouth in 1957. The 106ft (32-meter) long vessel, staffed with period-costumed interpreters who act the parts of the passengers and crew, vividly conveys the hardships of the 66-day voyage in 1620. (Note: if you're visiting both the *Mayflower II* and Plimoth Plantation, a combination ticket is available.)

Across the road from the Rock is **Coles Hill**, where, during their first winter, the Pilgrims secretly buried their dead at night to hide the truth about their fast-dwindling numbers from the Indians. Nearby is a large Massosoit statue.

Pilgrim Hall Museum Ⓑ (75 Court Street, Plymouth; www.pilgrimhall.org; tel: 508-746-1620; Feb–Dec daily 9.30am–4.30pm; charge), a Greek Revival building designed by Alexander Parris, has the country's largest collection of Pilgrim memorabilia, including Myles Standish's Bible and the cradle of

Peregrine White, who was born aboard the *Mayflower*.

Farther east, beyond Main Street, is **Burial Hill Ⓒ**, with gravestones dating back to the colony's founding. The most famous epitaph reads: 'Under this stone rests the ashes of Willm Bradford, a zealous Puritan & sincere Christian, Gov. of Ply. Col. from April 1621 to 1657 (the year he died, aged 69) except 5 yrs. which he declined.' The hill was the site of the Pilgrims' first meetinghouse, fort, and watchtower. South of Burial Hill is the replica **Jenney House Museum Ⓓ** (6 Spring Lane; www.jenneygristmill.org; tel: 508-747-4544; tours Apr–Nov Mon–Sat 9am–5pm; charge), where corn is still ground as in the days of the Pilgrims. The **Jabez Howland House Ⓔ** at 33 Sandwich Street (tel: 508-746-9590; Memorial Day–Columbus Day daily 10am–4.30pm; charge) is the only surviving house in Plymouth in which a *Mayflower* Pilgrim actually lived.

Plimoth Plantation

The year is always 1627 at **Plimoth Plantation** (www.plimoth.org; tel:

ABOVE: statue of Massosoit near Plymouth Rock.
BELOW: Old Ship Meeting House.

TIP

Distances between communities are short, and you can travel the entire Cape, with frequent stops, in a day. But it's better to take your time. Most visitors make one township their base, though some prefer to mosey from town to town. Each has its own distinctive character, but they have one thing in common: all are close to superb beaches.

BELOW: Plimoth Plantation.

508-746-1622; late Mar–late Nov daily 9am–5pm; charge), 3 miles (5km) south of the Rock, where interpreters dressed in Pilgrim costumes and speaking in Old English dialects assume the roles of specific historical residents of the colony. Query Mistress Alden about Captain Standish and she may well respond: 'Oh, he lives next door and there are some, sir, who feel he is not the easiest man with whom to deal.' Question the same Mistress Alden or Captain Standish about Paul Revere or George Washington and they will look at you with incomprehension. The interpreters do not simply stand around waiting for questions but go about their 1627 work and interact with one another. Even the livestock is painstakingly backbred to approximate 17th-century barnyard beasts. Another part of the site is a **Wampanoag Homesite**, where visitors learn about Wampanoag

culture and history, and the particular story of one Wampanoag man, Hobbamock.

Cape Cod

Leave Plymouth on Route 3, and head south 17 miles (27km) to reach the **Sagamore Bridge**, which soars across the **Cape Cod Canal**. Beyond lies a land of marshes and meadows, pines and cranberry bogs and, above all, beaches.

For Henry David Thoreau, Cape Cod was 'the bared and bended arm of Massachusetts.' The **Upper Cape**, comprising the towns of Sandwich, Falmouth, and Woods Hole, constitutes the upper arm beyond the canal; the **Mid-Cape**, which stretches from Hyannis to Orleans and which includes the towns of Chatham, Harwich, Brewster, Dennis, Yarmouth, and Barnstable, takes in the elbow; and the **Lower Cape** – that part generally likened to the forearm, stretching northward to end

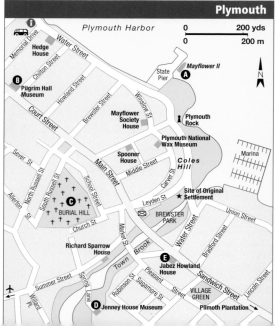

Plymouth

Plymouth Harbor

0   200 yds
0   200 m

Memorial Drive
Water Street
Hedge House
Chilton Street
B Pilgrim Hall Museum
Howland Street
Court Street
Brewster Street
Winslow St
State Pier
A Mayflower II
Mayflower Society House
Plymouth Rock
Plymouth National Wax Museum
Spooner House
Coles Hill
Marina
Sever St
North Russell St
South Russell St
Middle Street
Carver Street
Site of Original Settlement
Allerton St
C BURIAL HILL
School Street
Leyden St
BREWSTER PARK
Union Street
Church St
Main Street
Market St
Water Street
Bradford Street
Richard Sparrow House
Town Brook
E Jabez Howland House
Sandwich Street
Lincoln St
Summer Street
Spring Lane
Robinson St
Sagamore St
Pleasant
VILLAGE GREEN
Willard Pl.
D Jenney House Museum
Plimoth Plantation

with the 'sandy fist' of Provincetown – includes the towns of Eastham, Wellfleet, and Truro.

The Sagamore Bridge opens onto Route 6 (the Mid-Cape Highway), which runs first east and then north and ends, after about 60 miles (almost 100km), at Provincetown. This is the quickest route to take, but much more intriguing is Route 6A (the old King's Highway). It parallels, more or less, Route 6 and passes through many of the Cape's prettiest villages, most with weathered cedarshingle saltbox houses and a whitesteepled church.

The Cape has about 300 miles (nearly 500km) of sandy beaches, some backed by dunes rising 100ft (30 meters) or more. Thunderous surf pounds the Atlantic side of the Upper Cape, while gentler waters prevail in **Cape Cod Bay**. Slightly rougher are **Buzzards Bay**, to the southwest of the Upper Cape, and **Nantucket Sound**, to the south of the Mid-Cape.

Leisure activities

Because the Cape is so narrow, it is possible to spend the morning in roaring surf and, half an hour later, loll in placid, shallow waters. (Parking permits are required at some beaches, but are easily obtained; for the expansive beaches and dunelands of the Cape Cod National Seashore, the best bet for those spending more than a couple of days is to buy a season permit).

The Cape's 365 ponds are home to brown, rainbow, and brook trout, white and yellow perch, and black bass. A non-resident Massachusetts license is required for freshwater fishing, but not for surfcasting from ocean beaches, where striped bass and bluefish are the favorite quarry. 'Party boats,' which go out onto the bay for trips of several hours, are a popular fishing option; a number of them sail from MacMillan Wharf in Provincetown.

Nearly 40 golf courses dot the Cape. The greatest concentration is in the largest two towns of **Barnstable** ❸ and **Falmouth.** Only about a dozen courses are strictly private.

Each community has set aside special areas for bicycling, but cyclists really come into their own on the **Cape Cod Rail Trail**, a paved recreational trail that runs on an abandoned railroad bed for 26 miles (42km) from Route 134 in Dennis to Wellfleet. Its route passes quintessential Cape scenery and several cultural and historical sites. The **Salt Pond Visitor Center** of the **Cape Cod National Seashore** is right off the trail in Eastham.

Sandwich ❹, the town that glass built and the first community reached after crossing the canal, is a good place to be if the weather is bad. It's a lovely little village with numerous museums. Colorful utility and decorative glassware once made here is showcased in the **Sandwich Glass**

ABOVE: Nantucket Harbor Lighthouse.
BELOW: Plimouth Plantation.

ABOVE: summer activities in Cape Cod.

TIP

If you wish to travel to Provincetown directly and avoid the town's notorious traffic, a high-speed ferry operates from Boston's Long Wharf to Provincetown from May–Oct, tel: 617-227-4321; there's also air service from Boston.

in rhododendrons and daylilies. It houses an eclectic collection of Americana in several buildings. A replica of a round Shaker Barn contains a magnificent collection of antique cars dating from 1899 to 1937 (Gary Cooper's 1930 Duesenberg is the star). The American History Museum replica is filled with antique firearms, flags, Native American artifacts, and 2,000 miniature soldiers. The Art Museum has a fine collection of folk art, including Cape-crafted antique decoys and more than 100 Currier and Ives prints. And there's a working 1912 carousel for the kids.

Twenty-eight miles (45km) farther along Route 6A, near the elbow of the Cape, is **Brewster ❺**, another rainy-day favorite. The **Stony Brook Grist Mill** still grinds corn as it did in 1663. During April and May, schools of alewives (herring) returning from the Atlantic struggle in the millstream to leap up ladders that will lead them to the tranquil mill-ponds where they spawn.

The Lower Cape

In 1961, in order to preserve the beauty of the Cape and to highlight a number of natural and historic sights, the ocean shorelines of six towns – Chatham, Orleans, Eastham, Wellfleet, Truro, and Provincetown – were dedicated as the **Cape Cod National Seashore ❻** (CCNS) under the aegis of the National Park Service. Visitor centers, offering displays, films, and natural history interpretive programs, are located just off Route 6 at Eastham (**Salt Pond**, daily 9am–4.30pm) and at Provincetown (**Province Lands**, early May–late Oct daily 9am–5pm). The view of dunes and ocean from the upper deck of Province Lands is spectacular.

The **Marconi Area** (South Wellfleet), where Guglielmo Marconi sent the first radio signal across the Atlantic (1903), is part of the CCNS. At **Race Point** in Provincetown, visit

Museum (129 Main Street; www.sandwichglassmuseum.org; tel: 508-888-0251; Feb–Mar Wed–Sun 9.30am–4pm, Apr–Dec daily 9.30am–5pm; charge).

Several interesting historic sites border Shawme Pond. These include the **Hoxie House** at 18 Water Street, which, with its 17th-century furnishings, is believed to be the oldest (1637) house on the Cape. The **Thornton Burgess Museum** (4 Water Street; www.thorntonburgess.org; tel: 508-888-4668; Jun–mid-Oct Mon–Thur 10am–4pm; Fri–Sat 10am–1pm; donation) memorializes the beloved children's author (*Peter Cottontail* and other animal favorites) and Sandwich native, Thornton Burgess. At **Dexter's Grist Mill**, in use since the 1650s, you can see cornmeal being stone-ground and buy the delicious finished product.

Best of all is the **Heritage Museum and Gardens** (67 Grove Street; tel: 508-888-3300; mid-Apr–Oct daily 10am–5pm, Jul–Aug Wed 10am–8pm; charge), located on 76 acres (31 hectares) of gardens rich the **Life Saving Museum**, which displays the crude equipment used to rescue mariners from the hundreds of vessels once wrecked along this stretch of coast.

What attracts most people to the CCNS, however, are its magnificent beaches, sprawling, desert-like dunes, and heather-covered highlands, resembling, in Thoreau's words, a 'Turkey carpet' in autumn. The best oceanside beaches are **Nauset** (Orleans), **Nauset Light** (Eastham), **Marconi** (South Wellfleet), **Head of the Meadow** (Truro), **Provincetown** and, above all, **Longnook** (Truro). Arrive early to find parking at any of these spots – and bring a tolerance for bracing water temperatures.

Provincetown's popular beaches are **Herring Cove**, about a mile from town and whose southeast section is predominantly gay, and **Race Point**, a few miles north of the town. Then there is **Long Point**, gained by walking across a mile-long causeway beginning at the west end of Commercial Street, near the Provincetown Inn. Near the start of the causeway a commemorative stone notes that it was 'somewhere near here' that the Pilgrims first landed (no, it wasn't at Plymouth, as you'll see below).

Provincetown ❼

Provincetown, at the very tip of the Cape, is a three-ring, often raucous circus. Thick with crafts shops, art galleries, stores (both elegant and tawdry), and restaurants, 'P-town' combines a long-standing community of Portuguese fishing folk, a large gay population, and, during the summer, hordes of tourists. And yet serious artists maintain a tradition that started in 1899 with the founding of the Cape Cod School of Art.

Commercial Street parallels the harbor and is the center of activity. Parallel and just inland is **Bradford Street**. Near Bradford Street on High Poll Hill Road is the **Pilgrim**

Monument and Provincetown Museum (www.pilgrim-monument. org; tel: 508-487-1310; Apr–Nov daily 9am–5pm, June–Sep 15 until 7pm; charge). The monument commemorates the Pilgrims' stop in Provincetown in 1620 for six weeks before they moved on to Plymouth because of its more protected harbor and better water supplies. A slim and stately affair adapted from the Torre del Mangia in Siena and built in the early 1900s, the monument is the tallest all-granite structure in the country. It towers 252ft (77 meters) above the town and can be ascended (no elevators, but a tolerable climb via 116 steps and 60 gentle ramps) for a grand view of the Lower Cape. The museum at the base of the monument is strong on local history and commemorates the Arctic explorations of townsman Donald MacMillan. Works of local artists are on show in the **Provincetown Art Association & Museum** (460 Commercial Street; www.paam.org; tel: 508-487-1750; Memorial Day–Sept Mon–Thur 11am–8pm, Fri 11am–10pm, Sat–Sun 11am–5pm,

'Here a man may stand, and put all America behind him.'
Henry David Thoreau, after strolling at Race Point

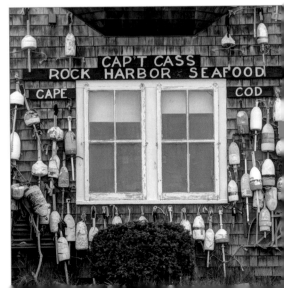

BELOW: Cap't Cass Rock Harbor Seafood is a local institution on Cape Cod's Rock Harbor.

ABOVE: the Old Harbor Lifesaving Station in Cape Cod.

Oct–Memorial Day Thur–Sun noon–5pm; charge, free Fri evening).

Chatham to Hyannis Port

Leaving Provincetown, backtrack for 28 miles (45km) on Route 6 to the traffic circle at **Orleans** and take Route 28 for 9 miles (14km) south to **Chatham ⑧**, at the Cape's elbow. Though not without shops, galleries, inns, and restaurants, Chatham is everything Provincetown isn't – quiet, sedate, and more like an old-money Maine resort. (For excitement, head for the observation deck above the Fish Pier to watch the fishing boats return in early afternoon.)

The 1752 **Old Atwood House Museum** (347 Stage Harbor Road; tel: 508-945-2493; June–Sept Tue–Sat 1–4pm) offers local history and seafaring exhibits and a remarkable series of paintings of local residents by Alice Stallknecht Wight.

From Chatham, continue west on State 28 along the Cape's South Shore, passing **Harwich ⑨**, where cranberries were first commercially cultivated. Old Harwich, incorporated in 1694, has resisted the overdevelopment

that has plagued other towns, and its Winchmere harbor is one of the prettiest on the Cape.

After an overbuilt commercial stretch, you reach **Hyannis ⑩** after 17 miles (27km). It and neighboring Hyannis Port are the commercial center and transportation hub of the Mid-Cape, with scheduled airline services to Boston, Martha's Vineyard, and Nantucket and ferries to the two islands. A vintage train provides a one-hour sightseeing ride to Sandwich or to Buzzards Bay.

Oddly, the magnet at **Hyannis Port** is the private Kennedy Compound, which isn't visible from the road (harbor cruise boats do advertise a glimpse). Visit, instead, the **Kennedy Memorial**, located on Lewis Bay (a pleasant walk); the **John F. Kennedy Museum**, on Main Street (tel: 508-790-3077), is primarily a photo gallery.

History and oceanography

A further 17 miles (27km) on Route 28 leads to elegant **Falmouth ⑪**, whose delightful green is surrounded by 18th- and 19th-century houses shaded by graceful elms. The Falmouth Historical Society's **Museums on the Green** (55 and 65 Palmer Avenue; www.falmouthhistoricalsociety.org; tel: 508-548-4857; early June–early Oct Tue–Fri 10am–4pm, Sat 10am–1pm; charge) include two 18th-century houses that feature furniture, fine art, textiles, and exhibits on whaling times and pre-Civil War medicine. Eight miles (13km) beyond Falmouth, at the southernmost tip of the Cape, is **Woods Hole**, famous for its **Oceanographic Institute** (tel: 508-289-2252). From here, ferries leave for Martha's Vineyard.

Leave Woods Hole on Route 28 and travel north for 17 miles (27km) to Bourne at the canal. Either cross the canal by Bourne Bridge and drive east on Route 6 to join Route 3, or take Route 6 along the south side of the canal, crossing at Sagamore Bridge.

SHOPPING

The Derby Street Shoppes (98 Derby Street) in Hingham feature 78 retailers, boutiques, and eateries. Provincetown's Commercial Street has a smattering of gift shops and high-end designers' outposts.

Gifts

Pulp
307-A Commercial St, Provincetown
Tel: 508-847-8070
www.pulpdc.com
A one-stop shop for sassy gifts and stationery. Also has candles, coffee-table books, and a smattering of oddball items.

Women's Clothing and Shoes

Crossing Main
5 Main St, Hingham
Tel: 781-740-0500
www.crossingmain.com
Clothes, shoes, and accessories from upscale fashion lines such as Hugo Boss, Loeffler Randall, Milly, Paige, and Vera Wang.

Gia B.
91 Derby St, Hingham
Tel: 781-749-5510
www.giaboutique.com
One of many chic boutiques in the Derby Street Shoppes, with elegant mainstays such as Trina Turk and Tory Burch.

RESTAURANTS, BARS AND CAFES

Many of the restaurants below have limited hours and/or are closed off-season (generally Oct–May). Be sure to call ahead at those times.

Chillingsworth
2449 Main St, Route 6A
Tel: 508-896-3640
www.chillingsworth.com
D Tue–Sun, L Fri–Sun, Br Sun
$$$$
Often cited as the finest dining spot on the Cape, the restaurant/inn (three guest rooms) is in the 300-year-old Chillingsworth Foster estate on six landscaped acres (2.4 hectares), and specializes in French and American cuisine. Enjoy a seven-course table d'hôte menu in the luxurious main restaurant or a lighter à la carte menu in the bright, airy bistro.

Atlantica
Cohasset Harbor Resort, 44 Border St
Tel: 781-383-0900
www.cohassetharborresort.com
D Tue–Sun mid-June–Oct
$$–$$$
With a fabulous harbor view, an outstanding raw bar, and a varied menu including maple-hardwood-grilled meats and fish with an assortment of sauces (bourbon peach glaze, garlic herb aioli, blood-orange *gastrique*), this is a fine place on a clear summer's eve.

Coonamessett Inn
311 Gifford St
Tel: 508-548-2300
www.capecodrestaurants.org
L & D daily **$$$**
In a 200-year-old inn on six manicured acres (2.4 hectares), this Cape perennial serves regional specialties such as grilled pork loin chops with peach compote, and baked Chatham scrod. Sunday brunch is a standout.

Tosca
14 North St
Tel: 781-740-0080
www.toscahingham.com
D Tue–Sun **$$$**
Italian-inspired cuisine with an American influence is served in a renovated 1910 Granary Marketplace building. The setting, with exposed brick, mahogany tiles, and an open kitchen, is decidedly theatrical.

The Paddock
20 Scudder Ave
Tel: 508-775-7677
www.paddockcapecod.com
mid-Apr–June D Tue–Sun, July–mid-Nov L & D daily, closed mid-Nov–mid-April **$$**
Linens, candlelight, and fresh flowers set the mood in this dining room, which has been serving contemporary American cuisine for more than 40 years. Look for polenta crab cakes, a large selection of fresh fish, and prime beef.

Isaac's on the Waterfront
114 Water St
Tel: 508-830-0001
www.isaacsdining.com
L & D daily **$$**
With a magnificent view of Plymouth Harbor, and a deft touch with seafood dishes, Isaac's has become one of Plymouth's most popular dining spots for both couples and families. Beef and poultry are also on the menu.

Napi's
7 Freeman St
Tel: 800-571-6274
www.napis-restaurant.com
L daily Oct–Apr, D daily year-round **$$**
Built from a hodgepodge of salvaged materials, furnished with antiques, and decorated with works by local artists, this offbeat establishment's menu is every bit as eclectic – linguine and clams, Brazilian shrimp, and Thai chicken and shrimp.

Dan'l Webster Inn Spa
149 Main St
Tel: 508-888-3622 or 800-444-3566
www.danlwebsterinn.com
B, L, & D daily **$$–$$$**
The four dining rooms in this 300-year-old inn are elegant and candlelit, but don't expect just the usual standard Yankee fare: the menu includes sophisticated dishes such as hazelnut-encrusted rack of pork and artichoke and mascarpone ravioli.

Prices for a three-course dinner per person, with tax and tip:

$ = under $25
$$ = $25–50
$$$ = $50–75
$$$$ = over $75

RIGHT: A freshly cooked Cape Cod lobster

INSIGHT GUIDES **TRAVEL TIPS**
BOSTON

TRANSPORTATION

GETTING THERE AND GETTING AROUND

GETTING THERE

By Air

Boston Logan International Airport is the largest transportation center in New England, handling dozens of domestic and international airlines. It is the northern terminal of the busy New York–Boston run.

Logan has five terminals (A–E), four of which are passenger terminals. Note that domestic and international flights of the same airline do not necessarily use the same terminal. There is a free shuttle bus service between the terminals.

Airlines that fly to Boston include: Aer Lingus, Air Canada, Air France, Alitalia, American, British Airways, Delta, Lufthansa, US Airways, and Virgin Atlantic.

There is an American Express Currency Exchange in terminals A, B, C, and E, and ATMs in terminals A, B, C, and E. **Free** wireless **internet** access is available throughout the airport for use on laptops and certain mobile phones. On your device, look for the network 'logan-wifi'. Charging stations are also built into many of the seating areas. Terminals A and C have Kidport areas, where children can play.

Hotel reservation information is available at the information booths in each terminal. **Hotels** near the airport include the Hyatt Harborside (tel: 568-1234) and Hilton Boston Logan Airport (tel: 568-6700).

By Rail

Boston is a part of several passenger train routes operated by Amtrak (tel: 800-872-7245, for the hearing-impaired 800-523-6590; www.amtrak.com). The Amtrak Downeaster trains to New Hampshire and Maine arrive and depart from North Station; all other passenger trains arrive at South Station (and stop at Back Bay Station), coming from New York, Washington, DC, and Philadelphia, with connections from all points in the nationwide Amtrak system.

Trains travel between New York and Boston daily on the Northeast Regional route, with travel times of around 4–4.5 hours, but the Acela high-speed train makes the journey in 3.5 hours. South Station is also the eastern terminus for Amtrak's Lake Shore Limited, which travels daily between Chicago and Boston by way of Cleveland, Buffalo, Rochester, and Albany. One train daily makes the journey in 20 hours.

By Bus

Several intercity bus companies serve Boston. The two largest,

Greyhound (tel: 526-1800/800-231-2222; www.greyhound.com) and Peter Pan (tel: 800-343-9999; www.peterpanbus.com), have frequent daily services from New York City and Albany, as well as services from points within New England. Greyhound serves the entire United States and parts of Canada.

Nearby destinations are served by smaller bus companies such as C & J Trailways, Concord Trailways, and Plymouth & Brockton. All converge at South Station. Both Greyhound and Peter Pan also have terminals at Riverside in Newton, on the 'D' Branch of the Green Line.

By Car

From the west:
Route I-90 (Mass. Pike) is the clearest route inbound, and feeds directly into the Ted Williams Tunnel to Logan Airport and points north. Three major exits before Williams Tunnel:
Exits 18–20 (Cambridge/Allston)

are best for Cambridge and Charles River locations.

Exit 22 (Prudential Center/Copley Square) is best for Back Bay, Fenway, Kenmore Square, and Boston Common (via Boylston, Charles, Beacon, Park, and Tremont streets).

Exit 24 (Expressway/Downtown) is best for Downtown and Liberty Tunnel (former Central Artery, now underground) access.

From the south:

Routes I-95, 24 and 3 all 'feed' into Route I-93 inbound. Two major exits are:

Kneeland Street/Chinatown – best for Back Bay, Theater District, and Boston Common Visitor Center (via Kneeland, Charles, Beacon, Park, and Tremont streets).

Dock Square – best for Airport, North End, Waterfront, and Faneuil Hall Marketplace.

From the north:

Routes 1 and I-93 enter Boston on elevated highway structures. Major exits:

Storrow Drive – best for Back Bay, Beacon Hill, Cambridge, and Boston Common Visitor Center (via Government Center exit and Cambridge Street, which becomes Tremont Street).

High Street – for Downtown.

Kneeland Street – best for Chinatown and Theater District.

Car Rentals

Car rentals can be arranged at the ground level of all terminals. Firms represented include: **Avis** (tel: 561-3500/800-331-1084); **Budget** (tel: 497-3733/800-527-0700); **Dollar** (tel: 634-0006/800-800-4000); **Enterprise** (tel: 561-4488/800-261-7331); **Hertz** (tel: 569-7272/800-654-3131); **National** (tel: 569-6700/877-222-9058); **Thrifty** (tel: 568-0100/800-847-4389).

Drivers must be at least 21 to rent a car; some renters specify 25. Rental agencies have offices throughout the city. Your hotel can help make arrangements, or a listing of agencies is available from the Greater Boston Convention & Visitors Bureau, tel: 536-4100. A valid driver's license and credit card are required.

If you are driving from Logan to Downtown Boston, you can use either the **Sumner Tunnel** or the **Ted Williams Tunnel**. Both have a $3.50 inbound fee, and no outbound fee. Opinions differ as to which is faster, but the Williams, which is newer, can save a few

minutes – especially if you are heading west or south. When bad traffic delays occur at the tunnels, take Route 1A North to Route 16 to Route 1 South and cross the **Tobin Bridge** into Boston.

GETTING AROUND

To and from the Airport

Logan, just 3 miles (5km) from Downtown Boston, is closer to town than any other major airport: this refers to distance and not to time. Traffic can back up at the tunnels under the harbor that connect airport to city.

The **MBTA Blue Line** from Airport Station is the fastest and cheapest way to Downtown and to many other places. Free shuttle buses run between airport terminals and the subway station.

Cabs are located outside each terminal. Fares to Downtown should average about $30–40, provided there are no major traffic jams. Several major bus companies, including Peter Pan, Concord Trailways, and Vermont Transit, serve many outlying suburbs and distant destinations.

AIRLINE TELEPHONE NUMBERS AND WEBSITES

Call Logan's public information office on: 800-235-6426 or 561-1800 (www.massport.com) for your airline's current terminal, as airlines often move about.

Some useful telephone numbers include:

Aer Lingus, tel: 800-474-7424, www.aerlingus.ie
Air Canada, tel: 888-247-2262, www.aircanada.ca
Air France, tel: 800-237-2747, www.airfrance.com
AirTran, tel: 800-247-8726, www.airtran.com
Alaska Airlines, tel: 800-252-7522, www.alaskaair.com
Alitalia, tel: 800-223-5730, www.alitaliausa.com
American Airways, tel: 800-

433-7300, www.aa.com
British Airways, tel: 800-247-9297, www.british-airways.com
Cape Air, tel: 800-352-0714, www.flycapeair.com
Delta, tel: 800-221-1212, www.delta.com
Iberia, tel: 800-772-4642, www.Iberia.com
Iceland Air, tel: 800-223-5500, www.icelandair.com
JetBlue Airways, tel: 800-538-2583, www.JetBlue.com
Lufthansa, tel: 800-645-3880, www.lufthansa.com
PenAir, 800-448-4226, www.penair.com
Porter Airlines, tel: 888-619-8622, www.flyporter.com
SATA (Azores Express), tel:

800-762-9995, www.sata.pt
Southwest, tel: 800-435-9792, www.southwest.com
Spirit Airlines, tel: 800-772-7117, www.spiritair.com
Sun Country, tel: 800-359-6786, www.suncountry.com
Swiss, tel: 877-359-7947, www.swiss.com
TACV, tel: 866-359-8228, www.flytacv.com
United Airlines, tel: 800-241-6522, www.ual.com
US Airways, tel: 800-428-4322, www.usairways.com
Virgin America, tel: 877-359-8474, www.virginamerica.com
Virgin Atlantic Airways, tel: 800-862-8621, www.virginatlantic.com

ABOVE: college students on the Boston 'T'.

A delightful way to approach the city and especially useful for those staying in Downtown hotels (Fairmont Battery Wharf, Boston Harbor, Boston Marriott Long Wharf, Langham Hotel, Residence Inn by Marriott Boston Harbor on Tudor Wharf, Millennium Bostonian – see Accommodations listings, from page 241) is by **water taxi** (see page 239).

A free shuttle bus operates between the airport ferry dock and all of the airline terminals. For up-to-date information on airport **traffic conditions**, call Massport's Ground Transportation Hotline (tel: 800-235-6426) or review updated flight information on: www.massport.com.

Orientation

Boston, it's justly claimed, is a walker's city – a good thing, for it is certainly not a driver's city. The city planners, as Emerson noted, were the cows, and it has been suggested that the Puritan belief in predestination extended even to urban design. Streets appeared where Providence chose to lay them – along cow paths, Native American trails and colonial wagon tracks – and are linked by crooked little alleys.

City planners, however, did come into their own in the middle of the 19th century, and as a result the Back Bay and, to a lesser extent, the South End have impeccable grid systems.

If you attempt to drive in the city and feel frustrated and inadequate, be consoled that many Bostonians feel the same way. Being faced by cars coming the wrong way on a one-way street, being stuck in a traffic jam, getting lost and then being unable to find a parking space is about par for the course. It's said that indicating a turn is considered 'giving information to the enemy.'

Public Transportation

Rapid Transit

Massachusetts Bay Transportation Authority (MBTA; www.mbta. com). For general information and customer service tel: 222-3200/1-800-392-6100; for the hearing impaired tel: 222-5146; weekdays 6.30am–8pm, weekends 7.30am–6pm. For MBTA police emergency tel: 222-1212.

For easy reference, see the subway map on page 289.

Ever since it was inaugurated in 1897, the subway (nowadays the rapid transit or, more usually, the 'T') has been a source of amusement for Bostonians. One ditty, 'The Man Who Never Returned,' tells of poor Charlie who was 'doomed to ride forever 'neath the streets of Boston' because he lacked the nickel fare necessary to alight.

However, despite severe overcrowding during rush hours, the 'T' is a fairly efficient and user-friendly system.

The five rapid transit lines – Red, Green, Orange, Blue, and Silver – that radiate out from Downtown Boston cling to the name 'subway' even though all lines run above ground for part of their route, and the Silver Line is actually served by buses.

There are more than 75 rapid transit stations, usually named for a nearby square, street, or landmark. In addition, Green Line trains stop at many street corners along the surface portion of their routes. All five lines intersect in Downtown Boston. Transfers between lines, at no extra charge, are possible at:

Park Street – Red and Green Lines (with an underground walkway to the Orange Line at Downtown Crossing).
Downtown Crossing – Red and Orange Lines (with an underground walkway to the Green Line at Park Street).
Government Center – Blue and Green Lines.
State – Blue and Orange Lines.
Haymarket and North Station – Green and Orange Lines. (This connection is considerably more convenient at Haymarket than at North Station.)

'Inbound' is always toward Downtown Boston – Park Street, Downtown Crossing and Government Center. 'Outbound' means away from Downtown. Outside of central Boston, both the Red and Green Lines have branches. Check the sign on the front of the train. Green Line trains (also called streetcars or simply cars) carry letters to indicate different branches: B – Boston College; C – Cleveland Circle; D – Riverside; E – Heath Street or Arborway. A red line through the letter on a sign means that the train goes only part of the way on that particular branch.

The 'T''s old token turnstiles have been replaced with new fare gates. Before approaching the fare gate, you must buy a paper CharlieTicket at a ticket-vending machine. Select the type of ticket you wish to purchase and pay by cash, credit card, or debit card.

The adult fare for the 'T' using a paper ticket is $2.50. An alternative to buying a paper ticket is to purchase a plastic, reusable, reloadable CharlieCard at select locations; the adult fare when using the CharlieCard is $2. Approach the turnstile and insert your paper ticket into the slot or tap your CharlieCard against the card target, and the gate will open.

The Rapid Transit operates 20 hours a day – from shortly after 5am until past 1am. On Sundays, service begins about 40 minutes later. Last trains leave Downtown Boston at 12.45am.

For information on the MBTA discount pass, see Discount Passes, page 257.

By Bus

The majority of the MBTA's 160-plus bus routes operate feeder services linking subway stations to neighborhoods not directly served by the rapid transit system. Some crosstown routes connect stations on different subway lines without going into Downtown. Only a few MBTA buses actually enter Downtown Boston, and most of these are express buses from outlying areas.

One service that visitors might wish to use is Route 1, which travels along Massachusetts Avenue (at the western end of the Back Bay) across the Charles River to MIT and onto Harvard Square.

The basic MBTA bus fare is $2 ($1.50 with a CharlieCard), seniors 75¢, students (through high school) 75¢, and children under 12 are free with a paying adult. On a few relatively long routes, charges are higher. Inner Express fares are $4.50, Outer Express fares are $6.50. Exact change is required on buses.

Commuter Rail

The MBTA Commuter Rail extends from Downtown Boston to communities across New England, including tourist destinations such as Concord, Lowell, Salem, Ipswich, Gloucester, and Rockport. In addition, Amtrak's Downeaster route

TAXICABS

Taxi stands are common at popular tourist sites. Metered rates are $2.60 for the first seventh of a mile and $0.40 for each seventh of a mile thereafter. Idling/waiting time is charged $28.00 per hour. Tolls for bridges and tunnels are paid by the passenger, including a $2.75 toll for all trips from Boston proper to Logan Airport and North Shore Communities. For destinations outside the city, flat rates may be charged. For a list of cities covered by metered and flat rates, see: www.cityofboston.gov/police/hackney. There is no extra fare for additional passengers. Tipping is not mandatory, but it is a brave (or callous) soul who does not add 15 percent to the fare.

Companies authorized by the city of Boston are:
Top Cab, tel: 266-4800
Boston Cab Association, tel: 536-3200
ITOA Cab Association, tel: 825-4000
City Cab Association, tel: 536-5100
Metro Cab, tel: 782-5500
Tunnel Taxi, tel: 567-2700
617TaxiCab, 829-4222

serves Portland, Maine.

Trains to the north and northwest of Boston depart from **North Station**, while trains to points south and west of the city leave from **South Station**. For information, tel: 222-3200.

Commuter rail fares are zoned according to distance (refer to zone maps and prices at: www.mbta.com/fares_and_passes/rail/). Tickets are sold at the railway stations, on the MBTA website, and on the train (tickets purchased on the train may have a $1–2 surcharge).

Commuter Boat

Several water taxis offer year-round service between Boston Logan Airport, waterfront hotels, waterfront attractions, and Boston Harbor wharves, including:
Harbor Express (tel: 222-6999), which connects the Quincy Shipyard and Hull to Boston and Logan Airport via high-speed catamaran.
City Water Taxi (tel: 422-0392; www.citywatertaxi.com), which also continues on to Pier 4 in Charlestown for visits to the USS Constitution warship.
Rowes Wharf Taxi (tel: 406-8584; www.roweswharfwatertaxi.com).

Disabled Travelers

See Disabled Travelers in A–Z section, page 259.

Driving

Parking

Conveniently located public parking facilities are found throughout the city, including at Government Center; Post Office Square; the Public Garden; the Prudential Center; and on Clarendon Street near the John Hancock Tower. Private lots are scattered around.

It is better by far to use the subway and bus services provided by the MBTA (Massachusetts Bay Transportation Authority).

Limousine Services

Carey Limousine, tel: 623-8700.
Commonwealth Limousine, tel: 787-5575.
Fifth Avenue, tel: 884-2600.
LTI Worldwide Limousine Service, tel: 381-0180.

Cycling

Boston has plenty of dedicated trails that are good for cyclists and rollerbladers, including along the banks of the Charles or through Olmsted's Emerald Necklace. Boston also has a bike-share scheme, Hubway, launched in 2011 (www.thehubway.com). See also Sightseeing Tours, page 255, and Participant Sports, page 256.

ACCOMMODATIONS

SOME THINGS TO CONSIDER BEFORE YOU BOOK THE ROOM

Choosing Accommodations

The city of Boston is well endowed with hotels, ranging from grand landmarks and opulent outposts of luxury brands, to sophisticated boutique hotels, to more subdued mid-level chains. The metropolitan area has tens of thousands of hotel rooms, of which almost half are in Boston and Cambridge. Bed-and-breakfast accommodations are increasingly popular and can be of a high standard. There are also affordable, no-frills youth hostels. Booking for all types of accommodations can be done over the phone or internet.

Location is obviously a main consideration when choosing lodging. The Back Bay, Waterfront, and Downtown neighborhoods are packed with hotels of the luxury, business, and basic chain varieties; Beacon Hill is host to a fine array of luxury boutique hotels. Some visitors prefer the rarefied academic atmosphere of Cambridge, a 10- to 20-minute trip from Boston, easily reached by public transportation.

Another alternative is to stay in one of the many hotels in Greater or Metropolitan Boston and join the MBTA (Massachusetts Bay Transportation Authority) commuters for a 30–40-minute journey every morning and evening.

These suburban hotels, most of which belong to major chains, tend to be less expensive than city-center hotels, which is not insignificant given the high cost of rooms in central Boston.

The average hotel room price in Boston tops $200 per night, and hotel tax in the Boston area is 12.45 percent (which includes a sales tax, local lodging tax, and convention center tax). Deals and discounts can often be found through the individual hotels and websites, such as www.kayak. com, www.travelocity.com, www. hotels.com, www.priceline.com, www.orbitz.com, and www.hotwire. com. Prices can vary greatly by season. During summer months, many colleges in the area rent rooms in their dormitories.

All Boston hotels are required to be non-smoking.

Major Chains

Best Western, www.bestwestern. com, tel: 800-780-7234
Days Inn, www.daysinn.com, tel: 800-329-7466
Hilton, www.hilton.com, tel: 800-HILTONS
Hyatt, www.hyatt.com, tel: 888-591-1234
InterContinental, www.intercontinental.com, tel: 877-834-3613
Kimpton, www.kimptonhotels. com, tel: 800-KIMPTON

Marriott, www.marriott.com, tel: 888-236-2427
Radisson, www.radisson.com, tel: 800-395-7046

Hostels and 'Y's

Youth hostels offer basic and clean accommodations for very little money. Generally, guests under 18 must be accompanied by a parent or legal guardian.
Hostelling International Boston – Fenway
19 Stuart St
Tel: 536-9455
www.bostonhostel.org
40Berkeley
40 Berkeley St
Tel: 375-2524
www.40berkeley.com

Rentals

If you are staying in the area for an extended period, it may be more economical to choose a short- or long-term rental. Among the agencies that offer this service are:
A B&B Agency of Boston
47 Commercial Wharf
Tel: 720-3540/800-248-9262
www.boston-bnbagency.com
AAA Corporate Rentals
120 Milk St
Tel: 357-6900/800-487-5020
www.furnishedapt.com
Airbnb
www.airbnb.com

TRANSPORTATION

ACCOMMODATIONS

ACTIVITIES

A – Z

BEACON HILL AND BOSTON COMMON

XV Beacon
15 Beacon St
Tel: 670-1500
www.xvbeacon.com
 [p272, D3]
Classic opulence and high-tech toys unite in this sophisticated boutique hotel. Handsome rooms in the 1903 Beaux Arts building feature a working gas fireplace, Frette linens, cashmere throws, fresh flowers, heated towel racks, complimentary internet, and surround-sound stereo. Round-the-clock room service from on-site Mooo steakhouse is available, as are complimentary personalized in-residence cards and complimentary in-town Lexus courtesy service. Well-behaved dogs of all sizes are welcome. **$$$$**

Beacon Hill Hotel
25 Charles St
Tel: 723-7575
www.beaconhillhotel.com
[p268, C1]
Just steps from Boston Common, this modern yet historical hotel offers great views of Charles Street and Beacon Hill. The privately owned converted 1830s townhouse has 12 rooms and a suite, all of which were renovated in 2011 and now feature colorful bedding, plantation shutters, LED flat-screen TVs, black-and-white photographs, and complimentary internet access. The popular Beacon Hill Bistro is on site, serving executive chef Joshua Lewin's French bistro cuisine. **$$$**

Holiday Inn, Beacon Hill
5 Blossom St
Tel: 742-7630
www.hisboston.com
[p266, C4]
At the foot of the 'wrong' side of Beacon Hill, but next to Massachusetts General Hospital and steps from the river, this dependable hotel offers 303 rooms, free internet, and the on-site Foster's Bar & Grill. **$$$**

John Jeffries House
14 David G. Mugar Way
Tel: 367-1866
www.johnjeffrieshouse.com
[p266, B4]
Accommodations at this comfortable, 46-room bed-and-breakfast inn range from studios to deluxe suites; all have baths, phones, and TVs, and most have kitchenettes. Elegant common

rooms and an elevator are further draws. **$$**

Onyx Hotel
155 Portland St
Tel: 557-9955
www.onyxhotel.com
[p272, E1]
This modern, eco-friendly, and pet-friendly boutique hotel is conveniently nestled on a side street near Faneuil Hall and North Station. The 112 rooms are boldly decorated (think black-and-white checkered carpet, red-orange accents and animal-print bathrobes), and include high-tech amenities like an iHome sound system and flat-screen TV. Frette linens and Gilchrist & Soames bath amenities up the sophistication level further. A complimentary evening wine hour is hosted daily. **$$$**

DOWNTOWN

Harborside Inn
185 State St
Tel: 723-7500/888-723-7565
www.harborsideinnboston.com
[p272, F3]
The 98 rooms in this renovated 19th-century

warehouse offer simple teakwood furnishings, wall-mounted LCD flat-screen TVs, and nautical accents. The lack of frills is made up for by the prime location near

Faneuil Hall and the friendly staff. **$$**

Nine Zero
90 Tremont St
Tel: 772-5800
www.ninezero.com
[p272, D3]

Just off Boston Common, the ultra-hip Nine Zero is one of Boston's sleekest boutique hotels, offering a perfect balance of modern design and comfort. The 190 stylishly urban rooms offer an array of high-tech/high-speed amenities, custom-designed beds, billowy

BELOW: the opulent XV Beacon.

PRICE CATEGORIES

A very approximate guide to current room rates for a standard double per night is:

$$$$ = over $300
$$$ = $200–300
$$ = $125–200
$ = under $125

down comforters, and Aveda bath products. Socialize at the trendy on-site KO Prime steakhouse and daily hosted happy hours in the lobby. **$$$$**

Omni Parker House Hotel
60 School St
Tel: 227-8600
www.omnihotels.com
⑧ [p272, E3]
The country's oldest continuously operating

hotel (since 1854), across from Boston Common, completed a $30 million overhaul in 2008. Blending past and present, 551 guest rooms feature cherrywood furnishings, richly colored fabrics, LCD flatscreen TVs, and internet access. Also on site are a 24-hour gym and the historic Parker's restaurant, home of the Boston cream pie. **$$$**

Ritz-Carlton, Boston Common
10 Avery St
Tel: 574-7100/
800-241-3333
www.ritzcarlton.com
⑨ [p272, D4]
Located just off the Common, this sleek luxury hotel completed an $11 million renovation in 2008. The 193 elegant rooms – including 43 spacious suites – feature HD flat-

screen TVs, Bose radios, marble baths with separate showers, Frette linens, and pieces from a $1 million contemporary art collection. The hotel is home to the Artisan Bistro restaurant and Avery bar, and the 100,000-sq-ft (9,000-sq-meter) Sports Club/LA is accessible from hotel elevators. **$$$$**

NORTH END AND WATERFRONT

Boston Harbor Hotel
70 Rowes Wharf
Tel: 439-7000
www.bhh.com
⑩ [p272, F3]
Board the airport water shuttle at Logan and, seven minutes later, step into an ultra-luxurious waterside hotel. The 230 rooms feature distinctly Boston decor, and each has either a harbor or skyline view. A museum-quality art collection decorates public areas, and Meritage offers superb New American dining. **$$$$**

Boston Marriott Hotel Long Wharf
296 State St, Long Wharf
Tel: 227-0800
www.marriott.com
⑪ [p272, F2]
Situated at the waterfront next to the Aquar-

ium and within a minute's walk of Quincy Market. Many of the 397 rooms and 15 suites have panoramic views of the harbor; all feature internet access and a flat-screen TV. Ten PURE rooms offer a unique clean-air environment for the allergen-sensitive. **$$$$**

Fairmont Battery Wharf
3 Battery Wharf
Tel: 994-9000
www.fairmont.com/batterywharf
⑫ [p272, F1]
This sophisticated urban retreat, which opened in 2008, is on the historic Battery Wharf, close to the North End. The 150 spacious and elegant guest rooms – including 30 suites – feature large

work areas, flat-screen HD TVs and marble baths. The hotel's common areas house dramatic glass installations by Nikolas Weinstein, and the on-site Exhale Spa has 12 treatment rooms and a yoga studio. Water taxi service is available. **$$$$**

Millennium Bostonian Hotel
26 North St at Faneuil Hall
Tel: 523-3600
www.millenniumhotels.com
⑬ [p272, E2]
Following a $24 million refit, the Millennium Bostonian is a stylish, central retreat. Rooms and suites feature contemporary decor, HD TVs, Frette linens, and some have balconies. Rooms overlooking Quincy Market can be noisy, but the location

is incomparable. On-site North 26 restaurant dishes up progressive American cuisine. **$$$$**

Seaport Hotel
1 Seaport Lane
Tel: 800-440-3318
www.seaporthotel.com
⑭ [p268, E2]
Close to the World Trade Center and South Station, this waterfront hotel has state-of-the-art guest rooms with marble baths, work desks, Bose Wave music systems, and free internet access. The luxurious health club includes a dreamy 50ft (15-meter) heated pool and extensive exercise facilities. Aura Restaurant is on site. Pets under 50lbs (23kg) are welcome. **$$$$**

CHARLESTOWN

The Constitution Inn
150 Third Ave
Tel: 241-8400/
800-495-9622
www.constitutioninn.com
⑮ [p266, E1]

This former YMCA is just five blocks from the USS *Constitution* (known as 'Old Ironsides') and has 147 plainly but comfortably furnished rooms

with air conditioning and some kitchenettes. The fitness center includes an indoor heated pool, sauna, weight room, and bas-

ketball court. **$**

Residence Inn by Marriott Boston Harbor on Tudor Wharf
34–44 Charles River Ave
Tel: 242-9000

www.marriott.com/bostw
⑯ [p266, D2]
All 168 suites at this waterfront hotel offer views of the harbor or Downtown and have fully equipped kitchens. There's a heated indoor pool, fitness room, and complimentary hot breakfast buffet. A private water taxi ($15) transports guests to Logan Airport and other harbor destinations. **$$**

BACK BAY AND FENWAY

463 Beacon Street Guest House
Tel: 617-536-1302
www.463beacon.com
⑰ [p270, E2]
A great hotel alternative for stays of a week or longer, this turn-of-the-20th-century brownstone close to Massachusetts Avenue has comfortable rooms with private baths, phones, TVs and air conditioning; many have kitchenettes or full kitchens. Rooms are available by the night. **$$**

Boston Hotel Buckminster
645 Beacon St
Tel: 236-7050/800-727-2825
www.bostonhotelbuckminster.com
⑱ [p270, E2]

Built in 1897, this pet-friendly hotel has 67 rooms and 49 suites. All have private baths and one to three beds (the one-bed units fall into the Inexpensive price range) and offer either a view of Kenmore Square or the skyline. A Continental breakfast is included. **$$**

Boston Marriott Copley Place Hotel
110 Huntington Ave
Tel: 236-5800
www.marriott.com
⑲ [p268, B3]
This large, reliable hotel with over 1,100 handsome rooms is linked by indoor passages to the Copley Place mall and to the Prudential Center. **$$$$**

Boston Park Plaza Hotel & Towers
50 Park Plaza
Tel: 426-2000
www.bostonparkplaza.com
⑳ [p268, C2]
A popular spot for conventions, this elite, historic hotel near Boston Common has a spacious, elegant, chandeliered lobby, 950 guest rooms with flat-screen plasma TVs, nine restaurants and lounges, and a 24-hour fitness center. The hotel hosts an afternoon tea and is home to a tea sommelier. **$$$$**

The Eliot Suite Hotel
370 Commonwealth Ave
Tel: 267-1607/800-44-ELIOT
www.eliothotel.com
㉑ [p270, E2]
A charmingly chic European-style boutique hotel offers 95 elegantly furnished rooms and suites (some with kitchenettes and sitting areas), and Ken Oringer's Clio and Uni Sashimi Bar, two of the city's finest restaurants. **$$$$**

The Fairmont Copley Plaza
138 St James Ave
Tel: 267-5300/866-540-4417
www.fairmont.com
㉒ [p268, B2]
With an opulent lobby and 383 European-style rooms, many with handsome period furnishings, this palatial 1912 hotel overlooking Copley Square remains *la grande dame* of Boston hotels, offering gracious service and elegant

accommodations. The Fairmont Gold club level features a private lounge, and seven culturally themed suites celebrate Boston history with specially designed artwork. The new elegant Oak Long Bar + Kitchen features a farm-to-table American menu. **$$$$**

Four Seasons Hotel Boston
200 Boylston St
Tel: 338-4400
www.fourseasons.com
㉓ [p268, C2]
Elegant simplicity, old-world Boston charm, and impeccable service are hallmarks of this 15-story, 273-room red-brick hotel overlooking the Public Garden. The spacious, sumptuous accommodations feature marble bathrooms, glass-topped desks, and bay windows, many with views of the Public Garden, Beacon Hill, and the State House. Complimentary house car drop-off service is offered within 2 miles (3km) of the hotel. The hotel also features an indoor swimming pool, whirlpool, and sauna. **$$$$**

BELOW: the Lenox, a Boston fixture since 1900.

PRICE CATEGORIES

A very approximate guide to current room rates for a standard double per night is:

$$$$ = over $300
$$$ = $200–300
$$ = $125–200
$ = under $125

TRANSPORTATION

ACCOMMODATIONS

ACTIVITIES

A – Z

Howard Johnson Hotel Fenway
1271 Boylston St
Tel: 267-8300
www.hojo.com
㉔ [p270, D3]
Close to Fenway Park, this hotel has simple accommodations (some rooms with private balconies), a pool, free high-speed internet, and a Chinese restaurant. **$$**

The Lenox Hotel
61 Exeter St
Tel: 536-5300/800-225-7676
www.lenoxhotel.com
㉕ [p268, A2]
Understated elegance and attention to detail define this 214-room hotel, a Boston fixture since 1900. Rooms are decorated in French provincial, oriental, or colonial decor. The corner rooms are particularly spacious, and an entire floor is dedicated to PURE allergy-friendly rooms. City Table serves

New England seasonal fare, and cozy City Bar offers signature cocktails and small plates. **$$$$**

Mandarin Oriental, Boston
776 Boylston St
Tel: 535-8888
㉖ [p268, A2]
Opened in 2008 at a central Bay Back address, this ultra-luxurious hotel combines classic Bostonian residential elegance with refined oriental influences. The 148 guest rooms – including 12 suites – feature Frette linens, spacious granite bathrooms, and all the latest technologies; the spa combines Asian healing philosophy with signature treatments incorporating New England herbs. Additional draws include the sophisticated Asana restaurant, the chic M

Bar & Lounge, a fitness center, and direct access to the Prudential Center and shops at Copley Plaza. **$$$$**

The MidTown Hotel
220 Huntington Ave
Tel: 262-1000/800-343-1177
www.midtownhotel.com
㉗ [p268, A3]
Conveniently located near Symphony Hall, the Christian Science complex, and the Prudential Center, this standard 159-room motel has an outdoor pool, and adjoining and connecting rooms are available. **$$**

Newbury Guest House
261 Newbury St
Tel: 437-7666/800-437-7668
www.newburyguesthouse.com
㉘ [p268, A2]
Three 1880s single-family Victorian homes were renovated to create this elegant, 32-room inn, which features free

internet and a hot buffet breakfast. Right on the heart of Newbury Street shops; the inn has quieter rooms in the back. Wheelchair-accessible. **$$**

Taj Boston
15 Arlington Street
Tel: 536-5700/877-482-5267
㉙ [p268, B2]
Overlooking the Public Garden at Arlington and Newbury streets, the elegant Taj Boston is renowned for its classic and traditional style (it opened in 1927) and excellent service. There are 273 rooms, including 44 suites with wood-burning fireplaces, a fitness center and two restaurants. Complimentary car service is offered to the Financial District, and original art and antiques are displayed throughout the hotel. **$$$$**

THE SOUTH END

Chandler Inn
26 Chandler St
Tel: 482-3450/800-842-3450
www.chandlerinn.com
㉚ [p268, C3]
Located between Copley Square and Park Square, this small, gay-friendly hotel features 56 sophisticated and comfortable rooms (some designed by Dennis Duffy, others by Eric

Roseff) with work desks, satellite televisions, and data ports. Some rooms are quite small, as are the baths, but the ambience is good. **$$**

Clarendon Square Inn
198 West Brookline St
Tel: 536-2229
www.clarendonsquare.com
㉛ [p268, B3]
This beautifully appointed, gay-friendly

c.1860 Victorian B&B offers the amenities of a small luxury hotel and the warmth of a small inn. Rooms accommodate up to three people and have wireless internet, DVD players, and views of the Boston skyline. There's a rooftop hot tub. **$$**

Nolan House B&B
10 G St

Tel: 269-1550/800-383-1550
www.nolanhouse.com
㉜ [p268, D4]
The three guest rooms in this c.1860 non-smoking Victorian home are air conditioned and comfortably furnished. There's free parking, a full breakfast, and bus service right outside the door. Rooms have shared or private baths. **$**

CAMBRIDGE

A Friendly Inn at Harvard Square
1673 Cambridge St
Tel: 547-7851
www.afinow.com/afi

㉝ [p272, C1]
Describing itself as 'the intelligent choice for those who want their brains stimulated and

not their wallets' – this is a comfortable inn with free parking. All rooms have private baths, phones, air con-

ditioning, TV, and wireless internet access. **$**

Charles Hotel
1 Bennett St
Tel. 864-1200

www.charleshotel.com
34 [p272, A2]
A touch of class on the edge of Harvard Square: rooms are appointed with commissioned artwork and high-tech amenities, and offer views of Harvard Square, Cambridge, or Boston. The Regattabar is one of the best jazz venues in the region. A shopping mall is attached to the hotel, and the Square's shops and restaurants are at the doorstep. **$$$$**
DoubleTree Guest Suites
400 Soldiers Field Rd, Boston
Tel: 783-0090
www.doubletreehotels.com
35 [p272, B4]
On the river, next to the Harvard Business School, this is a great hotel for families. All 310 suites have two rooms, each with a telephone and TV, and a living room with a sofa bed. Harvard Square is a 15-minute stroll away, and the Scullers Jazz Club is on site. **$$**
The Harvard Square Hotel
110 Mount Auburn St
Tel: 864-5200
www.hotelsinharvardsquare.com
36 [p272, A2]
Newly renovated with modern decor, a larger lobby and a Starbucks café, this six-floor, 73-room hotel in the heart of Harvard Square offers on-site car rentals, free in-room internet, and business services. Parking is $35 for overnight guests and a $20 daily rate. **$$**
Hyatt Regency
575 Memorial Drive
Tel: 492-1234

www.cambridge.hyatt.com
37 [p270, C1]
The 'pyramid on the Charles,' with its striking glass atrium, is closer to MIT than to Harvard and just across the bridge from Boston University. Some of the 469 rooms offer great views of the river and Boston skyline; some also have balconies. Indoor lap pool with sundeck, sauna, and eucalyptus steam rooms. **$$$**
The Inn at Harvard
1201 Massachusetts Ave
Tel: 491-2222
www.hotelsinharvardsquare.com
38 [p272, C2]
Designed by Harvard graduate Graham Gund, this four-story Georgian-style hotel's architecture blends in with the university. The 113 rooms, built around a four-story sunlit atrium, are pleasantly appointed with a mixture of old-world beauty and modern-day convenience. A restaurant is on the premises. **$$**
Kendall Hotel
350 Main St
Tel: 577-1300
www.kendallhotel.com
39 [p266, A4]
In a handsomely renovated, 1893 Victorian firehouse steps from the Kendall/MIT Red Line 'T' stop, this boutique hotel has 73 rooms and 4 one-bedroom luxury suites, some with Jacuzzi baths. Underground parking is available. **$$**
Hotel Marlowe
25 Edwin H. Land Blvd
Tel: 868-8000/800-825-7040
www.hotelmarlowe.com
40 [p266, B3]
This eclectic and vibrant Kimpton boutique hotel

ABOVE: the Sheraton Commander Hotel, Cambridge.

near the banks of the Charles River combines high-tech amenities with family- and pet-friendly services. There are 236 guest rooms and suites, and a fitness center. **$$$$**
Mary Prentiss Inn
6 Prentiss St
Tel: 661-2929
www.maryprentissinn.com
41 [p272, B1]
This restored neoclassical Greek Revival inn dates from 1843 and is on the National Register of Historical Places. The 20 rooms have exposed beams, shutters, and antiques; some have wood-burning fireplaces and Jacuzzis. Additional attractions are the full breakfast, afternoon tea, and lush outdoor deck. **$$**
Royal Sonesta
5 Cambridge Parkway
Tel: 806-4200
www.sonesta.com
42 [p266, B3]
The 400 rooms on the Cambridge banks of the

Charles River offer great views of the Boston skyline. The hotel is close to the Science Museum and practically next door is the Cambridge-Side Galleria, a popular shopping mall. Free shuttle service into Boston and Harvard Square. **$$$**
Sheraton Commander
16 Garden St
Tel: 547-4800/800-325-3535
www.starwoodhotels.com/sheraton
43 [p272, A1]
This old-fashioned landmark near Harvard Square has 174 rooms, some with Boston rockers, four-poster beds, and kitchenettes. **$$**

PRICE CATEGORIES

A very approximate guide to current room rates for a standard double per night is:

$$$$ = over $300
$$$ = $200–300
$$ = $125–200
$ = under $125

WEST OF BOSTON

Concord

Concord's Colonial Inn
48 Monument Square
Tel: 978-371-1533/800-370-9200
www.concordscolonialinn.com
This historically significant inn has 56 rooms with colonial country-style decor and modern amenities. Fifteen of the 56 rooms are in the 1716 main building (which is included on the National Register of Historic Places). The rest of the rooms are in a newer wing and cottages. **$$**

Hawthorne Inn B&B
462 Lexington Rd
Tel: 978-369-5610
www.concordmass.com
This historic inn has seven antiques-filled rooms well furnished with artwork, private baths, air conditioning, phones, and data ports. The Emerson Room has a gas log fire. Children are welcome. **$$**

Northbridge Inn
21 Monument St
Tel: 978-371-0014/888-530-0007
www.northbridgeinn.com
This 1885 in-town lodging has six spacious, one- and two-bedroom suites with country decor, queen beds, tiled baths, kitchens, TVs, telephones, and data ports. A full hot breakfast is available. **$$$**

Sudbury Center

Longfellow's Wayside Inn
72 Wayside Inn Rd
Tel: 978-443-1776/800-339-1776
www.wayside.org
The country's oldest operating inn (1716), a two-story building first restored by Henry Ford and, after a fire, by the Ford Foundation, has 10 charming antiques-filled rooms and is close to Lexington and Concord. The restaurant serves hearty Yankee fare. **$$**

NORTH OF BOSTON

Gloucester

Bass Rocks Ocean Inn
107 Atlantic Rd
Tel: 978-283-7600/888-802-7666
www.bassrocksoceaninn.com
Three houses comprise this inn. The two-story Oceanfront and Seaside houses offer sweeping views of the sea. The main house (the Stacey House) is on the National Register of Historic Places. Bikes are available for guests. There's an outdoor pool and rooftop sundeck. **$$$**

Cape Ann Motor Inn
33 Rockport Rd
Tel: 978-281-2900/800-464-VIEW
www.capeannmotorinn.com
This year-round three-story property offers oceanfront rooms with balconies overlooking Long Beach and with views of Thatcher Island lighthouses. Each room has a TV, double bed and sofa pullout, and private bath; some have a kitchenette. Rates include breakfast, coffee and pastries. Pets are accepted. **$$**

Marblehead

Harbor Light Inn
58 Washington St
Tel: 781-631-2186
www.harborlightinn.com
Located in the heart of the harbor district, this formally and elegantly decorated, 21-room inn has a 19th-century addition built around an 18th-century house. Decor ranges from traditional to contemporary. Rooms feature private baths, Wi-fi, body products, and air conditioning, and many also have a fireplace, whirlpool tub, sundeck, or patio. **$$$$**

Marblehead Inn
264 Pleasant St
Tel: 781-639-9999/800-399-5843
www.marbleheadinn.com
Marblehead Inn has 10 spacious, two-room suites with country Victorian-style furnishings, kitchenettes, private baths, and most with Jacuzzi tubs. A Continental breakfast is included. **$$**

Newburyport

Clark Currier Inn
45 Green St
Tel: 978-465-8363
www.clarkcurrierinn.com
A dignified, three-story 1803 shipbuilder's home in the Federal mode. Many of the eight rooms (all with private bath, internet, and air conditioning) feature pumpkin-pine floors, pencil-post beds and other antique furnishings. The parlor, with its fireplace, is very comfortable and cozy. **$$**

Garrison Inn
11 Brown Square
Tel: 978-499-8500
www.garrisoninn.com
Garrison Inn is a small, sophisticated boutique luxury hotel in a four-story former Federalist residence (c.1803). The 24 rooms are decorated in a neutral palette with warm woods and reproduction antiques, and feature private baths and the latest technologies. Some have fireplaces. David's Tavern serves good eclectic American fare nightly. **$$**

Rockport

Sally Webster Inn
34 Mount Pleasant St
Tel: 978-546-9251/877-546-9251
www.sallywebster.com
This small and quaint inn has seven antiques-filled guest rooms. All have private baths and cable TV; several feature wide-board pine floors

PRICE CATEGORIES

A very approximate guide to current room rates for a standard double per night is:

$$$$ = over $300
$$$ = $200–300
$$ = $125–200
$ = under $125

and canopy beds. There is also a living room with a fireplace, and breakfast is served out on the terrace in good weather. **$$**

Seaward Inn and Cottages
44 Marmion Way
Tel: 978-546-3741/877-473-9273
www.seawardinn.com
A welcoming Cape Ann summerhouse turned B&B, perched on a beautifully landscaped, 5-acre (2-hectare) seaside ledge. There are nine rooms in the main inn with ocean and garden views, two nearby houses, and adjacent cottages. The grounds include a natural, spring-fed outdoor swimming pool, and a lawn for bocce, croquet and ping-pong. A complimentary full breakfast is provided. **$$$**

Hawthorne Hotel
18 Washington Square West
Tel: 978-744-4080/800-729-7829
www.hawthornehotel.com
The city's only full-service hotel is a renovated Federal-style lodging at the edge of the Green. All 93 rooms – including six suites – have 18th-century reproduction furnishings and modern amenities. There is a business center, fitness center, and complimentary Wi-fi. Nathaniel's Restaurant serves a lively jazz brunch buffet and the Tavern has casual fare. **$$$**

The Salem Inn
7 Summer St
Tel: 978-741-0680/800-446-2995
www.saleminnma.com
This Downtown inn is actually a collection of three restored, historic buildings constructed between 1834 and 1874. Many of the 40 rooms have fireplaces (operable Nov–Apr), oversized whirlpool baths, and/or canopy beds. All rooms have TV and phones, and each of the inns has a parlor with a fireplace. Free continental breakfast and Wi-fi. **$$**

Stonehedge Inn and Spa
160 Pawtucket Blvd
Tel: 978-649-4400
www.stonehedgeinnandspa.com
Luxurious rooms, an outstanding wine cellar, the Left Bank wine-themed restaurant, and a first-class spa are hallmarks of this non-smoking, European-style luxury inn set in 36 acres (15 hectares) of woodland near the town of Lowell. Many of the 30 suites, which are elegantly decorated with French country-style furnishings, have fireplaces, Jacuzzis, and balconies with pleasant views. **$$$$**

SOUTH SHORE AND CAPE COD

Many lodgings on the Cape are seasonal and require a minimum stay, especially on weekends and holidays. Be sure to call ahead for reservations. Note that summer and winter prices can vary greatly.

Beechwood Inn
2839 Main St, Route 6A
Tel: 508-362-6618/800-609-6618
www.beechwoodinn.com
Two of the six guest rooms in this homey, three-story, 1853 Queen Anne home have fireplaces; all are furnished with antiques. The parlor is pure Victorian, and the porch is a lovely spot to while away a few hours on a Cape Cod vacation. **$$**

Captain Freeman Inn
15 Breakwater Rd
Tel: 508-896-7481/800-843-4664
www.captainfreemaninn.com
A luxurious 1860s shipbuilder's home on Cape Cod with 14 antiques-filled spacious rooms (some with whirlpool tub and fireplace) and a heated, outdoor pool. Bicycles are available for guests, and a full breakfast is included. **$$$**

Old Sea Pines Inn
2553 Main St, Route 6A
Tel: 508-896-6114
www.oldseapinesinn.com
Rooms at this 1907, non-smoking Shingle-style mansion, once a girls' boarding school, range from small with shared bath, to spacious suites with fireplaces. Two of the 24 rooms are suitable for families. Rates include breakfast and internet. There's a summer dinner theater on the premises. **$**

Chatham Bars Inn
297 Shore Rd
Tel: 508-945-0096/800-527-4884

BELOW: one of the cozy cottages at the Chatham Bars Inn resort on Cape Cod.

www.chathambarsinn.com
This grand 22-acre (9-hectare), 217-room resort has a main inn, outlying cottages (many with fireplaces, private decks, and ocean-view patios), specialty spa suites with saunas and built-in massage tables, and a private beach. Rooms feature Aveda bath products, Bose Wave radios, Nespresso coffeemakers, and internet access. There's also a fine dining room, entertainment, and complimentary supervised summer children's activities. **$$$$**

Chatham Tides Waterfront Lodging
394 Pleasant St
Tel: 508-432-0379
www.chathamtides.com
A variety of accommodations are available, including simple motel rooms with efficiency kitchens, suites, and townhouses with private sundecks (weekly rentals only in summer). Private beach on Nantucket Sound. **$$$**

Cohasset

Cohasset Harbor Inn
44 Border St
Tel: 781-383-6650/800-252-5287
www.cohassetharborresort.com
Beautifully situated overlooking the harbor, this year-round inn offers a variety of accommodations including standard rooms, mini-suites, and spacious suites overlooking the water. Atlantica Restaurant serves dinner Tue–Sun; the casual Olde Salt Restaurant offers alfresco dining daily for lunch and dinner. **$$**

Falmouth

The Captain's Manor Inn
27 W. Main St
Tel: 508-338-7336
www.captainsmanorinn.com
This 1849 National Register Italianate villa, built by a seafarer to please a homesick wife, has large, handsome high-ceilinged rooms, and knowledgeable hosts. Well-supervised children aged 12 and older are welcome. **$$**

Coonamessett Inn
311 Gifford St
Tel: 508-548-2300
www.capecodrestaurants.org/coonamessett
Set in 6 acres (2.4 hectares) of grounds, this lovely inn is more than 200 years old and features one and two-bedroom suites. The rooms are unfussy, and many overlook the lovely pond and gardens. Off-season rates are inexpensive. **$$**

Mariner Motel
555 Main St
Tel: 508-548-1331/800-233-2939
www.marinermotel.com
A non-smoking, family-friendly motel a short walk from the Vineyard ferry, this place has 30 pleasant rooms and an outdoor pool. **$**

Martha's Vineyard

Charlotte Inn
27 S. Summer St, Edgartown
Tel: 508-627-4751
www.thecharlotteinn.com
An exquisite country inn shaded by linden and chestnut trees, with five buildings (from 18th-century to new) decorated with antiques and Edwardian flair – 19th-century oil paintings, burnished mahogany paneling, and deep hunter greens. Children over 14 are welcome. **$$$**

The Edgartown Inn
56 N. Water St, Edgartown
Tel: 508-627-4794
www.edgartowninn.com
Built in 1798 for a whaling captain and an inn for over 150 years, this non-smoking property has welcomed Daniel Webster and Nathaniel Hawthorne as guests. Accommodations, in the inn and two outbuildings, include private and shared baths. **$$**

Nantucket

Jared Coffin House
29 Broad St
Tel: 508-228-2400/800-248-2405
One of the oldest inns in Nantucket, this year-round historic inn in the heart of the historic district offers single bedrooms and two-room suites with radio and TV in the original building, a three-story 1845 mansion, as well as in five other historic buildings. A room with a loft is well suited to families. All rooms have air conditioning. **$$**

The Wauwinet Inn
120 Wauwinet Rd
Tel: 508-228-0145/800-426-8718
www.wauwinet.com
Nantucket's most elegant inn is 9 miles (14km) from the center of town and has 35 well-furnished rooms and cottages (some in the dunes and many with water views). The restaurant, Toppers, is excellent, and the rate includes breakfast. Closed in winter. **$$$$**

Sandwich

Dan'l Webster Inn Spa
149 Main St
Tel: 508-888-3622/800-444-3566

www.danlwebsterinn.com
Daniel Webster really did stay here, but today the non-smoking, year-round inn blends colonial charm with contemporary amenities. Many of the rooms have canopy or four-poster beds; some have fireplaces and two-person showers, whirlpools, and private balconies. A full-service spa is on site. **$$**

Earl of Sandwich Motel
378 Route 6A
Tel: 508-888-1415/800-442-3275
www.earlofsandwich.com
This quiet, year-round motel features standard and upscale units, and lovely grounds with an outdoor swimming pool. A Continental breakfast is included. **$**

West Dennis

Lighthouse Inn
1 Lighthouse Rd
Tel: 508-398-2244
www.lighthouseinn.com
A lighthouse-turned-inn, this 9-acre (3.6-hectare), old-fashioned seaside resort has been operated by the Stone family since 1938. There are 61 cottages and rooms (all with air conditioning and refrigerator and many with ocean views and wood-burning fireplaces) and a private beach. Supervised activities for children aged three and over are provided in July and August. **$$$**

PRICE CATEGORIES

A very approximate guide to current room rates for a standard double per night is:

$$$$ = over $300
$$$ = $200–300
$$ = $125–200
$ = under $125

TRANSPORTATION

ACTIVITIES

FESTIVALS, THE ARTS, NIGHTLIFE, TOURS AND SPORT

ACCOMMODATIONS

CALENDAR OF EVENTS

Public holidays are marked with an H. For more details of events, phone the City of Boston Special Events Line: 635-3911; www.city ofboston.gov/arts.

January

Chinese New Year, end of January or early February, is celebrated in Chinatown. Tel: 888-733-2678; www.BostonUSA. com and www.chinatownmain street.org.

February

Boston Wine Expo, the nation's largest trade and consumer wine event, showcasing more than 185 wine exhibitors and over 1,800 wines, is held at the Seaport World Trade Center. Tel: 877-946-3976; www.wine-expos. com/Wine/Expo.
New England Boat Show, Boston Convention and Exhibition Center. The oldest and largest boating marketplace in New England showcases powerboats, cruising sailboats, and more than 250 exhibits of marine accessories. Tel: 472-1442; www.newenglandboat show.com.

March

Harpoon St Patrick's Festival, early March. Irish food, beer, and music. Tel: 888-427-7666.
New England Spring Flower Show, a week-long event at Bayside Expo held in the second week, is the nation's oldest annual flower exhibition. Tel: 933-4900; www.masshort. org.
St Patrick's Day Parade and Evacuation Day. South Boston's 3.2-mile (5km) gala, held on a Sunday near March 17, begins on Broadway at 1pm and features floats, pipe bands, and marching bands.

April

Patriots' Day Reenactments, over Patriots' Day H weekend, take place in Concord and Lexington; www.battleroad.org.
Lantern service at Old North Church, the Sunday before Apr 19, commemorates Paul Revere's famous ride. Tel: 523-6676; www.oldnorth.com.
Boston Marathon, the 26-mile world-renowned event, begins in Hopkinton and ends at Copley Square. Third Monday of month. Tel: 236-1652; www.baa.org/races/boston-marathon.aspx.

May

Boston Pops. Commencement of a two-month Tue–Sat (8.30pm) season at Symphony Hall begins mid-May. Tel: 888-266-7575; www.bso.org.
Lilac Sunday, mid-May. The air at the Arnold Arboretum is fragrant with the aroma from several varieties of varicolored lilacs in bloom. Tel: 384-5209; http://arboretum. harvard.edu.
Memorial Day H, Monday of last weekend in May.

June

Free Friday Evening Flicks at the Hatch Shell on Memorial Drive. www.hatchshell.com.
Boston Pride, first week. A lesbian and gay pride festival, which includes a flag-raising at City Hall, an Aids Walk around Charles River Basin, concerts, pageants, block parties, and a parade. Tel: 262-9405; www.bostonpride.org.
Boston Harborfest. Maritime and colonial festival, with daily events at locations throughout the city the week before July 4th; includes the popular Chowderfest. Tel: 227-1528; www.boston harborfest.com.
Blessing of the Fleet, on the last weekend, takes place at both Gloucester and Provincetown: activities peak on Sunday.

ACTIVITIES

A – Z

July

Boston Pops: free outdoor concerts at the Hatch Memorial Shell on the Esplanade. Tel: 888-266-1200; www.bso.org.
Independence Day H. **Fourth of July celebrations** include a reading of 'Old Ironsides' docked balcony of Old State House; waterfront activities marked by the turn-around of 'Old Ironsides' docked at the Charlestown Naval Yard; an evening **Pops Concert** at Hatch Shell on the Esplanade, culminating with the *1812 Overture* accompanied by cannons and fireworks (arrive early and bring a blanket or chairs).
ArtBeat, the third weekend of the month, celebrates the arts with musicians, exhibits, and performers in Davis Square, Somerville. Tel: 625-6000, ext. 2985; www.somervillearts council.org.
The North End lives up to its 'Little Italy' reputation with brass bands, religious processions, and street food in several weekend festivals during the month.

August

The North End continues its religious processions and feasts.
Feast of the Blessed Sacrament, in New Bedford the last weekend of the month, is the country's largest Portuguese cultural event, with music, entertainment, and parades; www. portuguesefeast.com.
August Moon Festival, the first week of August. Chinatown celebrates with prancing lions and dragons, food, and martial arts displays. Tel: 888-733-2678; www.BostonUSA.com and www. chinatownmainstreet.org.
Gloucester Waterfront Festival, in mid-August, includes a lobster bake, and exhibits. Tel: 978-283-1601; www.capeannvacations. com.

September

Labor Day H, first Monday.
Boston Tattoo Convention, at the Boston Center for the Arts, 539 Tremont Street, hosts hundreds of tattoo artists, contests, vendors, and entertainment.

www.bostontattooconvention. com.
Boston Film Festival, premieres feature films, documentaries and shorts, and hosts discussions. Tel: 523-8388; www.bostonfilm-festival.org.

October

Columbus Day Parade, on the Sunday closest to Oct 12. Tel: 635-3911; www.cityofboston.gov/ arts.
Harvard Square Oktoberfest. In mid-month the Square becomes a Bavarian township for a week-end, with oompah bands, dancers, ethnic food, and a beer garden. Regional artists and merchants attend. Tel: 491-3434; www.harvardsquare.com.
Head of the Charles Regatta, in the middle of the month, is the world's largest two-day rowing event. Tel: 868-6200; www.hocr. org.
Salem comes alive (or plays dead) throughout the second part of the month with Halloween happenings. Tel: 978-744-0991; www.hauntedhappenings.com.

November

Veterans' Day Parade, on the Sunday nearest Nov 11. Tel: 635-4500; www.cityofboston. gov/arts.
Thanksgiving H, fourth Thursday.

December

Christmas Tree Lightings, the first weekend at the Prudential Center (tel: 800-746-7778), and Boston Common (tel: 635 4500).
Boston Tea Party Reenactment, in the Old South Meeting House on or near the 16th, recounts Boston's patriots' protest of King George III's taxations without representation. Tel: 482-6439; www. oldsouthmeetinghouse.org.
First Night, on the 31st, citywide revels celebrating art and community start in the afternoon and continue until the small hours. Tel: 542-1399; www.firstnight.org.

CHILDREN'S ACTIVITIES

Popular places include:
Children's Museum, 300 Congress Street, tel: 426-6500, www.bostonchildrensmuseum. org, is packed with interactive exhibits, and will particularly engage those up to 10 years of age. Open daily.
Franklin Park Zoo, 1 Franklin Park Road, Jamaica Plain, tel: 541-5466, www.zoonewengland.com, is home to a host of creatures including gorillas, leopards, lions, as well as the more pettable animals at Franklin Farm. Open daily.
Museum of Science, Science Park, tel: 723-2500, has more than 600 interactive exhibits featuring live animal and physical science demonstrations. A visit to the Mugar Omni Theater (with five-story IMAX screen)

and Planetarium are highlights. Open daily.
New England Aquarium, 1 Central Wharf, tel: 973-5200. A four-story ocean tank with sharks, turtles, penguins, and moray eels is the centerpiece of this state-of-the-art aquarium. The six-story IMAX screen provides an amazing fish-eye view of the sea. Open daily.
USS *Constitution* and Museum, Charlestown Navy Yard, tel: 426-1812. There's little damage that even the most energetic kid can do to 'Old Ironsides,' the 1797 warship. Costumed guides are on deck to answer questions. Open Apr–Oct Tue–Sun, Nov–Mar Thur–Sun. Free. See Child-Friendly Tours, page 258.

THE ARTS

BosTix isBoston's only half-price, day-of-show ticket outlet and information source for theater, dance, and music events. For information: tel: 262-8632; www. bostix.org, www.artsboston.org. Many upcoming events are listed on: www.bostonusa.com (tel: 888-733-2678).

Church Music

Emmanuel Church
15 Newbury St, tel: 536-3356. Sunday morning's 10am service, Sept–May, may include a cantata by J.S. Bach. The church hosts a program of evening concerts.
King's Chapel
58 Tremont St, tel: 523-1749. Events include a Sunday concert series at 5pm and a Tuesday recital series at 12.15pm which might feature jazz, folk, classical, or medieval music.

Classical Music

Asbefits the 'Athens of America,' Boston is a seriously musical city. The city's prominence in education helps: playing, singing, and dancing – for your pleasure and their own – are students from most of the more than 50 colleges and universities in Greater Boston.
Boston Camerata
45 Ash Street, Auburndale, tel: 262-2092; www.bostoncamerata com. America's foremost early music ensemble, led by Anne Azéma, performs at various venues.
Boston Cecilia
1773 Beacon St; tel: 232-4540. Professional musicians perform hits of the Baroque era using period instruments, as well as more contemporary works.
Boston Landmarks Orchestra
10 Guest St., Ste. 280; tel: 987-2000; www.landmarksorchestra. org. Free classical music concerts at Boston's landmarks.

Boston Philharmonic
295 Huntington Avenue, #210; tel: 236-0999; www.bostonphil. org. For more than 25 years Benjamin Zander has been conducting this orchestra, made up of professionals, amateurs, and students. A whole season might be devoted to a single composer. Performances are at Jordan Hall and Harvard University's Sanders Theatre.
Boston Pops
Symphony Hall, 301 Massachusetts Avenue; tel: 266-1200; www.bso.org.
The orchestra Arthur Fiedler made famous, with a host of guest musicians, performs light favorites from May to mid-July; the Fourth of July concert on the Esplanade is an annual highlight.
Boston Symphony Orchestra
Symphony Hall, 301 Massachusetts Avenue; tel: 266-1200; www.bso.org.
One of America's 'Big Five' orchestras, now led by James Levine of Metropolitan Opera fame, performs in acoustically sublime Symphony Hall Oct–Apr.
Cambridge Society for Early Music
Tel: 489-2062; www.csem.org. Solo, chamber, choral and orchestral music from the Middle Ages through the early 19th century is performed using historically appropriate instruments at small halls and intimate venues throughout the area.
Handel and Haydn Society
300 Massachusetts Avenue; tel: 266-3605; www.handelandhadyn. org. America's oldest musical organization, which debuted in 1815, performs Baroque and Classical at Symphony Hall and Jordan Hall.

Comedy Clubs

Few cities in the nation harbor as many comedy clubs as Boston. Some serve light snacks as well as drinks (bar and tables); all have a cover charge, and at some the show is continuous while at

others there are discrete show-time hours, especially when big names perform. Most clubs have an admission fee, and an 'open mike' night when the audience may take to the stage.
Comedy Studio
Hong Kong Restaurant, 1238 Massachusetts Avenue, Cambridge; tel: 661-6507; www.the comedystudio.com. Dinner and a show, which might be a magic act, stand-up comedy, or a rather racy comedy-debate.
Improv Asylum
216 Hanover Street; tel: 263-6887; www.improvasylum.com. Improvisation and sketch comedy.
ImprovBoston
40 Prospect Street, Cambridge; tel: 576-1253; www.improvboston. com. A creative troupe whips up humorous routines Tue–Sun.
Nick's Comedy Stop
100 Warrenton Street; tel: 482-0930; www.nickscomedystop.com. The city's longest-running comedy club hosts stars on their way up as well as many who have already arrived. Thur–Sat.
Wilbur Theatre
246 Tremont Street; tel: 800-745-3000; www.thewilburtheatre.com. Opened in 1914, this intimate and elegantly restored theater is now home of the Comedy Connection, and hosts both comedy and musical talent.

Cultural Events Venues

Cambridge Multicultural Arts Center
41 Second Street, Cambridge; tel: 577-4100; www.cmacusa. org. The city's ornate arts center is the perfect setting for an ongoing series of musical events, dance performances, and plays.
Hatch Shell
The Esplanade; tel: 626-4970. Renowned for its free May–September concerts and dance performances, the most famous of which are the Boston (Symphony) Pops concerts in July.

ABOVE: Boston Symphony Hall.

Isabella Stewart Gardner Museum

280 The Fenway; tel: 566-1401, box office 278-5156; www.gardnermuseum.org. Chamber music concerts in the Tapestry Room at 1.30pm on Sundays from September to April.

Museum of Fine Arts

465 Huntington Avenue; tel: 369-3306; www.mfa.org. Hosts a year-long music program with a wide variety of performers.

New England Conservatory of Music

290 Huntington Avenue; tel: 585-1100; http://necmusic.edu. Acclaimed music conservatory that houses Jordan Hall, one of the country's finest concert halls. The NEC presents lectures, seminars, and classical, jazz, and improvisation music concerts.

Sanders Theatre

Memorial Hall, Cambridge and Quincy streets, Cambridge; tel: 496-2222. This 1,200-seat theater, renowned for its quirky Victorian architecture and fine acoustics and sightlines, has hosted a variety of musical and literary events for more than a century.

Symphony Hall

301 Massachusetts Avenue; tel: 266-1200; www.bso.org. Home of the Boston Symphony Orchestra, which presents winter concerts and moves to Tanglewood (in Lenox) during the summer, letting the Boston Pops take over. The Symphony Hall is used to stage a range of other classical performances, including a celebrity program.

Dance

José Mateo Ballet Theatre

400 Harvard Street, Cambridge; tel: 354-7467; www.ballettheatre.org. José Mateo's troupe is the only ballet company in New England to produce an entire repertoire by its own resident choreographer.

Boston Ballet

19 Clarendon St; tel: 695-6950; www.bostonballet.org. The city's premier dance company; the troupe presents classical, neoclassical and contemporary works. Their Christmas holiday *Nutcracker* is a perennial favorite.

Jazz

Berklee Performance Center

136 Massachusetts Avenue; tel: 747-8890, box office 747-2261; www.berklee.edu/BPC. Owned by the Berklee School of Music, this 1,200-seat auditorium is best known for its jazz concerts. Excellent musical events, keenly priced, are mounted by students and faculty.

Movie Theaters

The city and suburbs have a fair number of cinemas, many with multiple screens. The Boston Public Library, tel: 536-5400, and the Museum of Fine Arts, tel: 267-9300, regularly show classics. Some commercial cinemas in the city are:

Allston Cinemas

214 Harvard Avenue, Allston; tel: 277-2140. Two screens.

Brattle Theatre

40 Brattle Street, Harvard Square, Cambridge; tel: 876-6837. Art house, foreign, and classics all feature at this funky former theater, which also hosts film festivals and author readings.

Coolidge Corner Movie Theatre

290 Harvard St, Brookline; tel: 734-2500. Boston's oldest art house shows independent and foreign films on its one screen.

Kendall Square Cinema

1 Kendall Square, Cambridge; tel: 499-1996. Independents and first-runs.

Loews Boston Common

175 Tremont Street; tel: 423-5801. A state-of-the-art, stadium-seating theater with 19 screens.

Loews Harvard Square

10 Church Street, Cambridge; tel: 864-4580. Five screens for Harvard sophisticates.

Somerville Theatre

55 Davis Square; tel: 625-4088. First- and second-run films at reduced prices.

Opera

Boston Lyric Opera

45 Franklin Street; tel: 542-4912; www.blo.org. Fully staged productions from a varied repertoire using world-class emerging singers and internationally acclaimed directors and designers.

Opera Boston

25 Kingston St, 3R; tel: 451-3388; www.operaboston.org. An acclaimed, innovative professional opera company presents fully staged performances at the Cutler Majestic Theatre in the Theater District.

Rock and Pop Concerts

Bank of America Pavilion
290 Northern Avenue, Wharf 8, South Boston; tel: 728-1600.
This enormous white marquee at the waterfront, which seats 5,000, is a glorious venue May– September for rock, country, jazz, and pop.

Orpheum Theatre
1 Hamilton Place; tel: 482-0106; www.orpheumtheatreboston.com.
The historic 1852 Music Hall has been refurbished and now presents big names.

TD Garden
Causeway Street; tel: 624-1000; www.tdgarden.com.
Venue, seating nearly 20,000, for rock and pop concerts, ice shows, circuses, along with hockey and basketball events.

Wang Center for the Performing Arts
270 Tremont Street; tel: 482-9393, box office 866-348-9738; www.citicenter.org/theatres/wang.
A huge auditorium showcases headliner performing artists.

Theater

Boston theater runs the gamut from Broadway shows to amateur and professional college productions by way of repertory and experimental theater. It has long played the role of a try-out town for pre-Broadway productions.

ACT Roxbury
184 Dudley St; tel: 541-3900.
Cultural and economic development program sponsors a host of activities, including art and history tours, a film festival, open studios, and an arts series.

American Repertory Theater
Loeb Drama Center, 64 Brattle Street, Cambridge; tel: 495-6228; www.americanrepertorytheater.org.
The ever-controversial ART, Harvard's repertory troupe, presents neglected past works, as well as new American plays and modern interpretations of the classics.

Boston Center for the Arts
539 Tremont Street; tel: 426-5000; www.bcaonline.com.

Hosts experimental theater at venues throughout the city.

Charles Playhouse
74 Warrenton St; tel: 426-6912.
Home of the long-running and now renowned Blue Man Group art troupe.

Colonial Theatre
106 Boylston Street; tel: 426-9366; www.bostonscolonialtheatre.com.
Boston's oldest theater, with a richly restored early 20th-century proscenium, features pre- and post-Broadway productions.

Cutler Majestic Theatre
219 Tremont St, Theater District; tel: 800-233-3123; www.maj.org.
This jewel box of a theater, which belongs to Emerson College, has been lovingly restored. It presents accomplished productions of musicals by Emerson students and other performances.

Huntington Theatre Company/ Boston University Theatre
264 Huntington Avenue; tel: 266-0800; www.huntingtontheatre.org.
The acclaimed resident company mounts seven professional productions each season, from *The 39 Steps* to operettas by Gilbert & Sullivan to plays by Lillian Hellman.

Lyric Stage
140 Clarendon Street; tel: 585-5678; www.lyricstage.com. Boston's oldest residential professional theater company presents serious 20th-century plays, including New England and American premieres.

The Opera House
539 Washington Street; tel: 800-982-2787; www.bostonoperahouse.com. The city's 1928 Opera House has been restored to its former glory and now hosts dazzling Broadway-quality performances such as *The Lion King* and *Dirty Dancing*.

Publick Theatre
Christian Herter Park, 1175 Soldiers Field Road, Brighton; tel: 454-1444; www.publicktheatre.com. Boston's oldest resident theater company performs Shakespeare under the Stars (summer only) on the banks of the Charles River.

Shubert Theatre
265 Tremont St; tel: 482-9393; www.citicenter.org/theatres/shubert.
This 1910 theater is frequently the setting for pre-Broadway tryouts and touring Broadway companies.

NIGHTLIFE

Boston's several hundred thousand students ensure the city has a busy nightlife. Bars, nightclubs, discos, and comedy clubs abound in both Boston, especially in the Back Bay, and Cambridge. Most remain open until 2am, although Cambridge nightspots tend to close earlier than their Boston counterparts. Those under 21 cannot be served liquor, but many clubs admit customers 19 years and older on certain nights. It's best to call ahead and check an establishment's age policy.

Gay Scene

Mostly in the South End. Many mainstream bars designate one night a week as Gay Night. For listings check *Bay Windows* (www.baywindows.com), a gay paper available in major bookstores.

Fritz
Chandler Inn, 26 Chandler Street; tel: 482-3450. Friendly gay neighborhood sports bar that serves brunch until 3pm weekends.

Jacques Cabaret
70 Broadway; tel: 426-8902; www.jacquescabaret.com. Drag shows nightly at 10pm, and live alternative music downstairs Friday and Saturday nights. Attracts both gay and straight audiences.

Ramrod/Machine
1254 Boylston Street; tel: 266-2986. A long-popular venue, Ramrod demands leather and Levi's. The enormous dance hall (Machine) plays dance and techno and attracts a lively mixed crowd on Fridays and Saturdays.

Live Music Venues

Black Rose
160 State Street; tel: 742-2286. A classic Irish pub, close to Faneuil Hall Marketplace, which teems with Boston businesspeople primed to unwind. Live Irish music nightly and weekend afternoons.

Club Passim
7 Palmer Place, Cambridge; tel: 492-7679; www.clubpassim.org. Enjoy folk and acoustic performers in the oldest folk club in the country, where Joan Baez had her first break and musicians including Taj Mahal and Shawn Colvin launched their careers. A vegetarian restaurant and coffeehouse continues serving during the nightly show. No alcohol.

Common Ground
85 Harvard Avenue, Allston; tel: 783-2071. Funk, soul, rock, pop, ska, Celtic, and R&B mingle at this sports bar/Irish pub. The Irish pizza is topped with mashed potatoes, cheddar cheese, and bacon.

House of Blues
15 Landsdowne St; tel: 888-693-2583; www.houseofblues.com/boston. Come for the great bands and great sound quality.

Middle East
472 Massachusetts Avenue, Cambridge; tel: 864-3278. Dine on ethnic cuisine then catch a local band on the rise. Rock, indie, folk, and more.

The Plough and Stars
912 Massachusetts Avenue, Cambridge; tel: 441-3455. A tiny but beloved Irish bar with a wide range of music, from bodhran to bluegrass.

Regattabar
Charles Hotel, 1 Bennett Street, Cambridge; tel: 661-5000. An upmarket bar featuring top jazz names. You must buy tickets beforehand at www.regattabar jazz.com.

Ryles Jazz Club
212 Hampshire Street, Cambridge; tel: 876-9330; www.ryles-jazz.com. A great venue for jazz, blues, Brazilian and Latin music.

Scullers Jazz Club
Doubletree Guest Suites Hotel, 400 Soldiers Field Road; tel: 562-4111; www.scullersjazz.com. This long-time favorite, in a room with a panoramic view of the Charles River, attracts top names. Advance reservations recommended.

Wally's Café
472 Massachusetts Avenue, South End; tel: 424-1408; www.wallyscafe.com. This hole-in-the-wall bar, Boston's longest-running jazz joint, is much frequented by students. No food, no cover, no credit cards, but lots of beer and fine music.

Nightclubs

The club scene is in constant flux. Two areas where there is some

For those in search of a serious game on the green baize or for those just wanting to hang out and have fun, try the following:

Flattop Johnny's
1 Kendall Square, Building 200, Cambridge; tel: 494-9565; http://flattopjohnnys.com.
Microbrewed beer served to the sound of alternative rock at the ultra-hip hall's 12 tables. Half-price pool on Sundays, nine-ball tournament Sun 4pm and Mon 7pm, and free after 9pm on Weds. Burgers, sandwiches, snacks. Mon–Wed 4pm–1am, Thur–Sun 3pm–1am.

Jillian's and Lucky Strike
145 Ipswich Street; tel: 437-0300; www.jilliansboston.com. Home to three floors of bars, billiards, arcade games, darts, ping-pong, and the Lucky Strike bowling alley. Mon–Sat 11am–2am, Sun noon–2am; Mon–Thur, 18 and over after 8pm, Fri–Sat 21 and over after 8pm.

degree of continuity are Landsdowne Street in the Fenway, which attracts a younger, edgier crowd, and Boylston Place ('the Alley') near the Theater District, which attracts executive types. Some clubs are open only Wednesday or Thursday through Sunday.

Great Scott
1222 Commonwealth Ave; tel: 566-9014; www.greatscott boston.com.
Up-and-coming bands, a friendly crowd, and a Friday night indie-electro-britpop dance party.

Paradise Rock Club
967 Commonwealth Avenue; tel: 562-8800; www.thedise.com. One of Boston's premier rock-and-roll clubs for over 30 years and the first US venue where U2 performed. Up-and-coming artists are now the specialty, such as Ray LaMontagne, and Dresden Dolls.

BELOW: Club Passim, an epicenter of folk and acoustic music.

Roxy
279 Tremont Street; tel: 338-7699, www.royaleboston.com. Come on weekends to dance to big DJs or hear live music in a spacious hall, once a hotel ballroom. Drinks are pricey.

SIGHTSEEING TOURS

Bike Tours

Boston Bike Tours
Tel: 308-5902; www.bostonbiketours.com. Bicycles and helmets are provided for these three- to four-hour tours, which leave from the Visitor Information Center on Boston Common. All ages welcome.
Urban AdvenTours
103 Atlantic Ave; tel: 233-7595/800-979-3370; www.urbanadventours.com. Guided bicycle tours of Downtown, Fenway, the Charles River, and sunset tours. Daily tours offered 10am, 2pm, and 6pm.

Boat Tours and Cruises

Bay State Cruise Company
200 Seaport Boulevard; tel: 877-783-3779; www.baystatecruises.com. The *Provincetown III* catamaran speeds to Provincetown in 90 minutes. Music/dance cruises leave Friday and Saturday evenings for those 21 and older.
Boston Duck Tours
Leave from Prudential Center, Museum of Science, and New England Aquarium; tel: 267-3825; www.bostonducktours.com. Narrated historic tours of

PUBLIC ATTRACTIONS

For public tennis courts, swimming pools, and skating rinks, contact the Department of Conservation and Recreation, 251 Causeway Street, Suite 600; tel: 626-1250; www.mass.gov/dcr.

the city and Charles River aboard World War II vintage amphibious vehicles.
Boston Harbor Cruises
1 Long Wharf; tel: 227-4321 or 877-733-9425; www.bostonharborcruises.com. Three-hour whale-watching, sightseeing, sunset, and lighthouse cruises, a ferry to Provincetown, and a wild 'Codzilla' tour.
The Charles Riverboat Co.
CambridgeSide Galleria, 100 CambridgeSide Place; tel: 621-3002; www.charlesriverboat.com. One-hour narrated sightseeing cruises of the Charles River and Boston Harbor (daily mid-May–mid-Oct) and sunset cruises (June–Aug).
Massachusetts Bay Lines
Rowes Wharf; tel: 542-8000; www.massbaylines.com. Three- to four-hour music and whale-watching cruises; whales are guaranteed or guests receive a free ticket for another cruise.
New England Aquarium
Central Wharf; tel: 973-5200; www.neaq.org. Three- to four-hour whale-watching cruises to Stellwagen Bank. Boats leave from the aquarium's wharf (mid-Apr–mid-Sept Mon–Fri 9.30am/1.30pm, Sat–Sun 10am/2pm, limited schedule early Apr and mid-Sept–mid-Oct). If whales aren't sighted, you get a free ticket for another cruise.
Odyssey Cruises
Rowes Wharf; tel: 866-307-2469; www.odysseycruises.com. Elegant sightseeing, dinner/dancing, and midnight cruises.

Bus Tours

Bus companies run daily tours in summer in Boston and its environs, and also farther afield.
Gray Line Boston Cape Cod
16 South Charles Street; tel: 720-6342 or 781-986-6100; www.grayline.com. Tours of Greater Boston, Lexington, Concord, Cambridge, Plymouth, Salem, Cape Cod, and Newport, Rhode Island, depart from several Downtown hotels.

Gray Line Sightseeing
Tel: 720-6342/800-343-1328; www.brushhilltours.com. Air-conditioned coaches stop at more than a dozen historic sites, including Harvard University, and allow unlimited reboarding on later buses.

Trolley Tours

Beantown Trolley and Harbor Cruise
14–16 S. Charles Street; tel: 720-6342; www.beantowntrolley.com. Two-hour narrated tour aboard a trackless trolley includes stops at the Museum of Fine Arts and the Seaport District. Visitors are picked up at hotels, and can get off and on as they wish. Price includes harbor cruise May–Oct.
Old Town Trolley
380 Dorchester Avenue; tel: 269-8018; www.historictours.com. Cruises along Beacon Hill, Newbury Street, Downtown, the waterfront, and Bunker Hill Pavilion, passing close to many Freedom Trail sites. The tour lasts 90 minutes, but passengers can alight and board a later trolley. The company also offers a two-hour **Ghosts and Gravestones tour**, which includes historic burial grounds.

Walking Tours

Both Boston and Cambridge are ideal for walking. Many walking tours, both general and for the specialist, are available.
Boston African-American Historical Park
14 Beacon Street; tel: 742-5415; www.nps.gov/boaf. Free 90-minute tour of the 1.5-mile (2.6km) Black Heritage Trail. Memorial Day–Labor Day Mon–Sat 10am, noon, and 2pm (reservations for groups of five or more) and Labor Day–Memorial Day, Mon–Sat 2pm (reservations required).
Boston by Foot
77 N. Washington Street; tel: 367-2345; www.bostonbyfoot.com. Ninety-minute walks include tours of: Beacon Hill, the Freedom Trail, Literary Landmarks, the

North End, and the Victorian Back Bay. A 60-minute Boston by Little Feet tour is geared for ages 6–12 (see page 258). Call ahead.

Boston National Historical Park
Boston National Historical Park Visitor Center, 15 State Street; tel: 242-5642; www.nps.gov/bost. Free 90-minute, ranger-led tours visit the heart of the Freedom Trail. Tours limited to 30 people.

Boston Walks
Tel: 489-5020; www.walkboston. org. Varied themed walking tours.

North End Italian Market Tours
6 Charter Street; tel: 523-6032; www.bostonfoodtours.com. Visit the butcher, baker, and cheesemaker, and taste the best local food.

SPORT

BosTix is Boston's only half-price, day-of-show ticket outlet and information source for sporting events (see page 251).

Participant Sports

Canoeing

Charles River Canoe and Kayak Center
A green-roofed kiosk is located at Artesani Park, off Soldiers Field Road; tel: 965-5110. Canoes, kayaks, and rowing shells for hire. Instruction available. June–Aug daily, late Apr–May and Sept–early Oct Fri–Sun only.

South Bridge Boat House
496 Main Street, Concord; tel: 978-369-9438. Canoes and rowboats for exploring the Sudbury, Assabet, and Concord rivers. Apr–Oct Mon–Fri 10am–one hour before dusk, Sat–Sun 9am–one hour before dusk.

Cycling

Bikes may be rented, in the warmer months, from:

Ata Cycle
1773 Massachusetts Avenue, Cambridge; tel: 354-0907; www. atabike.com.

Back Bay Bicycles
366 Commonwealth Avenue; tel: 247-2336; http://backbay bicycles.com.

Community Bicycle Supply
496 Tremont Street; tel: 542-8623; www.communitybicycle. com.

Golf

Massachusetts Golf Association
Tel: 774-430-9100/800-356-2201. Represents nearly 400 clubs in the state and will provide up-to-date information on which courses are open to the public.

One public 18-hole course supervised by the Parks and Recreation Department is: William J. Devine Golf Course, 1 Circuit Drive, Franklin Park; tel: 265-4084.

Sailing

Sailing small boats on the Charles River Basin is a tradition. Less tranquil, but more exciting, is sailing in the harbor.

Community Boating Inc.
21 David Mugar Way; tel: 523-1038; dock: 523-9763. Become a temporary member, prove you can sail, and 100 sailboats, windsurfers and kayaks await you. One-day sailboat fee $75; one-day kayak fee $35. Apr–Oct Mon–Fri 1pm–sunset, Sat–Sun 9am–sunset.

Jamaica Pond Boathouse
507 Jamaicaway; tel: 522-5061. Sailboats and rowboats for hire in summer for sailing on a pretty lake.

Spectator Sports

Baseball

Boston Red Sox
Fenway Park, 4 Yawkey Way; tel: 733-7699; boston.redsox.mlb. com. This cozy park, built in 1912 and home to the 'Green Monster,' still has real grass. The Kenmore Square (Green Line of the 'T', branches B, C, D) and Fenway stations (Green Line, branch D) are close to the Park.

ANNUAL EVENTS

Each year Boston is host to two major sporting events:

Boston Marathon, tel: Boston Athletic Association at 236-1652; www.bostonmarathon. org.
Held on the third Monday (Patriots' Day) in mid-April. The finish line is at Copley Square, but the Copley Station of the 'T' is closed on Marathon day. To reach the final stretch, take the Orange Line to Back Bay Station or the Green Line to Auditorium or Kenmore; or the Green Line (C branch) to any stop on Beacon Street.

Head of the Charles Regatta, tel: 864-8415; www.hocr.org. Held on the second-to-last Saturday and Sunday of October, when thousands of oarspeople from all over the world race their shells on the Charles. Take the Red Line of the 'T' to Harvard Square and walk south on J.F. Kennedy Street to the river. Or board the Green Line (B branch) to Boston University campus and walk to the Boston University Bridge.

Basketball

Boston Celtics
TD Garden, Causeway Street; tel: 866-423 5849; www.nba.com/ celtics, www.tdgarden.com. Accessible by the Green or Orange lines of the 'T.'

Football

New England Patriots
Gillette Stadium, Foxboro; tel: stadium information 508-543-3900, tickets through Ticketmaster 800-745-3000; www.patriots.com. Special 'T' commuter trains to all Patriots home games from South Station (www.mbta.com/riding_ the_t/patriots).

Hockey

Boston Bruins
TD Garden, Causeway Street; tel: 624-2327; http://bruins.nhl.com, www.tdgarden.com.

A – Z

AN ALPHABETICAL SUMMARY OF PRACTICAL INFORMATION

A

Admission Charges

Museums charge entry fees for adults, and are generally discounted or free for children. Discounts are also sometimes available for seniors and students. Some museums and tours offer discounts for groups. Major museums often offer one free day per month, the day varying by museum – it is worth taking advantage of these if you can (see Free Museums, page 10). The **Boston City Pass** and **Go Boston card** provide discounted admission to multiple attractions (see Budgeting for Your Trip, right).

Age Restrictions

You must be at least 16 to drive in Massachusetts, even if you hold a valid license from another state, and at least 16 and a half to obtain a Massachusetts driver's license.

The legal drinking age in Massachusetts is 21, as in the rest of the United States. The legal age of consent is 16. You must be 21 years of age to rent a car; some companies will require you to be 25 or over.

B

Budgeting for Your Trip

Boston is an expensive city, but if you need to economize, there are numerous options.

Hotels

The average daily rate for hotels in Boston and Cambridge tops $200, and the sky's the limit for luxury hotels, which easily top $400 for a standard room. Some relatively inexpensive options are available (in the under-$150 range), but budget travelers will certainly want to check some of the many websites devoted to discounted lodgings. Among them are: www. kayak.com, www.travelocity.com, www.hotels.com, www.priceline. com, www.orbitz.com, and www. hotwire.com. Hotel rates fluctuate with the seasons and demand. If your travel time is flexible, call the hotel and ask them when their rates are 'off season.' Many colleges and universities in the area rent rooms in their dormitories during the summer months, when students are not present. Hostelling International also opened a new 450-bed hostel in Boston in 2012.

Dining

Mainstream tourist restaurants can be costly, but there are also inexpensive places, including ethnic restaurants in Chinatown, pizza and sandwich shops, and affordable places in Cambridge's Central Square and Inman Square areas. A glass of house wine is generally in the $7–10 range, and a beer several dollars less. A main course at an inexpensive restaurant will be less than $10, moderately priced restaurants will set you back $15–30, and expensive restaurants offer entrées for around $30–50.

Transportation

Transportation options include taxis, the 'T' subway, and buses. A taxi from the Boston Logan Airport to Downtown is around $30–40. A ride on the 'T' is $2.50 for adults, $1 for seniors, $1 for students, and free for children under 12. A bus ride costs $2, $0.75 for seniors, $0.75 for students, and free for children under 12. *See below for information on the MBTA Visitor Pass.*

Discount Passes

BosTix Ticket Booth Faneuil Hall (near the West End Entrance of Quincy Market) and Copley Square (corner of Boylston and Dartmouth streets); tel: 262-8632, ext. 229; www.bostix.org.

ABOVE: a Red Sox rally outside the New City Hall.

Tickets and information for over 100 entertainment and cultural attractions. Day-of, half-price theater tickets are sold. Tue–Sat 10am–6pm, Sun 11am–4pm. Cash and credit cards accepted. **Boston CityPass.** Tel: 888-330-5008; www.citypass.com/boston. Save nearly 50 percent on admission to five famous attractions: the Museum of Fine Arts, Museum of Science, New England Aquarium, Skywalk Observatory at the Prudential Center, and either the Harvard Museum of Natural History or Revolutionary Boston at the Old State House. The pass ($46 adults, $29 children) is good for nine consecutive days, and sold at all attractions included in the pass.

Go Boston Card. Tel: 866-628-9027; www.smartdestinations. com. These one-, two-, three-, five-, or seven-day pre-paid visitor passes offer unlimited admission to more than 50 attractions and tours, including the Hop-on/Hop-off Beantown Trolley, Whale Watch, the Swan Boats, Isabella Stewart Gardner Museum, Fenway Park Tour, Samuel Adams Brewery Tour, and the Museum of Fine Arts. Cards are on sale at the Boston Common, Prudential Center and Faneuil Hall visitor information centers, and BosTix ticket booths *(see above)*. A one-

day pass is $60 for adults and $40 for children.

Family Friendly Value Pass Download the voucher at www.bostonusa.com/images/stories/pdfs/visitor/family_friendly.pdf for dozens of discounts to attractions and restaurants (like two-for-one ice cream at Quincy Market or a free kid's ticket to the Franklin Park Zoo). Discounts change seasonally.

MBTA Visitor Pass Tel: 888-844-0355; www.mbta.com. A one-day LinkPass ($11) or weekly LinkPass ($18) can be purchased for unlimited travel on the 'T,' local buses, the Inner Harbor Ferry, and Commuter Rail Zone 1A. Passes can be purchased at the Back Bay, Downtown Crossing, North Station, and South Station. Visit the website for a full list of sales locations.

C

Children

There are loads of museums to explore, shops to visit, and activities geared specially to children. The Visitors Bureau's *Kids Love Boston* Guide, available for $4.99, includes an illustrated guidebook written especially for kids, a Travel Planner, and an illustrated kids' map of Massachusetts. It can be ordered online at www.BostonUSA.com. See also Children's Activities, page 250.

Child Care

Many hotels offer child-care services, which charge by the hour. Ask at the front desk.

Parents in a Pinch, Inc., 45 Bartlett Crescent, Brookline, tel: 739-5437/800-688-4697, www.parentsinapinch.com, offers in-room hotel care for children of all ages, with a minimum stay of four hours. Charges start at $15 per hour, plus a daily placement fee.

Child-Friendly Tours

Boston by Little Feet, tel: 367-2345, www.bostonbyfoot.com.

Geared for ages 6–12, the hour-long tour stops at 10 sites along the Freedom Trail. Meets at the Samuel Adams statue on Congress Street. Tour times: May–Oct Fri–Sat 10am, Sun 2pm, Apr call for times. The cost is $8. Meet 10 minutes before the tour's start time at the Samuel Adams statue in front of Faneuil Hall. No reservations are necessary, and tours are offered rain or shine.

Clothing

Many stores throughout the area cater to children. Among them: **Baby Gap**, Copley Place, 100 Huntington Avenue; tel: 247-1754. Sells a wide range of clothing basics.

Tadpole, 37 Clarendon Street; tel: 778-1788; www.shoptadpole.com. South End shop filled with high-end, modern clothing, furniture, toys, and gifts.

Climate

Part of the magic of Boston is that it is a land of seasons. The first snow may fall in November, and intermittent snow accompanied by cold weather – considerably below freezing – will usually continue well into March. The Charles River usually freezes over. Spring, which can be temperamental, spans March into May. This is when magnolias and lilacs bloom and magic fills the air. Summer

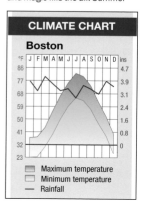

(June–September) can be very hot and humid with some real dog days, although most of the time the weather is just pleasantly hot – in the 70° to 80°F (21–27°C) range.

The fall encroaches gradually, usually with one last splurge of glorious 'Indian summer' days. Starting in September and 'peaking' in mid-October, resplendent fall colors can be enjoyed in the outskirts of Boston and even more so in the mountains of northern New England. In summary, Boston weather can be described in one word: erratic.

What to Wear

Boston is simultaneously more formal and less so than other parts of the country. The old-guard restaurants and hotels require proper dress, whereas in student enclaves, anything goes, including shorts, T-shirts, and athletic shoes. Plan ahead and call if necessary. It can get very cold in winter and hot and humid in summer.

When to Visit

Boston's weather is changeable. The best times to come may well be late spring and early fall (to enjoy the glorious autumnal New England foliage). Boston's coldest month is January, and the warmest month is July. Around November can be wet, so be prepared.

Crime and Safety

Boston is generally safe for tourists, though as a major city it has its fair share of crime. Be sure to use normal safety precautions: avoid showy displays of wealth in run-down areas, lock doors, don't leave valuables lying around, and avoid parks after sundown.

At time of writing, the US Department of Homeland Security (www.dhs.gov) has designated the terror alert status of 'orange,' or high, for all international and domestic flights in the USA. For safety updates, visit the www.travel.state.gov and www.fco.gov.uk.

ABOVE: street artists in Harvard Square.

Customs Regulations

What You Can Bring In

Visitors aged over 21 may take into the US:
– 200 cigarettes, 100 cigars (non-Cuban), or 3lbs (1.4kg) of smoking tobacco
– 1 liter of alcohol
– duty-free gifts worth up to $100
Do not bring in meat products, seeds, plants and fruits. Don't even think about bringing in narcotics. Customs agents in the US are very tough and efficient. For information: www.cbp.gov.

What You Can Take Out

The United States allows you to take out anything you wish, but consult the consulate or tourist authority of the country you are visiting next on its customs regulations for entrance.

D

Disabled Travelers

The MBTA (Massachusetts Bay Transportation Authority) has an excellent website (www.mbta.com) with information about transportation accessible to disabled travelers. For more information,

call the MBTA on 722-5123. The City of Boston's Commission for Persons with Disabilities can be reached on 635-3682 (TTY 635-2541). Elevators are standard in hotels.

E

Electricity

Boston homes have 'standard' electricity, which is 110 volts. European appliances require an adapter because European countries use 220–240 volts. Some hotel bathrooms have electrical outlets suitable for use with European appliances (220–240

EMERGENCIES

In the case of an emergency or serious accident, dial **911**. Your hotel or a taxi driver will be able to direct you to the nearest hotel.
Police, Ambulance, Fire 911
Credit cards lost or stolen:
AmEx, tel: 1-800-528-4800;
Diners Club/Carte Blanche,
tel: 1-800-234-6377; Master-Card, tel: 1-800-627-8372;
Visa, tel: 800-847-2911 (800-VISA-911).

volts), but it is useful to pack an adapter.

Embassies and Consulates

Australia: 150 East 42nd Street, 34th Floor, New York; tel: 212-315-6500.
Canada: 3 Copley Place, #400; tel: 262-3760.
Ireland: 535 Boylston Street; tel: 267-9330.
Israel: 20 Park Plaza, #1020; tel: 535-0200.
UK: One Memorial Drive, 15th floor, Cambridge; tel: 245-4500.

G

Gay and Lesbian

Boston is a progressive and gay-friendly New England destination, with a sizable and visible GLBT community. Massachusetts was the first state in the United States to legalize same-sex marriage, and Provincetown, outside Boston, is one of the most popular gay destinations in the country. Gay-oriented Bay Windows (www.baywindows.com) and EDGE Boston (www.edgeboston.com) are good local sources of information. The South End neighborhood is a hub for gay men, and

BELOW: a Greek Orthodox Priest in Harvard.

24-HOUR PHARMACIES

CVS, 587 Boylston Street, Boston; tel: 437-8414.
CVS, 36 White Street, Cambridge; tel: 876-5519.

Jamaica Plain has a large lesbian community. Gay bars are found particularly in the Theater District, South End, and the Fenway, and many other bars have designated 'gay' nights.

H

Health and Medical Care

Health care can be extremely expensive in the United States, and it is very strongly recommended to arrange your own medical insurance before setting off from home.
Massachusetts General Hospital, 55 Fruit Street, tel: 726-2000, operates a Medical Walk-In clinic (tel: 726-2707) Mon–Fri 8.30am–8pm, Sat–Sun 9.30am–4pm for non-emergency situations, and 24-hour emergency-room care for more serious conditions. The hospital's international Patient Center helps patients from overseas with appointments, transportation, and language interpretation services.
    Other facilities with 24-hour care include:
Brigham and Women's Hospital, 75 Francis Street, tel: 732-5500.
Children's Hospital, 300 Longwood Avenue, tel: 355-6000.
Tufts Medical Center, 800 Washington Street, tel: 636-5000.
    Other useful medical hotlines include:
Beth Israel Deaconess Hospital, tel: 667-7000.
Massachusetts Eye and Ear Infirmary, tel: 523-7900.
Tufts Dental School, 1 Kneeland Street, tel: 636-6828. Emergen-

cies Mon–Fri 9–10.30am and 1–2.30pm. Walk-in clinic with limited admissions.

Dentists

Dental Referral Service (tel: 800-511-8663) and **1-800-Dentist** (tel: 800-336-8422; www.1800dentist.com) provide free, round-the-clock recommendations.

I

Internet

Nearly all hotels have internet access, but you may have to pay a $10–15 daily fee. Harvard Square, in Cambridge, has free public Wi-fi. Many bookstores and cafés (especially Starbucks) also have free Wi-fi.
Boston Public Library, 700 Boylston Street; tel: 536-5400; www.bpl.org. Mon–Thur 9am–9pm, Fri–Sat 9am–5pm. The Library is a wireless hotspot; patrons using wireless devices may access the Library's internet service at the Central Library and at all branch locations. There are also computer workstations, with time limits that vary by location and demand.

M

Maps

Insight Guides' FlexiMap Boston is laminated for durability and easy folding, and contains travel information as well as exceptionally clear cartography.
    Freedom Trail and transportation maps are available at the Visitor Center at Boston Common.

Media

Print Newspaper

Boston Globe (www.boston.com), daily newspaper with

PUBLIC HOLIDAYS

All government offices, banks and post offices are closed on public holidays. Public transportation doesn't run as often on these days, but most shops, museums, and other attractions are open.

January New Year's Day; Martin Luther King Day (third Mon)
February President's Day (third Mon)
March/April Easter Sun
May Memorial Day (last Mon)
July Independence Day (4th)
September Labor Day (first Mon)
October Columbus Day
November Thanksgiving Day (fourth Thursday) and the following day
December Christmas Day (25th).

weekly calendar listings on Sundays.
The Boston Herald (www.boston herald.com), daily newspaper.
Improper Bostonian (www.improper.com), a free sophisticated biweekly digest with a good listings section.
Boston Magazine (www.bostonmagazine.com), a slick and informative monthly of local interest.

Online Newspaper

Christian Science Monitor (www.csmonitor.com), a prestigious daily newspaper, now online (with a weekly print version). Strong on international news.

Radio Stations

Radio stations in the area include:
WEEI, 850 AM: sports.
WRKO, 680 AM: talk.
WBZ, 1030 AM: news.
WODS 103.3: Top 40
WBUR, 90.9 FM: news.
WZLX, 100.7 FM: classic rock.

Television Stations

These include:
PBS, channel 2 (WGBH).

CBS, channel 4 (WBZ).
ABC, channel 5 (WCVB).
NBC, channel 7 (WHDH).
ESPN, channel 15 (ESPN).
CNN, channel 17 (CNN).
Fox, channel 25 (WXNE).
UPN, channel 38 (WSBK).
WB, channel 56 (WLVI).

Money

Credit and debit cards are accepted in most establishments. If in doubt, be sure to double-check before you order dinner or have your purchases tallied up. Traveler's checks are accepted in some places.

ATMs are found all over the city. Remember: if you use an ATM that is not associated with your bank, you may be charged a fee of several dollars.

O

Opening Hours

Most offices are open Mon–Fri 9am–5pm, although some offices open at 8am. Banks are open Mon–Fri 9am–3pm and often later. Saturday hours are generally 9am–1pm.

P

Postal Services

The main Post Office is at 25 Dorchester Avenue (tel: 654-5302; www.usps.gov), behind South Station. Hours are daily 6am–midnight. If you do not know where you will be staying, mail can be addressed to: General Delivery, Main Post Office, 25 Dorchester Avenue, Boston 02205.

The Post Office at Logan Airport is open until midnight. Stamps are available in vending machines in airports, hotels, stores, and bus and train stations.

R

Religious Services

Bostonians are tolerant of diverse beliefs. There is no official religion in the United States; in Boston, Catholicism is by far the most common religion, with nearly 40 percent of Bostonians identifying as Catholic. Protestantism (in particular, Episcopal, Baptist, and Unitarian Universalist denominations) and Judaism are present in smaller numbers.

T

Tax

The sales tax in Massachusetts is 6.25 percent, which is added at the register in stores and to the bill at restaurants. The hotel tax is 8.45 percent in Boston (5.7 percent elsewhere in the state), which is generally not included in prices quoted.

Telephone Codes

Area codes for Boston and its environs are **617** and **857**. You do not need to dial the area code if you are calling on a landline from within the same area. Area codes for Cape Cod, Martha's Vineyard, and Nantucket are **508** and **774**. The North Shore, including Cape Ann, use **978** and **351**. Towns to the south of Boston use **781** and **339**. Western Massachusetts is **413**. International dialing code: to call Boston from abroad, dial your country's exit code + 1 + 617 or 857 + number.

Time Zone

Boston runs on Eastern Standard Time. Every spring the clock is turned one hour ahead, and every fall one hour back. Boston is three hours ahead of Los Angeles, one hour ahead of Chicago, five hours behind London and 15 hours behind Tokyo.

Tipping

Tipping is voluntary, but very much expected. Gratuities are usually not automatically tallied into the bill, unless your restaurant party is large. Some guidelines:
• Waiters are usually given 18 percent of the bill. For above-average service, or in a better restaurant, tip 20 percent.
• Taxi cab drivers usually get 15 percent of the fare.
• Doormen, skycaps, and porters receive one dollar a bag.
• Hairdressers, manicurists, and masseurs usually receive 10–15 percent of the total charge.

Tourist Information

Boston National Historical Park. Faneuil Hall; tel: 242-5642; www.nps.gov/bost. Staffed by park rangers, the center offers visitor maps, brochures, free ranger-guided tours and information about Freedom Trail sites. Daily 9am–5pm.
Cambridge Visitor Information

WEBSITES

www.bostonusa.com Greater Boston Convention and Visitors Bureau's official site.
www.massvacation.com Massachusetts Office of Travel and Tourism's site provides information for the entire state.
www.mbta.com For up-to-date information about the transportation system.

www.massport.com All you need to know about Logan Airport.
www.capecodchamber.org Cape Cod Chamber of Commerce information.
www.visitNewEngland.com Information about the region.
www.northofboston.org Details of places to the north of the city.

Booth. In the center of Harvard Square; tel: 497-1630. Source of comprehensive Cambridge-specific information, including tours, maps, and brochures. Mon–Fri 9am–5pm, Sat 9am–4pm, Sun 9am–1pm.
Greater Boston Convention and Visitors Bureau. 2 Copley Place; tel: 536-4100/888-733-2678; www.bostonusa.com. Offers phone information for visitors, and maintains the Prudential Visitor Center on the west side of the Prudential Plaza, open Mon–Sat 9am–5pm, Sun 1–5pm, and the Boston Common Visitor Information Center, 147 Tremont Street. The booth here marks the start of the Freedom Trail, and is open daily, 9am–5pm.

Harvard University Information Office. Holyoke Center in Harvard Square, tel: 495-1573. Source of Harvard-specific information. Mon–Sat 9am–5pm.
Massachusetts Office of Travel and Tourism. 10 Park Plaza, Suite 4510; tel: 973-8500/800-227-6277; www.massvacation.com. 'MOTT' can supply details on the state, as well as day-trip information. Mon–Fri 9am–5pm. Booths at Greyhound Bus depot at South Station and at Logan Airport, Terminals A and E.

V

Visas and Passports

For up-to-date information on US entry regulations, visit http://travel.state.gov.
Tel: 202-663-1225.

W

Weights and Measures

The US uses the imperial system, and metric is rarely used. Some useful conversions:
1 inch = 2.54 centimeters
1 foot = 30.48 centimeters
1 mile = 1.609 kilometers
1 quart = 1.136 liters
1 ounce = 28.4 grams
1 pound = 0.453 kilograms
1 yard = 0.9144 meters

BELOW: lunch on the patio at the Boston Harbor Hotel.

FURTHER READING

Non-Fiction

About Boston, by David McCord. Boston's essence distilled into short, poetic chapters, written by a poet and educator who was honored by the city with the title Grand Bostonian. First published in 1948.

Bibles, Brahmins, and Bosses, by Thomas H. O'Connor. A concise, well-written history of the city.

Boston: A Topographical History, Third Enlarged Edition by Walter Muir Whitehall, and enlarged by Lawrence Kennedy. A vivid historical survey of Boston with a focus on physical changes, illustrated with old pictures and maps. First published in 1968.

Cityscapes of Boston, by Robert Campbell and Peter Vanderwarker. A Boston historical survey, beautifully illustrated with black-and-white images comparing sites in the past and present.

Dead Certainties: Unwarranted Speculations, by Simon Schama. Exploration of the gap between events and historical interpretation, focusing in part on the 1849 Parkman-Webster murder case.

The Houses of Boston's Back Bay, by Bainbridge Bunting. Seminal, immensely detailed review of Back Bay architecture.

The Islands of Boston Harbor, by Edward Rowe Snow, updated by Jeremy D'Entremont. History and legends of the Harbor Islands.

Lost Boston, by Jane Holtz Kay. A classic architectural history of Boston, handsomely illustrated and recently updated.

Paul Revere and the World He

Lived In, by Esther Forbes. Pulitzer Prize-winning account of Revere's life and the American Revolution.

The Proper Bostonians, by Cleveland Amory. Some very entertaining insights into the city's social framework.

Fiction

On Beauty, by Zadie Smith. Follows a mixed-race British/American family living in a fictional town outside Boston.

The Bostonians, by Henry James. A 19th-century satire of the city's radical and reformist circles.

The Friends of Eddie Coyle, by George Higgins. Part of a Boston-based series; other titles include *Cogan's Trade, Impostors, Outlaws, Penance for Jerry Kennedy*.

The Last Puritan, by George Santayana. The life of Puritan Oliver Alden, conflicted over his sense of duty and natural instincts.

The Late George Apley, by John P. Marquand. A 1937 satire of Boston upper-class society.

Little Women, by Louisa May Alcott. Four sisters – Meg, Jo, Beth and Amy March – grow up in 19th-century New England.

Mystic River, by Dennis Lehane. Three men united by tragedy. Set in grim, working-class Charlestown.

The Namesake, Jhumpa Lahiri. Cultural challenges are faced by Indians who move from Calcutta to Cambridge.

The Rise of Silas Lapham, by William Dean Howells. Rags-to-riches story, and accompanying moral dilemmas.

The Scarlet Letter, by Nathaniel Hawthorne. Adulteress Hester Pyrne struggles for repentance in 17th-century Puritan Boston.

For Children

Make Way for Ducklings, by Robert McCloskey. A family of ducks live in the Boston Public Garden's Lagoon.

The Trumpet of the Swan, by E.B. White. Story of a trumpeter swan born without a voice that learns to play the trumpet.

Other Insight Guides

Among nearly 200 companion books to this one are numerous guides covering the United States, from *Alaska* to *Hawaii*, and *New England* to *California*. One title, USA On the Road, suggests itineraries designed to explore every part of the country. **Insight City Guides** include *Chicago, Las Vegas, New York, San Francisco, Seattle*, and *Washington DC*.

Boston is one of the titles in the **Insight Step by Step** series. These books provide a series of timed itineraries, with recommended stops for lunch. The itineraries are plotted on an accompanying pullout map.

Insight Select Guides offer a collection of over 100 inspiring ideas for your stay in cities including *New York City, Chicago*, and *San Francisco*.

Durable and flexible, **Insight Fleximaps** include *Atlanta, Boston, Los Angeles, Miami, New York, San Diego, Seattle*, and *Washington DC*.

TRANSPORTATION

ACCOMMODATIONS

ACTIVITIES

A – Z

ART AND PHOTO CREDITS

BOSTON STREET ATLAS

The key map shows the area of Boston covered by the atlas section. An index of street names and places of interest shown on the maps can be found on the following pages. For each entry there is a page number and grid reference

Map Legend

Freeway with Junction	✈ ✈ Airport	▨ Freeway
Freeway (under construction)	† ✝ Church (ruins)	▨ Divided Highway
Divided Highway	† Monastery	Main Roads
Main Road	▙ ⌂ Castle (ruins)	
Secondary Road	⸪ Archaeological Site	Minor Roads
Minor Road	⚲ Cave	
Track	★ Place of Interest	Footpath
International Boundary	⌂ Mansion/Stately Home	Railroad
State Boundary	☼ Viewpoint	Pedestrian Area
National Park/Reserve	⚑ Beach	Important Building
Ferry Route		Park

Ⓜ Subway	
🚌 Bus Station	
❶ Tourist Information	
✉ Post Office	
⛪ Cathedral/Church	
☾ Mosque	
✡ Synagogue	
⚊ Statue/Monument	
⎮ Tower	
⍭ Lighthouse	

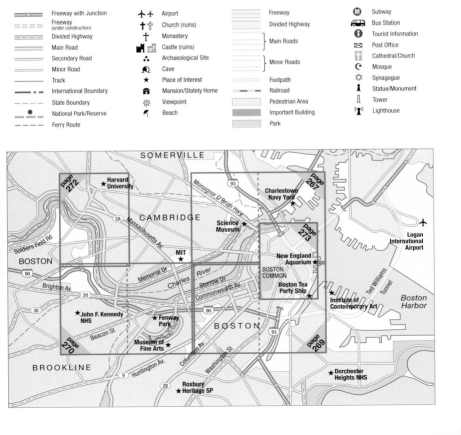

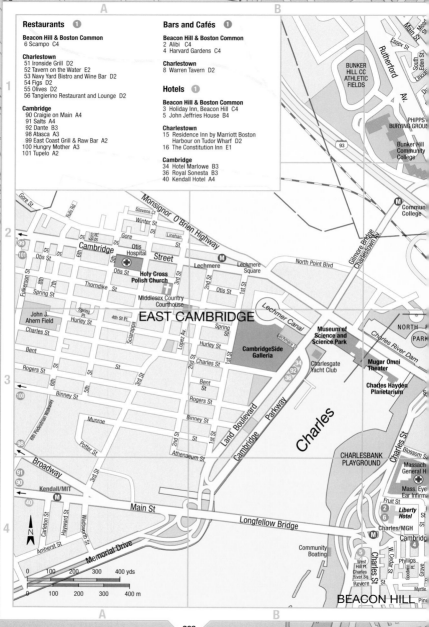

Restaurants ❶

Beacon Hill & Boston Common
6 Scampo C4

Charlestown
51 Ironside Grill D2
52 Tavern on the Water E2
53 Navy Yard Bistro and Wine Bar D2
54 Figs D2
55 Olives D2
56 Tangierino Restaurant and Lounge D2

Cambridge
90 Craigie on Main A4
91 Salts A4
92 Dante B3
98 Atasca A3
99 East Coast Grill & Raw Bar A2
100 Hungry Mother A3
101 Tupelo A2

Bars and Cafés ❶

Beacon Hill & Boston Common
2 Alibi C4
4 Harvard Gardens C4

Charlestown
8 Warren Tavern D2

Hotels ❶

Beacon Hill & Boston Common
3 Holiday Inn, Beacon Hill C4
5 John Jeffries House B4

Charlestown
15 Residence Inn by Marriott Boston
   Harbour on Tudor Wharf D2
16 The Constitution Inn E1

Cambridge
34 Hotel Marlowe B3
36 Royal Sonesta B3
40 Kendall Hotel A4

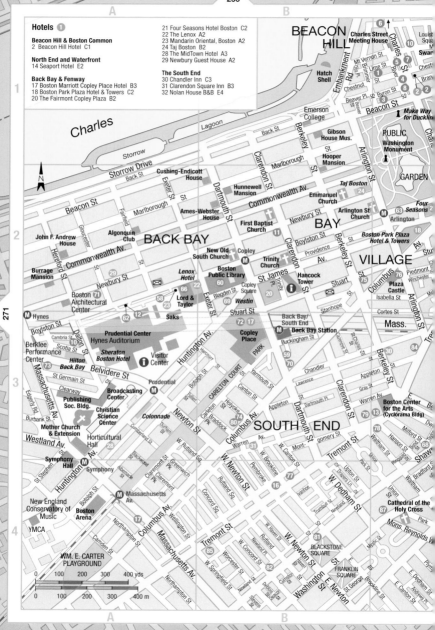

Hotels ❶

Beacon Hill & Boston Common
2 Beacon Hill Hotel C1

North End and Waterfront
14 Seaport Hotel E2

Back Bay & Fenway
17 Boston Marriott Copley Place Hotel B3
18 Boston Park Plaza Hotel & Towers C2
20 The Fairmont Copley Plaza B2

21 Four Seasons Hotel Boston C2
22 The Lenox A2
23 Mandarin Oriental, Boston A2
24 Taj Boston B2
28 The MidTown Hotel A3
29 Newbury Guest House A2

The South End
30 Chandler Inn C3
31 Clarendon Square Inn B3
32 Nolan House B&B E4

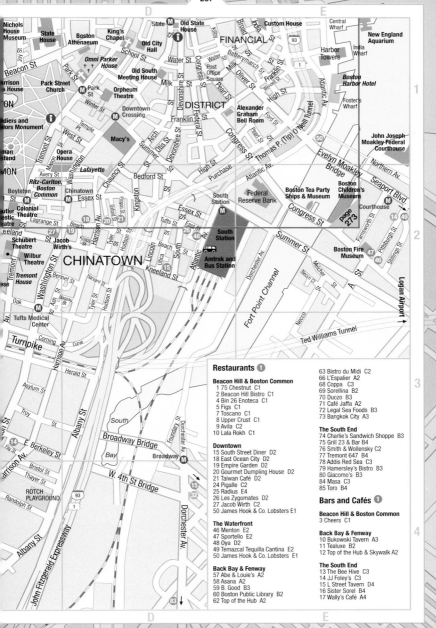

Restaurants ❶

Beacon Hill & Boston Common
1 75 Chestnut C1
2 Beacon Hill Bistro C1
4 Bin 26 Enoteca C1
5 Figs C1
7 Toscano C1
8 Upper Crust C1
9 Avila C2
10 Lala Rokh C1

Downtown
15 South Street Diner D2
18 East Ocean City D2
19 Empire Garden D2
20 Gourmet Dumpling House D2
21 Taiwan Café D2
24 Pigalle C2
25 Radius E4
26 Les Zygomates D2
27 Jacob Wirth C2
50 James Hook & Co. Lobsters E1

The Waterfront
46 Menton E2
47 Sportello E2
48 Oya D2
49 Temazcal Tequila Cantina E2
50 James Hook & Co. Lobsters E1

Back Bay & Fenway
57 Abe & Louie's A2
58 Asana A2
59 B. Good B3
60 Boston Public Library B2
62 Top of the Hub A2

63 Bistro du Midi C2
66 L'Espalier A2
68 Coppa C3
69 Sorellina B2
70 Duczo B3
71 Café Jaffa A2
72 Legal Sea Foods B3
73 Bangkok City A3

The South End
74 Charlie's Sandwich Shoppe B3
75 Grill 23 & Bar B4
76 Smith & Wollensky C2
77 Tremont 647 B4
78 Addis Red Sea C3
79 Hamersley's Bistro B3
80 Giacomo's B3
84 Masa C3
85 Toro B4

Bars and Cafés ❶

Beacon Hill & Boston Common
3 Cheers C1

Back Bay & Fenway
10 Bukowski Tavern A3
11 Tealuxe B2
12 Top of the Hub & Skywalk A2

The South End
13 The Bee Hive C3
14 JJ Foley's C3
15 L Street Tavern D4
16 Sister Sorel B4
17 Wally's Café A4

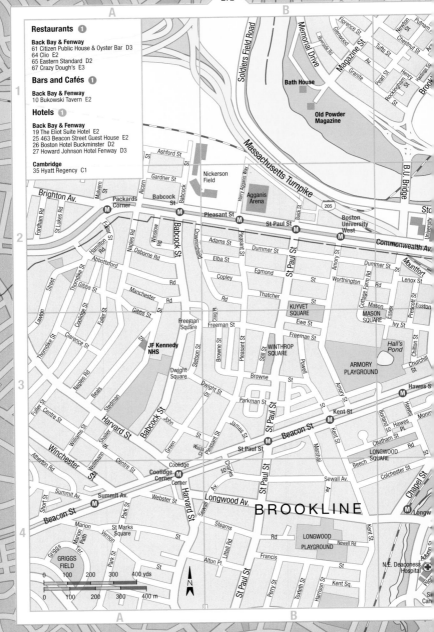

Restaurants ❶

Back Bay & Fenway
61 Citizen Public House & Oyster Bar D3
64 Clio E2
65 Eastern Standard D2
67 Crazy Dough's E3

Bars and Cafés ❶

Back Bay & Fenway
10 Bukowski Tavern E2

Hotels ❶

Back Bay & Fenway
19 The Eliot Suite Hotel E2
25 463 Beacon Street Guest House E2
26 Boston Hotel Buckminster D2
27 Howard Johnson Hotel Fenway D3

Cambridge
35 Hyatt Regency C1

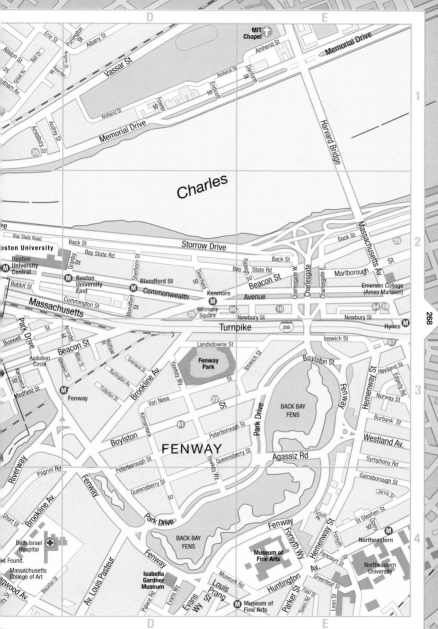

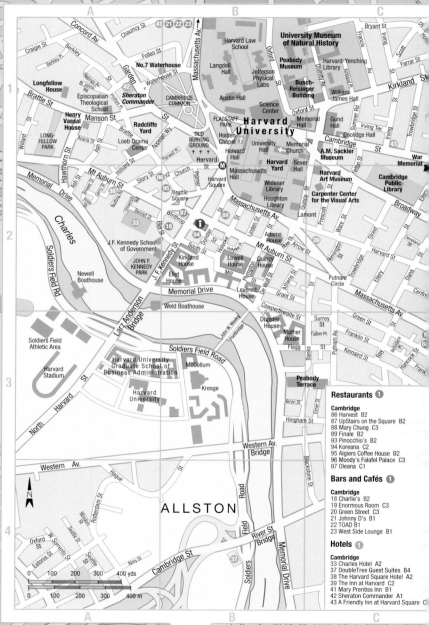

Restaurants ❶

Cambridge
86 Harvest B2
87 UpStairs on the Square B2
88 Mary Chung C3
89 Finale B2
93 Pinocchio's B2
94 Koreana C2
95 Algiers Coffee House B2
96 Moody's Falafel Palace C3
97 Oleana C1

Bars and Cafés ❶

Cambridge
18 Charlie's B2
19 Enormous Room C3
20 Green Street C3
21 Johnny D's B1
22 TOAD B1
23 West Side Lounge B1

Hotels ❶

Cambridge
33 Charles Hotel A2
37 DoubleTree Guest Suites B4
38 The Harvard Square Hotel A2
39 The Inn at Harvard C2
41 Mary Prentiss Inn B1
42 Sheraton Commander A1
43 A Friendly Inn at Harvard Square C1

267

Bars and Cafés ①

Beacon Hill & Boston Common
21st Amendment D3

Downtown
The Good Life E4
POSH BLU D4

The North End
Boston Beer Works E1
Goody Glover's E2

Hotels ①

Beacon Hill
XV Beacon D3
Onyx Hotel E1

Downtown
Nine Zero D3
Ritz-Carlton, Boston Common D4
Omni Parker House Hotel E3
Harborside Inn F3

North End and Waterfront
10 Boston Harbor Hotel F3
11 Boston Marriott Hotel
Long Wharf F2
12 Fairmont Battery Wharf F1
13 Millennium Bostonian Hotel E2

Restaurants ①

Beacon Hill & Boston Common
3 No. 9 Park D3

Downtown
11 Durgin Park F2
12 KO Prime D3
13 Milk Street Café E3
14 North 26 E2
16 Union Oyster House E2
17 Chau Chow City E4
22 Locke-Ober D3
23 Café Fleuri F3
25 Radius E4
28 Marliave E3
29 McCormick and Schmick's E2

The North End
30 Taranta E2
31 Antico Forno E2
32 Bacco E1
33 Bricco F2
34 Caffé Paradiso F2
35 Cantina Italiana F1
36 Dino's Café E1
37 Giacomo's F1
38 Lucca E2
39 Marco F2
40 Nebo E1
41 Regina Pizzeria F1
42 Trattoria di Monica F1
43 The Daily Catch F2
44 Neptune Oyster E2

The Waterfront
45 Meritage F3

50   100 150 200 yds

50   100 150   200 m

269

STREET INDEX

INDEX

RESTAURANTS

INSIGHT GUIDES

BOSTON

Project Editor
Sarah Sweeney
Series Manager
Rachel Lawrence
Art Editor
Lucy Johnston
Map Production
original cartography Berndtson
& Berndtson, updated by Apa
Cartography Department
Production
Tynan Dean, Linton Donaldson and
Rebeka Ellam

Distribution

UK
Dorling Kindersley Ltd
A Penguin Group company
80 Strand, London, WC2R 0RL
customerservice@dk.com

United States
Ingram Publisher Services
1 Ingram Boulevard, PO Box 3006,
La Vergne, TN 37086-1986
customer.service@ingrampublisher
services.com

Australia
Universal Publishers
PO Box 307
St Leonards NSW 1590
sales@universalpublishers.com.au

New Zealand
Brown Knows Publications
11 Artesia Close, Shamrock Park
Auckland, New Zealand 2016
sales@brownknows.co.nz

Worldwide
**Apa Publications GmbH & Co.
Verlag KG (Singapore branch)**
7030 Ang Mo Kio Avenue 5
08-65 Northstar @ AMK
Singapore 569880
apasin@singnet.com.sg

Printing

CTPS-China
© 2013 Apa Publications (UK) Ltd
All Rights Reserved

First Edition 1992
Fifth Edition 2013

ABOUT THIS BOOK

What makes an Insight Guide different? Since our first book pioneered the use of full-colour photography used creatively in travel guides in 1970, we have aimed to provide not only reliable information but also the key to a real understanding of a destination and its people.

Now, when the internet can supply inexhaustible (but not always reliable) facts, our books marry text and pictures to provide that more elusive quality: knowledge. To achieve this, they rely on the authority of locally based writers and photographers.

This new edition of *City Guide Boston* was commissioned by **Sarah Sweeney** and copyedited by **Kathryn Glendenning**. The book was thoroughly updated by **Barbara Rockwell**, a freelance arts and travel writer and a devoted city-lover, with a deep-rooted affection for all things Boston. Her U.S. travel expertise runs from coast to coast. She has written for various travel and lifestyle websites and contributed to Insight Guides' *Smart Guide San Francisco* and *Step-by-Step San Francisco*.

This edition builds on the success of earlier editions produced by **Brian Bell**, **Bill** and **Kay Scheller**, **Marcus Brooke**, and **Alan Andres**. The text of writers who contributed to previous editions has been updated for this book. They include **John Gattuso**, who wrote some of the History and Places chapters; **Michael Wentworth**, curator of painting and sculpture at the Boston Athenaeum, who wrote the original chapter on the visual arts; **William Schofield**, who invented the concept of the Freedom Trail; **Ken Mallory**, who contributed the chapter on the Harbor Islands; Cambridge-based urban planning writer, **Peter Strupp**, who wrote on architecture; **Jon Marcus**, who supplied the profiles of educational institutions; and **Dana Berg**, an artist and art historian.

The principal photographers were **Abe**, **Richard** and **Daniella Nowitz**, a family of photographers who captured the variety and character of this historical city.

The book was indexed by **Penny Phenix**.

SEND US YOUR THOUGHTS

We do our best to ensure the information in our books is as accurate and up-to-date as possible. The books are updated on a regular basis using local contacts, who painstakingly add, amend, and correct as required. However, some details (such as telephone numbers and opening times) are liable to change, and we are ultimately reliant on our readers to put us in the picture.

We welcome your feedback, especially your experience of using the book "on the road". Maybe we recommended a hotel that you liked (or another that you didn't), or you came across a great bar or new attraction that we missed.

We will acknowledge all contributions, and we'll offer an Insight Guide to the best letters received.

Please write to us at:
Insight Guides
PO Box 7910, London SE1 1WE
Or email us at:
insight@apaguide.co.uk

Boston Subway

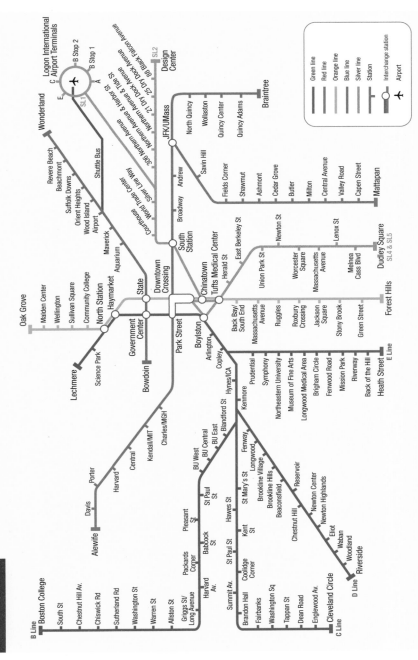

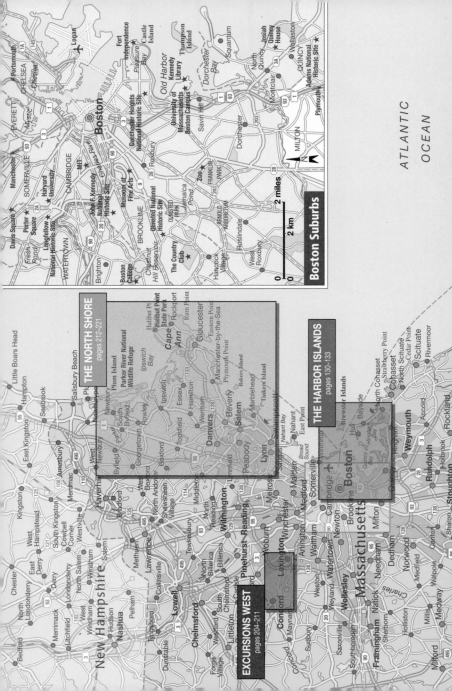

Boston Suburbs

*ATLANTIC
OCEAN*

New Hampshire

Massachusetts

Little Boars Head

Hampton

Seabrook

Salisbury Beach

Plum Island

Parker River National
Wildlife Refuge

Newbury

Ipswich
Bay

Cape
Ann

Rockport
Halibut Pt.
Halibut Point
State Park

Rum Point

Eastern Point

Gloucester

Manchester-by-the-Sea

Plymouth Point

Bakers Island

Marblehead

Tinkers Island

Salem

Beverly

Danvers

Wenham

Hamilton

Essex

Ipswich

Topsfield

Rowley

Georgetown

Byfield

South
Byfield

Boxford

North Andover

Lawrence

Methuen

Salem

Pelham

Hudson

Nashua

Lowell

Chelmsford

Billerica

Wilmington

Reading

Pinehurst

Lexington

Concord

Lincoln

Weston

Wayland

Sudbury

Maynard

Natick

Framingham

Wellesley

Needham

Dedham

Norwood

Norfolk

Medfield

Walpole

Sharon

Stoughton

Randolph

Weymouth

Hingham

Cohasset

Scituate

North Scituate

Rockland

Hanover

Abington

Brewster Islands

Hull

Quincy
Bay

Hingham
Bay

Nahant

Broad Sound

Winthrop

Boston

Cambridge

Somerville

Brookline

Milton

Quincy

Province Lands

Brant

THE ATLANTIC

EVERETT

CHELSEA

Logan

Fort
Independence

Castle
Island

Pleasure
Bay

Thompson
Island

Squantum

North
Quincy

Wollaston

QUINCY

Adams National
Historic Site

Josiah
Quincy
House

Dorchester
Bay

John F.
Kennedy
Library

University of
Massachusetts
Boston Campus

Savin Hill

Dorchester

Plymouth

Roxbury

Zoo

FRANKLIN
PARK

Jamaica
Pond

ARNOLD
ARBORETUM

Roslindale

West
Roxbury

Hancock
Village

MILTON

The Country
Club

Chestnut
Hill Reservoir

Boston
College

Brighton

WATERTOWN

National Historic Site

Longfellow
National Historic Site

Harvard
University

Porter
Square

Davis Square

Fresh
Pond

SOMERVILLE

Manchester

CAMBRIDGE

MIT

Charles River

John F. Kennedy
National
Historic Site

Museum of
Fine Arts

Dorchester Heights
National Historic Site

BROOKLINE

Olmsted National
Historic Site

Boston

N

0   2 miles

0   2 km